AFRICAN AMERICANS
IN THE WEST

Titles in ABC-CLIO's
CULTURES IN THE
AMERICAN WEST
Series

Scott C. Zeman, Series Editor

American Indians in the Early West, Sandra K. Mathews
Hispanics in the American West, Jorge Iber and Arnoldo De León
Women in the American West, Laura E. Woodworth-Ney

AFRICAN AMERICANS
IN THE WEST

Douglas Flamming

CULTURES IN THE AMERICAN WEST
Scott C. Zeman, Series Editor

A B C ⬬ C L I O

Santa Barbara, California • Denver, Colorado • Oxford, England

Library of Congress Cataloging-in-Publication Data

Flamming, Douglas.
  African Americans in the West / Douglas Flamming.
    p. cm.
  Includes bibliographical references and index.
  ISBN 978-1-59884-002-5 (alk. paper) — ISBN 978-1-59884-003-2 (ebook)
  1. African Americans—West (U.S.)—History.   2. African Americans—West
(U.S.)—Social conditions.   3. African Americans—West (U.S.)—Biography.
4. African American pioneers—West (U.S.)—History.   5. Frontier and pioneer
life—West (U.S.)   6. West (U.S.)—History.   7. West (U.S.)—Social conditions.
8. West (U.S.)—Biography.   I. Title.
  E185.925.F536   2009
  978'.0496073—dc22   2009016192

13 12 11 10 09   1 2 3 4 5

This book is also available on the World Wide Web as an eBook.
Visit www.abc-clio.com for details.

ABC-CLIO, LLC
130 Cremona Drive, P.O. Box 1911
Santa Barbara, California 93116-1911

This book is printed on acid-free paper ∞

Manufactured in the United States of America

To Mom and Dad

CONTENTS

CULTURES IN THE AMERICAN WEST

SERIES INTRODUCTION

Scott C. Zeman, Series Editor

In my classes on the history of the American West at the New Mexico Institute of Mining and Technology, we discuss the infamous Rock Springs Massacre of 1885 in which an angry mob killed 28 Chinese workers and forced the rest out of the Wyoming mining town. My students are always a bit surprised when I mention that right here at home in Socorro, New Mexico, at about the same time, nativists denounced Chinese immigrants. The local newspaper declared the "Chinese Must Go!" and in the nearby mining hamlet of Kelly (now a ghost town), an anti-Chinese riot broke out (the mob apparently was enraged by the hiring of a Chinese cook—fortunately, the cook escaped harm and the mob leader was killed by his own men).

During its mining-town heyday in the late 19th century, Socorro boasted a diverse population of Hispanos, Anglos, African Americans, Slavs, as well as Chinese. Today, Socorro is home to New Mexico Tech University, the National Radio Astronomy Observatory, and other affiliated high-tech enterprises. New Mexico Tech's student body includes East Indians, Norwegians, Czechs, Vietnamese, Russians, Kenyans, Colombians, *nuevo mexicanos*, Native Americans, and Anglos. I use this perhaps self-indulgent example because it highlights the multicultural nature and history of the region. It is impossible to imagine Socorro's history—just as it is with the rest of the West—without this simple fact. ABC-CLIO's

Cultures in the American West Series, of which this volume is part, takes the same point of departure: to understand the West—to make sense of it—we must adopt a view that accounts for the incredible variety of its peoples.

The volumes in this series follow the lead of the New Western History, which brought to the forefront of western historiography issues of race, ethnicity, and gender. To use the words of one of the school's foremost historians, Richard White, "The American West is a product of conquest and of the mixing of diverse groups of people. The West began when Europeans sought to conquer various areas of the continent and when people of Indian, European, Asian, and African ancestry began to meet within the territories west of the Missouri that would later be part of the United States. The West did not suddenly emerge; rather, it was gradually created" (*"It's Your Misfortune and None of My Own": A New History of the American West*, 4).

The volumes in the series take on the challenging task of demythologizing the most heavily mythologized region in the United States. In *Gunfighter Nation: The Myth of the Frontier in Twentieth-Century America*, Richard Slotkin's monumental study of the myth of the frontier in modern America, Slotkin argues that "according to this [frontier] myth-historiography, the conquest of the wilderness and the subjugation or displacement of the Native Americans who originally inhabited it have been the means to our achievement of a national identity, a democratic polity, an ever-expanding economy, and a phenomenally dynamic and 'progressive' civilization" (10). And, as Slotkin points out especially, "When history is translated into myth, the complexities of social and historical experiences are simplified and compressed into the action of representative individuals or 'heroes.'" The volumes in this series go far in helping deconstruct such a simplistic view of the history of the West.

Each volume in this series, written by experts in their respective fields, focuses on one of the many groups to call the West home. Volumes include discussions of origins, migrations, community development, and historical change, as well as short biographies. The volumes highlight key issues in the history of the groups, identify important historiographical concerns, and provide useful bibliographies.

Steven Danver of ABC-CLIO deserves the lion's share of the credit for this series. I would also like to thank him for being such a delight to work with. And thanks also to each of the authors of the volumes, without them this series would still be only an idea.

PREFACE

This book tells the story of African Americans in the West. It is a story that begins with slavery but moves toward freedom, and that is a story worth knowing. Perhaps it is the essential story of America itself: the story of getting free. For African Americans in the West, freedom was difficult to get, difficult to hold. But those who fought for it showed a level of courage and tenacity that can be downright inspiring—or at the very least instructive. Theirs was a story of striving, of heartbreak, of moving on and digging in. Theirs was a story of fighting the good fight. And it was a story of cold realities and enduring dreams. This book seeks to tell their story—the whole of it, from the colonial era to the present—in one manageable book, the kind of book that has a little zip in it.

The American West—the "West" explored here—has been two different things. It was, first of all, the western frontier of the United States, which expanded from the East Coast to the West Coast. This national expansion across the continent occurred in waves, and it occurred rapidly—beginning officially with the birth of the United States in 1783 and ending when the U.S. boundaries spanned the Pacific Coast in late 1848. The part of the nation most difficult for Americans to settle was the Great Plains, the dry and windy expanse between the Mississippi River Valley and the Rocky Mountains. Impatient as ever, Americans skipped over the Plains and pushed on to the Pacific. But by 1900, even the Great Plains had been settled by Americans. So the first American West—more a process than a place—actually came to an end; by about 1900, there was no more western frontier.

But another "West" remained. This is the western *region* of America—the left half of the American map. This part of the country developed differently from the rest of the nation. Life was different "out

West." The land itself had a lot to do with that: It is high and dry and ill-suited to the traditional family farm; there are vast distances between sources of water, between forested areas, between the beginning of an open space and the end of it. In this part of America, everything seems bigger and more intense—the sky, the sun, the clouds, the wind. Normal rainfall in the West would be considered a severe drought back East. The Rocky Mountains of the West make the Appalachian Mountains of the East look like hills. The West is a region of extremes, both geographically and po-litically, and it has a history of its own. Everyone knows that the Ameri-can South developed differently than the American North; the American West developed differently than either the North or the South—and that difference is part of the story told within.

An important contribution of this book is that it explores black west-ern history in both of these Wests. It begins by examining slavery on the moving frontier, and the ways in which the frontier ultimately and unexpectedly resulted in the abolition of slavery in America. And it con-tinues by examining African American life in the western *region*. Both the frontier and region were important for African Americans in the West. Indeed, as this book suggests, there is no way to understand the African American experience in the West without taking *both* of these Wests into account. This twofold treatment of African Americans in the West sets this book apart from other surveys of the black West, which focus on either the frontier or the region, without integrating the two.

This book is part of an innovative series designed by the publisher, ABC-CLIO. (Clio, by the way, was a figure in Greek mythology—the Muse of history!) The "Cultures in the American West" series includes books on most of the major social groups in the history of the West: Latinos, Native Americans, women as a group, and more. The books in the series have dif-ferent authors, of course, but all of the authors have agreed to adopt the same basic pattern of organization and chapter development. This is good for readers. It means, for example, that the volume on Hispanics will have a chapter structure similar to this volume on African Americans. So reading them all together will produce a cohesive understanding of these different groups and how their experiences in the West changed over time.

Twenty years ago, this survey on black history in the West could scarcely have been written. Historians had done very little research on blacks in the American West. They had focused on the history of slavery and on the rise of the northern ghettos—and not without good reason, for those critically important topics were in serious need of scholarly attention. In the process, though, historians of the African American experience missed the West, and historians of the West missed the African American experience. Fortunately for both fields of history, that trend has changed dramatically in the past generation. There is now an abundance of excellent historical studies of blacks in the West, and this book has benefited from those studies.

It has been a wonderful experience to do research in this field of history—an intellectual journey filled with unexpected challenges and endless wonders. And it has been a pleasure and privilege to convey that research in this book. To all students, welcome. And enjoy.

ACKNOWLEDGMENTS

I want to thank Steve Danver for inviting me to write this book for ABC-CLIO, for believing I could do it well, and for waiting patiently when I did more thinking than writing. Thanks, too, to James Sherman and everyone else at ABC-CLIO who carried the project to completion, including Christian Green, who oversaw the production of the book, and two very perceptive editors—Kim Kennedy White and Betsy Crist—whose hard work and sharp intelligence I will always appreciate.

Three talented undergraduate history majors at Georgia Tech provided superb research assistance for this study, and I am very grateful for their help. By the time this book is published, all three will have graduated and moved on to bigger and better things. To Stephen Brincks, Kristi Miller, and Leyna Palmer—sincerest thanks. Students like you make teaching worthwhile.

Indeed, I want to thank all of the students I have taught at Georgia Tech during the past decade. They have been smart, hard working, and intellectually curious, and they have made me a better teacher and scholar. Thanks also to Ronald Bayor, chair of my department—the School of History, Technology, and Society—for his support of my research. My colleagues Steven Usselman and Bill Winders have been unwaveringly enthusiastic about this project, and for that I am deeply grateful.

Closer to home, I want to thank my wife, Judith, and my children, Peter and Elizabeth, for all of the joy and love they have brought to my life and for all of the support and encouragement they have shown for this project. This book is dedicated to my parents, Jim and Shirley Flamming, both of whom were born out West. Their lives, it seems to me, have always reflected what is best and most beautiful about the American West.

Douglas Flamming
Georgia Institute of Technology

MAPS

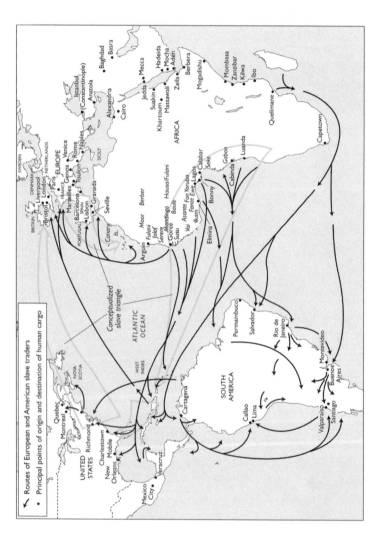

The transatlantic slave trade between Africa and the Americas began around 1520 and lasted for roughly 350 years. During that time, nearly 12 million black Africans were enslaved and shipped to the Americas in chains—a forced migration unparalleled in history. Virtually all western European nations engaged in the trade, and, as this map shows, the slave-trade routes were many and varied, with black Africans being sold into all parts of the Americas.

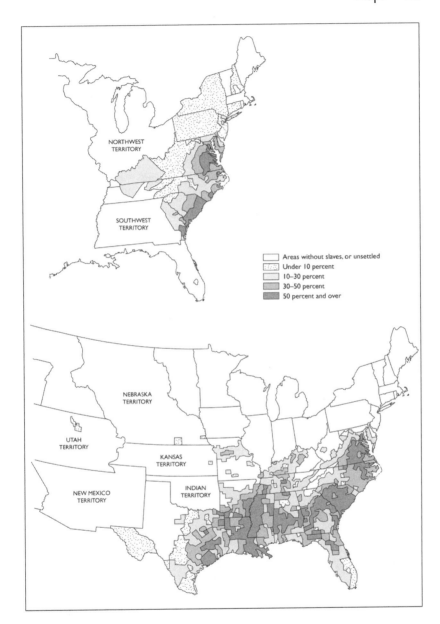

Areas without slaves, or unsettled
Under 10 percent
10–30 percent
30–50 percent
50 percent and over

Slavery and Frontier Expansion, 1790–1860: The map for 1790 (top) shows the concentration of slavery along the East Coast of the United States in the nation's early years. The map for 1860 illustrates the explosive expansion of slavery across the southern frontier. But slavery in America would expand no further, for the sectional conflict over slavery in the territories of the New West would lead to the Civil War between the free labor North and the slave South, a war that resulted in the abolition of slavery in the United States. (Adapted from McPherson, James M. Ordeal by Fire, *vol. 1: New York: Knopf, 1982, 29.)*

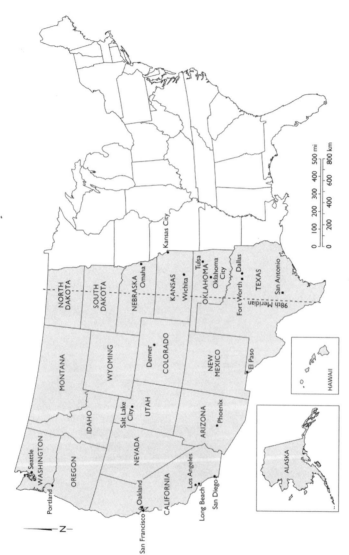

The Western region of the United States begins at roughly the 98th meridian, which is indicated on this map. The divide between the well-watered, heavily timbered East and the dry, open West is not so easily drawn as the line indicates, because the areas of Oklahoma, Kansas, and Nebraska that lay east of the 98th meridian are nonetheless mostly "Western" in climate, landscape, and culture. (Adapted from Taylor, Quintard. In Search of the Racial Frontier: African Americans in the American West, 1528–1990. New York: W.W. Norton, 1998, 20.)

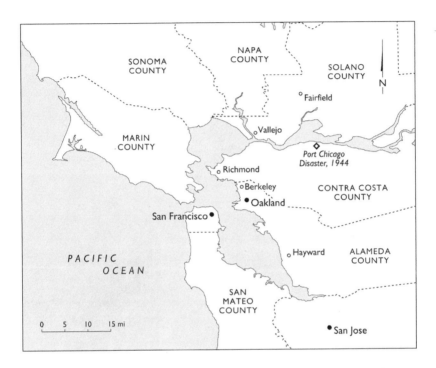

Prior to World War II, the San Francisco Bay area had small black communities in San Francisco, Oakland, and Richmond. Almost overnight, defense plants in the area swelled the size of those African American communities by the tens of thousands. The Kaiser Shipyards in Richmond were especially important in bringing African American workers to the Bay Area. The Port Chicago U.S. Navy munitions disaster of 1944, and the mutiny trials that followed, also occurred in the Bay Area. (Adapted from Gretchen Lemke-Santangelo. "Deindustrialization, Urban Poverty, and African American Community Mobilization in Oakland, 1945–1990s," *in* Seeking El Dorado: African Americans in California. *Seattle: University of Washington Press, 2001, 344.)*

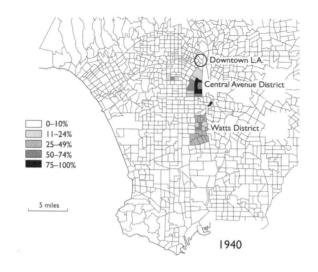

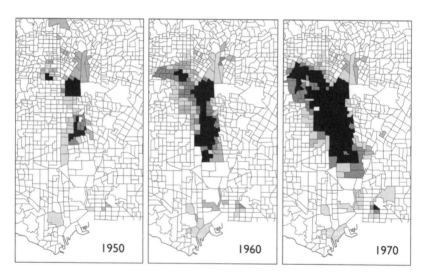

These maps provide snapshots of black neighborhood development in Los Angeles from 1940, right before World War II, to 1970, shortly after the Watts Rebellion. In 1940, most African Americans in Los Angeles lived in racially and ethnically diverse neighborhoods characteristic of western cities; Central Avenue and Watts were still two separate enclaves. The Second Great Migration, coupled with ongoing housing discrimination against African Americans, created the sprawling all-black ghetto of the 1960s. (Adapted from Josh Sides. L.A. City Limits: African American Los Angeles from the Great Depression to the Present. *Berkeley: University of California Press, 2003, 210–213.)*

THE AFRICAN AMERICAN WEST: GETTING STARTED

In September 1781, a group of unlikely settlers—46 of them in all—gathered on a dusty, open plain near a sandy river in *Alta California*, the northwestern province of New Spain. Poor but hopeful, these families had come to establish a pueblo on behalf of the Crown. They had made a long and difficult overland journey up from Mexico to build new lives for themselves. Colonial administrators wanted to create permanent settlements along the California coast, and the new village was part of that plan. The governor of California, Felipe de Neve, had recruited these families with promises of land and livestock. Now the day had finally arrived. Neve held a solemn ceremony, founding the pueblo for God and king and bestowing its official name: Our Lady the Queen of the Angels. A ceremonial cannon shot blasted the silence and then faded into desert hush.

And so Los Angeles was born. The 46 settlers who established Los Angeles were mostly of black-African descent. They were Afro-Spaniards. At least two families, the Quinterros and the Mesas, were considered "Negro," that is, strictly African. The rest were mestizos, with mixed lineages that included African, Indian, and Spanish. That was not so uncommon in New Spain, where Spanish women were few in number and Africans and Indians—most of whom were enslaved—far outnumbered the Spanish. Whether the pioneers who founded Los Angeles had been slaves before will probably never be known. But now, with the creation of Los Angeles in September 1781, they were free.

Six weeks later, all the way across the continent, another solemn ceremony took place: the surrender of the British Army to George Washington at Yorktown, Virginia. This stunning American victory effectively secured the independence of the United States—the independence that had been declared in 1776. The victory at Yorktown led to the 1783 Treaty of Paris. That peace treaty did more than recognize the independence of Great Britain's 13 colonies; it also gave the United States all English lands extending to the Mississippi River. Thus, the United States was born on the Atlantic but inherited a huge western frontier. By the time the ink was dry on the treaty, tens of thousands of Americans were already pushing beyond the Appalachian Mountains, locating their future toward the setting sun.

Many of these white Americans, however, saw black slavery as the foundation of their own liberty. In this view, whites could be free only if blacks were permanently entrapped at the bottom of society. That way, the poor whites would not always be in conflict with rich whites; there would be no class war among whites. The wealthy planters had Africans to do their labor, and the ordinary whites had an open chance to get ahead in the new republic, which allowed no hereditary titles and gave basic rights to even poor whites. But this was not the only view held by white people in the new nation. Others held that slavery was incompatible with the ideals upon which the United States was founded—equality at birth and the inalienable rights of life, liberty, and the pursuit of happiness. Looking west from Yorktown and other places along the Atlantic Coast, an immediate question was this: Would slavery be allowed to expand into the newly gained territories that lay west of the Appalachians?

These two opening stories—the founding of Los Angeles on the Pacific Coast and the founding of the United States on the Atlantic Coast—may seem like an odd pairing. But in fact they provide a fitting starting point for this book on African Americans in the West. The American West was, first of all, a frontier. The United States expanded from the East Coast to the Pacific, and its early history was bound up in the moving frontier. By 1850, however, the continent had been won, and Los Angeles had become part of the United States. But as the United States was expanding rapidly across the continent, a curious thing happened about halfway across: Americans ran into the Great Plains, where the climate and the land changed dramatically. From the Great Plains all the way to the Pacific, the environment was so vastly different from that in the American East that this western half of the continent developed differently. This

West became a distinctive section of the United States, a separate region within the nation—like the North and the South.

Both of these Wests—the frontier and the region—were critical to the historical experience of African Americans. The revolution had weakened slavery in America, because it highlighted the contradiction between America's demand for "liberty" and its reliance on slave labor. But the trans-Appalachian frontier revived slavery and made it stronger than ever. The frontier expanded the geographical area in which slavery existed, and it gave slaveholders greater power within the national government. This early frontier, then, was disastrous for African Americans.

But as frontier expansion continued to the Pacific, it brought challenges to slavery's further spread. Northerners began to fear that southern planters would take over the new western lands and block the opportunities for "free labor" there. In addition, the West beyond the 98th meridian—the arid West—was poorly suited to plantation agriculture, which contributed to the desperation of white southerners to open all of the West to slavery. Conflict between North and South over slavery's expansion to the West sparked the Civil War, which of course led to the demise of slavery in the United States. So although the early American frontier was a place of despair for African Americans, the great western region that lay beyond eventually became a symbol of emancipation and hope.

This book examines both of these black western experiences: the frontier of despair and the West of hope. As part of ABC-CLIO's book series on the multicultural West, it explores the meaning of the West for African Americans and how that meaning changed over time. It will follow the waves of black migration into the West—both forced and free—and will seek to untangle western myths from western realities. This introductory chapter defines the West(s), discusses the origins of African Americans, explains why the topic of black western history is important, and outlines how this book has been organized.

DEFINING THE WEST

Viewed from Yorktown, the history of the American West looks rather different than it does from the vantage point of Los Angeles. From Yorktown, the nation's story moves away into the distance, westward toward conquest. From Los Angeles, the United States seems at first a distant place, too far east to matter much—until it arrives and takes over the story. But definitions of the West are more complicated than even these two views suggest. What follow are brief discussions of four different ways to define the West: the West as an American frontier movement; the West as an American region; the west (lower case "w") as distinctive part of the world—the "western world"; and the West as an American ideal.

1. *The West as a Frontier*

Because the United States originated on the East Coast and expanded westward to the Pacific—a mostly undeveloped, not to say uninhabited, continent—America's frontier lay always to the west. The expanding frontier *was* "the West." When virtually all Americans lived east of the Appalachian Mountains, "the West" lay just beyond the next ridge. When Daniel Boone led pioneers through the Cumberland Gap into Tennessee and Kentucky, he was leading them into the West. And the Americans came; by the hundreds of thousands they poured into the trans-Appalachian frontier. Whites bought up the land, black slaves came in chains, and Indians found themselves surrounded and pushed off their homeland.

Newcomers filled the new West, confronted native tribes, established towns, and eventually turned the western frontier into a settled part of America. As the white pioneers saw it, they had replaced "savagery" with "civilization." By the time they had done so, the hunters and trappers and explorers among them had pushed even farther west, into the next frontier, into the next West, where new land and new Indians awaited. Before long, the explorers would be hired as guides by Americans seeking new opportunities on the frontier: drovers would come, then farmers, then town builders. Then the process would once again repeat itself: The line of frontier settlement moving ever-westward toward the Mississippi and ultimately beyond it.

The most famous American historian ever—Frederick Jackson Turner—saw this frontier process as the key to understanding the history of America. The essay that made him famous was published more than a century ago, but historians today (especially historians of the West) are still discussing it and debating it. "The Significance of the Frontier in American History," an article first presented in 1893, argued that the nation's frontier experience made it distinctively different from other nations. The

United States was not simply Europe transplanted in a new place. The people and institutions of Europe had been becoming less European and more "American" from their first forays into the western frontier.

With every new push into the western frontier, Turner believed, the forces of "civilization" confronted the realities of "savagery" and had no choice but to deal with it. (Yes, Turner used those very terms, and though they caused no stir among readers for many decades, they have been roundly criticized in the past half century as an indication of Turner's ethnocentric view of the world.) Coping with the dangers and uncertainties of both nature and Indians, Americans on the frontier were forced to adapt their traditional ways of thinking and behaving to their new environment. In order to survive, the people of the frontier had to become more self-reliant, more pragmatic, more democratic, more violent. Turner saw these character traits as the defining features of the American character, and they were, he insisted, a product of the frontier experience.

It is not necessary here to dwell on Turner's thesis, which has been critiqued and prodded from every angle imaginable. But it is important to know that his provocative argument and the endless debate it created has long influenced the way historians thought of "the West." From this perspective the West was not a single place, not a definable region. The West was the frontier, gradually, sometimes explosively, moving across the continent. When historians write about the West as a "process," that is what they mean: the West as the frontier process.

2. THE WEST AS A SPECIFIC REGION WITHIN THE UNITED STATES

Today, this way of thinking about the West is perhaps more familiar to readers than is the "frontier" West. Students today also need to know that the word "region" is a rather recent term, historically speaking. From the nation's beginnings through much of the 20th century, Americans used the term "section" as they now use the word "region." Throughout the 19th century, leading up to and following the Civil War, the word "section" usually carried political connotations—often antagonistic connotations. White southerners, for example, spoke of any legislation that targeted slavery (or later, Jim Crow) as "sectional legislation," that is, legislation that threatened the racial order of the southern section. Thus, there was a Northern section and a Southern section—and, it followed, a Western section.

One of the first historians to emphasize the importance of the West as a section was, ironically enough, Frederick Jackson Turner himself. One of his main points in "The Significance of the Frontier in American History" was to point out that the frontier era had in fact closed. The frontier had made the United States what it was, he wrote. What now would America become, he asked, in its post-frontier phase? He offered a preliminary answer in one of his last major essays, "The Significance of Section in American History," first presented in the late 1910s and published in the 1920s.

In "Significance of Section," Turner declared that three distinctive sections had developed in the United States: the North, the South, and the West. Yes, he admitted, the moving frontier had shaped America and created an enduring East-West divide, but, as it happened, the trans-Appalachian frontier had created not one "West" but rather conflicting frontiers—North and South. In the Old Northwest, the frontier process had created an expanding version of the Northeast—in effect a larger North. In the Old Southwest, the frontier process had created an expanding version of the South Atlantic—in effect a larger South. The frontier kept moving westward to the Pacific of course, and the Civil War should be seen as a dispute over which section (North or South) would win the vast new West. After the Civil War, the West as a section assumed its form, as rapid settlement erased the final lines of frontier settlement.

But time and place mattered, Turner emphasized. All sections of the United States had a frontier, but the particular circumstances of the frontier's final expansion made the western section qualitatively different from either the North or the South. The West had its own peculiar history, its own economic and political interests, as did the other two sections. There were overlapping interests and outlooks, to be sure, but what struck Turner was the distinctiveness of the three. Indeed, instead of highlighting American distinctiveness (as he had in his "Significance of the Frontier" essay), Turner now suggested that the United States had come to resemble Europe—with its continental ties and diverse cultures. He hoped America could operate like a League of Nations, in which North, South, and West would each respect the needs and interests of the other sections as they collectively developed appropriate economic policies for each region.

Turner was not replacing "frontier" with "section" as the driving force in American history. Rather, he saw them as two key stages in American development. He still believed the frontier had played a vital role in the making of America, but the frontier ran out of room, and the dynamics of expansion gave way to the dynamics of growth in the nation's three major sections. This, he argued, was the second great stage in national development.

If "the West" came to be a distinctive region within the nation, one obvious question is "Where did the West begin?" Did it begin at the Mississippi River? At the Missouri River? At the Rocky Mountains? Turner himself did not answer this question, but countless historians have tried. The most influential was Walter Prescott Webb, a child of the High Plains who located the West geographically and environmentally. His classic treatment was his 1931 book, *The Great Plains*, which offered a sophisticated and at times spirited analysis placing the transition point from East to West at the 98th meridian (that is, on any basic map, the longitudinal line corresponding to 98 degrees).

Beyond the 98th meridian, Webb showed, everything that eastern frontierspeople had become accustomed to simply disappeared from the land. The Eastern frontier was a well-timbered land, one seemingly endless forest; there was wood aplenty for building homes and barns, for building fires, and for constructing the myriad tools and implements needed on a farm. On this trans-Appalachian frontier there was plenty of water, too. This was a spring-fed country, with big rivers for transportation and trade and plenty of rain for crops and stock animals, for cooking, for washing, for drinking— enough water for anything! Then, about 400 miles west of the Mississippi, the people of the frontier came out of the woods and into the open. The trees thinned out, then essentially vanished from the land. The land rose; a hot wind blew without ceasing. The rain stopped.

By the time Americans reached the 98th meridian, the key fact of life was aridity—the lack of sufficient water for crops, for animals, for humans. In effect, the frontier process hit a wall it could not get around. The High Plains, or "Great American Desert" as early American maps called it, stretched for hundreds of miles westward, ending in real deserts or inhospitable mountains. Moreover, the Plains Indian tribes, having adopted the horse, roamed the High Plains as nomads, and, unlike most of the

Indian tribes back East, they proved an immovable barrier to American expansion.

Americans did push onward into the Far West, of course, but they went *across* the high plains with no intention of stopping. The Oregon Trail took thousands of families to the rich farming valleys of the far northwest. The California Trail, which cut off from the Oregon Trail, took hordes of gold prospectors to California. The Colorado gold rush of 1859 required miners to make a desperate trek across the full length of Kansas, and then eastern Colorado to boot, hundreds of miles of dust— not to mention direct competition with Plains Indians over very limited sources of wood and water. In effect, as Walter Prescott Webb pointed out, the frontier leapfrogged across the high plains to the Far West, leaving the interior West largely unsettled until the late 19th century—when the Industrial Revolution and the Indian Wars finally made it possible, or at least plausible, for Americans to settle the area.

The arid West, the West that begins at roughly the 98th meridian, is the West most historians ascribe to now. A recent survey of western historians showed that most agreed that the West "begins" with the high plains, that is, the 98th meridian. Environmental historians of the region, most forcefully Donald Worster, have emphasized the ongoing power of nature—of aridity—over human development, Industrial Revolution or no. Only a tiny nook of the region in the far Northwest—the Seattle and Portland area—gets more than 20 inches of precipitation per year, the amount of rain needed to raise basic farm crops without irrigation. What's more, the spring runoff from snowfall in the Rocky Mountains can't make up for the lack of rain; western rivers struggle to retain water as they wind through the high, dry plains and plateaus that bracket the mountains. Los Angeles is located on a river that has no chance of providing enough water for even a modestly sized city. For nearly a century, Los Angeles has acquired city water via sprawling aqueducts connected to rivers hundreds of miles distant. The issue of western water was there in the beginning, and it is with us still. More than any other factor, aridity has shaped the western region.

In this book, the West is defined first as a frontier and later as a region. This follows Turner's lead in defining region: the early frontier *was* indeed the American West, but once the frontier process had ended, the

West—the nation west of the 98th meridian—became a *section* in its own right. The ideas of "process" and "region" are not incompatible. Indeed, for understanding African American history, and especially African Americans and the West, this approach is absolutely necessary, as the chapters in this book aim to demonstrate.

3. THE "WESTERN WORLD"

At some point, almost all high school or college students take a course called "Western Civilization." These classes in "Western Civ" focus on the rise and expansion of European civilization and include an obligatory section on the Americas. The "Western world" is a shorthand phrase for the European societies that colonized most of the rest of the world and then served as the fountain of both industrialization and democratic government. It was a world dominated by white peoples, who controlled the labor of colored peoples; it was a world dominated by Christians, who fought among themselves, but who also sought to convert the rest of the world to that religion. People living outside America use the term "the west" (usually, by convention used with lower case "w") in this global sense more than Americans themselves, but everyone is familiar with the term. During the Cold War there were the eastern bloc countries, controlled by the Soviet Union, and the western bloc countries, controlled by the United States; and today, for example, anti-American sentiment among some Arab nations is sometimes put in these terms—as a condemnation of "Western" values.

This "global" use of the term "the west" will not be used much in this book, but it ought to be noted that European imperialism into the Americas had everything to do with the founding of Los Angeles in Spanish California and the Battle of Yorktown on the Atlantic Coast. All of this is connected.

Students sometimes ask, perceptively, why Euro-America was labeled as the "West" instead of "East"? The globe is round, after all, and every place on earth is east or west of someplace else. The answer, to make a long story short, is that the English were the ones who created a system for accurately measuring time and distance at sea, and they weren't shy about making that system the global standard. The key to the system was the calculation of longitude on the globe. For the benefit of those who slept through geography (and shame on you), the thin black lines that run east to west across any map indicate latitude. The lines running north to south on maps are indicators of longitude. Ships at sea could measure their latitude easily, using stars as their guide. Longitude was more difficult to measure—the stars were not much help—but eventually, shortly before the American Revolution, an Englishman discovered the key to the puzzle: distance could be measured by time, or, more precisely, by a special clock called a chronometer.

Longitude lines are called "meridians" and are measured in degrees—a random example being that Green Bay, Wisconsin, happens to be located at 88 degrees west longitude; or at the 88th meridian west. Time of day, distances from place to place, precise locations of things on earth—all of these measurements require longitude. And ground zero for time on earth—the prime meridian—is in London, England, or, to be precise, Greenwich, England, which precisely marks 0 degrees. There tourists may straddle a line on the ground and be living in two days at once! All places west of Greenwich are longitude "west," and the number gets larger the further west one goes. Same thing for anyplace east of Greenwich. East and west go their separate ways until they get halfway round the globe and run into one another at the 180th meridian (just west of Hawaii), which is called the International Date Line. (The standard time of day, just to close out the lesson, runs west from Greenwich and is calculated according to longitude. If it's noon in Greenwich, it's always midnight of that same day at the International Date Line.) The expansion of European powers across the Atlantic Ocean therefore led to the creation of the meridian system and inadvertently to a key definition of America's western region as that part of the nation lying west of the 98th meridian.

4. THE WEST AS AN IDEAL

"Eastward I go only by force," Thoreau wrote, "westward I go free." For African Americans of course, it was the other way around, at least until about 1850, when the West *did* become a place in which blacks could go free. And when that happened, African Americans began to see the possibilities for greater equality in the West. It was an idea deeply rooted in America's national culture. True, the West has been a moving frontier and it has been a distinctive region, but the West has also been an idea—a very big and powerful idea. First for Europeans and later for free Americans, the West represented unprecedented opportunity. Opportunity for what? For land, for a fresh start, for freedom from constraint, for gold and quick riches, for adventure, for a better life. Whether the western frontier lay just beyond the Appalachians, or whether there was no more frontier to conquer, the very idea that there was a "West" packed a powerful punch. The West became a place of dreams—a real place on earth where dreams might be chased down.

This idea was not held only by white Americans. As will be seen in the chapters that follow, African Americans eventually came to believe the region held singular promise for a better life. They gave voice to what I call the *Western Ideal*—the notion that the West offered the best chance for racial equality in the United States. When whites cheered about western equality, they almost invariably meant equality of opportunity among white people, but black westerners always emphasized equality of opportunity for African Americans, too. They sometimes emphasized their *American* selves to distinguish between themselves and the other racial and ethnic groups of the West—those that could be viewed as less American: Native American Indians, ethnic Mexicans, and Asian immigrants. Those groups, of course, had their own notions about the West, notions explored in the other volumes of this series.

The West was more than a frontier process or a place on the map. It was more than merely a unique section of the nation. It was also a powerful idea that, for 200 years, gripped the hearts and minds of Americans in a way that few other ideas ever would. In the beginning, blacks did not embrace this idea—and for good reason. By the late 19th century, however, they claimed the idea of western freedom as strongly as did any group in America, precisely because they had known the opposite of freedom in the most literal sense. African American interest in the West must be understood in this context.

WHY STUDY THE WEST?

The story of the American West is a ripping good tale. If nothing else, Western history is dramatic. The same can be said of African American history. Both offer historical episodes of unending fascination. So, when these two fields of history are brought together, the result is a story of

America's past that is filled with excitement, turmoil, opportunity, tragedy, and hope. Good stuff. Interesting reading.

There is more than entertainment to be had here, however. Studying history "for history's sake"—for the simple enjoyment of it—is a worthwhile use of anyone's time, but history also has a larger purpose. The history of African Americans in the West is *important*. Important? How? The answer is that history, generally, gives people a better sense of who they are as a people and a nation. Indeed, it is impossible to understand America and one's own place in it without first knowing how America got where it is today. And knowing *that* requires a serious evaluation of our nation's history. The payoff of historical study is a clearer perspective of the here and now—and that is no small payoff.

It is useful to note that the central themes for both African American history and Western history are basically the same: hope, opportunity, freedom. What did people hope for, and how could they fulfill those hopes? Where and how could Americans find new opportunities to fulfill their dreams? What did "freedom" mean, and how could one live free? And then, too, both fields of study confront the more difficult questions of the American past: Why were some Americans freer than others? Who had the power to grant or deny freedom? What happened when opportunities faded, when freedoms were taken away, when hope died? What did race have to do with it?

These important questions form the core not just of Western history and African American history; in a larger sense, they are the very heart of American history itself. The point here is that the history of African Americans in the West can be more than interesting. It can also have a significant influence on the way all of us think about life. It can shed light on how the past has given shape to the present, and perhaps it can help Americans to know where the nation can and should go from here.

AMERICANS OF AFRICAN DESCENT

A multicultural history of the West rests on a foundation of basic assumptions: (1) that there *were* identifiable racial and ethnic groups in western history, (2) that those groups persisted as groups because of external pressures and internal ties, (3) that those groups experienced the West in different ways, and (4) that those groups influenced western history even as they were shaped by it. All of these assumptions stand up to analytical scrutiny. They are accurate. Our tendency as Americans is to view freedom and opportunity as individual matters, and that view is not entirely wrong, but American history (including the western branch of it) has hinged largely on group identity and group law.

Three brief examples illustrate the point. First, only blacks could be made slaves. Not all African Americans were slaves, and not all nonblacks were fully free, but only African Americans were defined as chattel slaves. Second, when the U.S. Army forced the Cherokee to leave their ancestral land in Georgia in the late 1830s, the soldiers did not use a screening process to determine which Cherokees might be worthy of staying and which would have to go. No, the Cherokee were forced off their land as a group—and, not incidentally, were forced off by another identifiable sociopolitical group, namely, the white Americans who wanted Cherokee land and were powerful enough to take it. Third, until 1920, women in most states did not have the right to vote. Group identity, not individual liberty, dictated that policy. It might be worth noting here that women in most Western states—unlike their counterparts back East—were granted suffrage long before the 1920s. Either way, laws governing woman suffrage were group laws.

Until quite recently, group law in the United States abused the individual and collective rights of African Americans, and the story of blacks in the West is in large part a story about African Americans seeking to get free from bondage and second-class citizenship. But the question of group law raises questions about how and why particular individuals were categorized as part of certain groups. To put the question more simply: Just who were African Americans? That answer begins with the Atlantic slave trade.

Between roughly 1520 and 1870, three and a half centuries in which Europe's maritime nations ruled most of the world, nearly 12 million black Africans were captured, sold, and shipped in chains to the Americas. Between 9 and 10 million of those slaves were purchased upon arrival in the ports of South America, Central America, the Caribbean islands, and North America. Two facts follow. The first is that the infamous Middle Passage voyage from Africa to the Americas claimed the lives of 2 million Africans. The second is that the lands of the New World gained a huge population of people from sub-Saharan Africa. The many millions of people throughout the Americas who can claim "black" or "colored" ancestry are, at least in part, the descendents of these slaves.

Portugal, a small but strong naval power in the 16th century, created the African slave trade to the Americas not long after Columbus's famous voyage, and their principal destination would be the Portuguese colony of Brazil. Indeed, nearly 40 percent of all slaves sold in the Americas were sold to sugarcane planters in Brazil. The slave trade proved so profitable that other European powers wanted access. Spain, Portugal's primary maritime rival, eventually shouldered its way into the trade and eventually came to dominate it. In later centuries, the Dutch got a foothold; England and France both had their heydays in the trade.

England's 13 colonies on the North American mainland—those that would eventually become the United States—were established rather late in the process. Its first mainland colony (Virginia) was not founded until 1607, nearly a century after the African slave trade began, and its last (Georgia) was established more than a century later. Virginians purchased the first Africans sold in these colonies, when a small number of slaves were hauled into Jamestown in 1619. By the mid-17th century, black slavery had become a firmly established fact of life and law in the English colonies. The founder of the Georgia colony actually banned slavery at the start, but plantation-minded settlers soon gained control and jettisoned that idea; slavery quickly took hold there, as it had in all of the colonies.

From the beginnings of slavery in the Virginia colony until the United States legally closed the African trade in 1808, an estimated 645,000 slaves were sold in the seaports of the Atlantic Coast. This figure represented between 6 and 7 percent of the number of all slaves sold throughout the Americas during the slave-trading era. Most slaves were shipped directly from Africa, but some had already been "seasoned" in the West Indies. According to shipment records, most Africans purchased in the 13 colonies came from the Congo River region and from the areas northwest of the Congo: the Gold Coast, Windward Coast, and Senegambia. But even such specificity is not much help in identifying homelands, for these are all vast regions within themselves, and the Congo River trade ran deep into the African mainland. Historians continue to find evidence that planters in various parts of the United States favored slaves from select tribes, but the matter remains in dispute, in part because slave cargos were some-times mixed during transport, leaving the embarkation point in dispute, if indeed embarkation points had any connection to the slaves' original homes.

In the broadest sense, the Africans who were enslaved were part of the Bantu-speaking peoples of West Africa and central Africa. The Bantu first emerged along the long elbow-shaped coastline that defines the West Coast of central Africa. In antiquity, the Bantu people settled the lands near the central curve of this coastline, near the present-day nations of Nigeria and Cameroon. In time, the Bantu discovered the arts of agriculture, and their population grew accordingly. Some expanded into the lands that lay west and north, through what is now Liberia and up to present-day Sen-egal. Others spread east and south across the continent—overwhelming, conquering, and/or assimilating most of the other population groups that occupied sub-Saharan Africa. The Bantu were a dark-skinned people with tightly curled black hair and brown eyes, and their demographic expan-sion across Africa did not change these aspects of their general appearance very much.

Nonetheless, the Bantu people—or, more accurately, "peoples"—were far more diverse than the singular Bantu label suggests. By the time the European slavers hit Africa in the mid-16th century, the Bantu had evolved into hundreds of different socioeconomic groups, with different languages and dialects. Their physical features also diverged somewhat. Virtually all had dark eyes and tightly curled black hair; but some groups were generally taller than others, and complexions ranged from medium brown to virtually black. Think of these Bantu peoples as separate "eth-nic" group under the larger umbrella term of "black African"—as Italians and Germans are different ethnic groups under the umbrella term "white European." The Bantu peoples also exhibited variations in their levels of political organization, wealth, and power. Some lived in loosely defined communities, and others were part of identifiable tribal organizations that had greater numbers and resources. Still others were subjects of well-established kingdoms.

Different levels of political organization and historic ethnic animosi-ties among black Africans allowed European slave traders to play the different kingdoms, tribes, and communities against one another in the process of capturing and selling Africans into slavery. For example, a powerful African tribe might work in conjunction with Spanish slave traders to ensnare and market the people of weaker communities or rival tribes. In effect, some African groups worked as bounty hunters for the Europeans, gaining in return a variety of goods and services, including guns, metal tools, and money (in the form of jewels, gold, or other forms of currency)—which further empowered those groups to act as slavers. The tables could be turned, of course. As rival European powers forced their way into the trade, each newcomer found it useful to form alliances with the downtrodden tribes and pit them against the tribes that had been enslaving them, and so the hunters could become the hunted.

For our purposes, the details of this horrific process are less important than the result: slaves brought into the Americas were not merely "African slaves"; they were also an ethnically diverse population that had been violently uprooted and thrown together. Scholars of this diaspora often refer to the mixing of African peoples as a process of "creolization"—a term usually applied to the biological or cultural intermingling of Africans with Indians, or Africans with Europeans, or all three groups. But it is worth emphasizing that "creolization" also involved the intermingling of black Africans with other, quite different, black Africans—to say nothing of the multiple Indian and European groups that Africans mixed with. Africans forced to the shores of the Americas thus became, in effect, the first American melting pot. If the melting pot metaphor assumes a choice—a desire to assimilate into the dominant culture—then it will not do here, but if the metaphor is expanded to include enforced ethnic mixing, then it offers a useful way to remember that Africans with different languages, different customs, and different group affiliations had to find ways to coexist.

So although the history of African people in America would eventually include many "back to Africa" movements, and although many Africanisms continue to thrive in American culture, African Americans never had any single African place to go back to, no single African people to reconnect with, no single African culture to conserve. What's more, European powers carved up and colonized virtually all of Africa after the slave trade was abolished, further obliterating the homeland. The forced melting pot of American slavery and the European conquest of Africa itself made the slaves' African roots more difficult to trace. The African American longing for their homeland would survive, as would many African customs and beliefs, but the painful truth was that the African homeland would remain vaguely defined—more of a heartfelt longing than a realistic promised land. There was no homeland to return to, even if that were possible. That reality lent extra urgency to African American efforts to carve a niche for themselves in American life. Would the West provide such a place?

ABOUT THIS BOOK

A few final words are in order about how this book is arranged and what readers can expect from it. This book is not intended to be encyclopedic; it is an interpretive work that highlights major issues and trends. Not everything in black western history is included here. In each chapter, I have emphasized what I consider to be events of vital importance to an understanding of the African American experience in the West. Because this book covers large swaths of time and space in a single volume, the narrative moves at a rapid clip and sometimes this focus on major trends and events can make readers forget that real people were involved in all of this. To keep the human dimension in the forefront, each chapter begins with a personal story, a little vignette intended to reflect a major thesis in that chapter—a "human interest story" so to speak.

To keep these opening vignettes from feeling scattered and unconnected, each one is about someone moving to Los Angeles, California—from the story of the arrival of the founders that opens this chapter to the arrival of Shaquille O'Neal that opens chapter 9. The choice of Los Angeles was not difficult. By the early 20th century, it had emerged as the center of African American life and politics in the western region, and its influence continued to grow throughout the 20th century. To understand the black West, one has to understand the history of Los Angeles.

The chapters of the book are basically organized chronologically; they move forward through time in linear fashion, and each chapter covers a specific time period—not unlike the periodization one would find today in any basic textbook of U.S. history. Chapters 2 and 3 focus on the 19th century: the frontier of slavery, the rise of freedom in the West, and the development of black communities in the West during the decades following emancipation. Most of the remaining book, chapters 4 though 9, focuses squarely on the western region and carries the story of the black West through the 20th century. The final chapter discusses the historiography of African Americans in the West—that is, how historians have studied the topic and how that has changed over time—and closes with a brief suggestion about where the field of black western history is headed and what critical issues are currently facing African Americans in the region.

A note on some terms used within. In the English colonies and in America through the Civil War, black Americans generally referred to themselves as Africans, or Negroes, or colored. After the Civil War ended in 1865 and up until the civil rights movement peaked a century later, blacks used many names for themselves and used them interchangeably: Negro, colored, black, Afro-American, and "the Race," being the foremost among them. I use all of these terms interchangeably in this book, either as the historical context dictates or just to prevent repetition in the prose.

Blacks sometimes debated which term offered the best and most accurate appellation for themselves, but there was no consensus. With the sudden rise of the Black Power movement after 1965, young people denounced the term "Negro" as being old and conservative and insisted that "Black," usually with an upper case "B," was the only proper term, and it was used in political catch phrases of the day, such as "Black Is Beautiful." Later, the terms "Afro-American" and "African American" gradually came into use. They had been around a long time but seemed new at the time. Although one seldom hears them anymore, the terms probably used most often historically among blacks themselves have been "the Race" or "our people"—terms that denoted a powerful group identity and a shared past—as well as shared hopes for the future.

At the end of each chapter, there is a brief section that lists the basic history books I have relied upon for that chapter. I have deemed it important to keep these little historiographical essays as brief as possible and limited the lists almost exclusively to readily available books or to essays published in readily available books. For those interested in further study or research, these books should be sitting on the shelves of most college libraries or can be ordered easily enough through the library's interlibrary loan system. Many of the books listed in these sections are in fact available online—as electronic books on your library system or as inexpensive paperbacks available through amazon.com and other Internet booksellers. The aim has been to highlight the basic books that have not only been helpful to me in writing this book but also those that should be easily available to interested students. All of the books cited within the text or in the sources sections at the end of each chapter are given full citations in the Selected Bibliography at the end of this book.

Enough for introductory remarks. On to the story itself! Our story begins with a slave named Hannah, living on an ordinary cotton plantation in South Carolina in the antebellum era. The West will soon change her life dramatically: first for the worse, then for the better.

Chapter Two

FRONTIERS OF SLAVERY AND FREEDOM, 1815–1865

In 1846, a young woman named Hannah and her husband, Frank, were living with their children on a plantation in South Carolina. Although they were a family, they had no control over whether they could stay together. They were American slaves, and slaves had no legal right to marriage or family, no right to stay or go as they pleased. That reality forced Hannah and Frank apart in 1846, when their master died. A legal dispute over the estate ensued, and, as a result, the entire estate was put on the auction block. Frank was sold to one buyer; Hannah and her children to another.

Hannah and her children were sold into the West, to the cotton frontier of Mississippi. For African Americans in slavery, this was what "the West" meant before 1850. It meant families torn apart. It meant forced removal. It meant being "sold down the river." For black Americans, the first American frontiers did not mean freedom and opportunity over the next ridge.

Hannah was purchased by Rebecca Smith, the daughter of her former master and a wife and mother in her own right. Years earlier, Rebecca had married Robert Smith, not a very prosperous man, and they had moved west into the cotton frontier. In Mississippi, Robert had failed to gain the kind of wealth he envisioned—indeed he had not even become a landowner—but he did manage to buy a slave, Biddy Mason, who was originally from Georgia. Now, apparently at the request of Rebecca, Robert had purchased Hannah and her children and brought them to Mississippi.

But even as the cotton frontier had ensnared Hannah, the American West was about to expand westward with startling rapidity. The United

States had annexed Texas in 1845, and in 1846 it declared war on Mexico, with an eye toward taking a possession of Mexican lands all the way to the Pacific Ocean. And the United States did just that, winning the Southwest and California. At the same time, the United States officially obtained Oregon Territory from the British—bringing into the Union all of what is now Oregon, Washington, Idaho, and part of Montana and Wyoming. Suddenly, there was a "New West," and it all seemed a very long way from the South.

Hannah had scarcely arrived in Mississippi when the Smith household left Mississippi for this New West. Robert and Rebecca had recently converted to Mormonism, and when the Latter-day Saints decided to establish their new Zion at Salt Lake, the Smiths, along with other Mississippi Saints, decided to go. So, by the end of 1848, Hannah, Biddy Mason, and their children found themselves, along with about two dozen other slaves, in a most unlikely place: Utah.

But, as it turned out, Hannah's adventures in the New West had hardly begun. Soon, she was bound for California. Mormon leaders had decided to establish a colony in the Golden State, and why not: The entire nation, indeed much of the world, was talking California, the gold rush having erupted in 1849. The Mormon colony was not about gold, however, but cattle—and a settlement was targeted for the hilly grazing lands around San Bernardino, a village about 60 miles east of Los Angeles, which was itself still a small town with a Spanish-Mexican feel to it. Robert and Rebecca Smith had volunteered to be part of the San Bernardino colony, and so Hannah, Biddy, and their growing number of children moved from Utah to Southern California.

By the time they arrived, however, California had joined the Union as a free state. When slaveholders brought their slaves there with the intention of living in California, would the slaves remain slaves? The state constitution did not clearly address this point, but free blacks and white abolitionists in California tried to free the slaves who were brought to the state. Most of this antislavery activism occurred in northern California, where the gold rush population boom had brought the issue to the fore. But it was in sleepy Los Angeles that Hannah and Biddy and the Smiths found themselves at the center of a slavery controversy.

It happened this way: Living in Los Angeles was a black family—the Owens family—Robert and Minnie and their children, who had once been slaves in Texas. Robert had managed to purchase his own freedom and then Minnie's; then both worked until they purchased their three children. Once all of the family was freed in 1853, the Owens family left Texas and pushed westward to Los Angeles. Robert Owens may have been an early black cowboy in Texas, for in Los Angeles he established a livery stable and cattle business. His enterprise prospered and grew, and he hired both free blacks and Mexican vaqueros to run it. After the Mormons arrived in San Bernardino, Robert and Minnie Owens got to know Hannah and Biddy—or, if a romantic touch is not out of line, their son, along with another young black cowboy who worked with them, fell in love with two of Hannah and Biddy's daughters.

Whether or not Biddy and the other slaves knew California was a free state, Robert Smith continued to hold the women and their children as slaves near San Bernardino. For a time Smith prospered as a cattle rancher, but in the mid-1850s he had a falling out with the local Mormon leadership, who, in a legal suit, won possession of Smith's land and cattle, leaving him broke and disgruntled. As a result, he decided to leave California and move to Texas. His plan might have been to sell at least some of his slaves in Texas and to use that income to make a new start. When the Owens family got word that the Smiths would soon move to Texas, they acted to stop it.

With the help of sympathetic whites and the county sheriff, the Owens family was able to block the Smiths' departure until the legal status of their slaves could be ascertained. The Smiths and their slaves were camped outside Los Angeles, preparing for their trip to Texas, when Los Angeles County authorities arrived and took Hannah, Biddy, and their children into protective custody. The trial that followed was explosive. The presiding judge was by birth and upbringing a southerner. Indeed, he himself had owned slaves before he moved to California.

But that judge—Benjamin Hayes—sided with Biddy and Hannah. California, he said, was a free state, and no one in California could legally be held in the condition of slavery. Robert Smith, then, did not have the right to make them leave California and go to Texas, where he could claim them as slaves. Hayes ruled that Hannah, Biddy, and their children were, by California law, "forever free."

Hannah's story encapsulates the relationship between African American slaves and the expanding American frontier in the antebellum era. In the beginning, the western frontier was a place of bondage and despair for blacks, a place that divided slave families and infused new life into the slave system. It was a frontier of white opportunity and black bondage. The expanding frontier seemed to be striding westward hand-in-hand with the southern slave system. But the frontier did not stop at the Mississippi River, and when California entered the Union as a free state in 1850, the West took on a different meaning for African Americans. For African American slaves in the early 19th century, the western frontier stood for slavery, but by 1850, black Americans—slave and free alike—saw the new western lands in a different light. This West might bring what they so desperately needed and wanted: Freedom.

SLAVERY ON THE EARLY FRONTIER

Even as American revolutionaries began their War for Independence in the mid-1770s, a few hundred American pioneers had already pushed west of the Appalachian Mountains—in what would soon become Kentucky and Tennessee. The western population increased after the war, and by the time the Constitution had been ratified in 1789, Kentucky and Tennessee had a combined population of more than 100,000. But that was nothing. By 1810, Tennessee alone boasted a population of more than 250,000. Such eye-popping migration marked the rise of the trans-Appalachian frontier, a pioneering process that would continue, in waves of varying magnitude, through the antebellum era.

It was significant that both Kentucky and Tennessee were slaveholding areas, because that meant slavery and the American frontier experience were closely related from the start. White settlers were primarily concerned about getting land of their own and protecting themselves from the Indians who resisted white intrusion. Few questioned the legitimacy of slavery. The most famous American frontiersman of the era, Daniel Boone, known for his rugged individualism, bought as many as 10 black slaves to work the Boone family farm in frontier Missouri.

There were white opponents of slavery, to be sure. The American Revolution itself had called the morality of slavery into question because the natural rights ideals that propelled the revolution insisted that all people were born equally free and independent; the English repeatedly reminded their rebellious colonists about their hypocrisy on this point. The Northwest Ordinance of 1787 forbade slavery in lands north of the Ohio River, extending to the nation's western border, the Mississippi River. Still, whites on the frontier voiced little concern about the morality of slavery, whether or not they participated in it. From their point of view, there were more pressing issues, including the availability and price of land, Indian attacks, and the presence of English, French, and Spanish interlopers, who had their own eyes on American lands and who saw advantages to making alliances with Indians to keep American settlers out.

Events in the 1810s dramatically changed the relationship between slavery and the American frontier. The United States' victory over Great Britain in the War of 1812–1815 effectively ended England's attempts to thwart American expansion westward. In Europe, Napoleon's demise signaled the end of any French power plays in the Mississippi River backcountry. Spain also left the North American continent, surrendering Florida to the United States in 1819 and granting independence to Mexico in 1821. Thus, American Indians lost all of their European allies and any real hope of resisting white-American expansion between the Appalachian Mountains and the Mississippi River. Before the decade ended, eastern Indians had lost huge tracts of land. In poured the Americans.

There were two sections of this trans-Appalachian frontier. North of the Ohio River was the Northwest (what historians call the Old Northwest)—primarily Ohio, Indiana, and Illinois. Slavery was not allowed here. South of the Ohio River were the slave states and territories: Tennessee and Kentucky, of course, and what would eventually become the states of Florida, Alabama, Mississippi, Louisiana, and Arkansas. In the frontier period, this region was called the "Southwest" (what historians call the Old Southwest), although later in the antebellum period everyone simply called it "the South."

The population of this Old Southwest exploded after 1815 and included white pioneers and black slaves. Alabama offers the most extreme example. In 1810, about 9,000 people lived there; by 1830, the population of Alabama had topped 300,000. During the same period, Mississippi's population grew from 30,000 to 130,000. In Tennessee, a more established state, the population boom was no less intense—from 262,000 in 1810 to more than 680,000 in 1830.

The creation and rapid adoption of the cotton gin in the 1810s played an important role in the expansion of the slave frontier. The cotton gin made it possible for slave owners to produce a profitable commercial crop in the interior lands of the Old Southwest. That crop was short-staple cotton. The cotton plant produces its fibers—the cotton ball that puffs out of the pod—with seeds still stuck in the fibers. Before those fibers can be woven into yarn, the seeds must be removed. Removing seeds from short-staple cotton by hand was far too difficult and time consuming for cotton to be a profitable commercial crop. There *was* a brand of cotton, called "long-staple," from which seeds could be easily extracted, but it could grow in very few environments—such as Georgia's Sea Islands. The cotton gin—a simple, relatively inexpensive machine—could quickly strip the seeds from the fiber of short-staple cotton. And short-staple cotton, it turned out, was perfectly suited to much of the interior South. The cotton gin, coupled with newly available lands and ambitious slaveholders, rapidly pushed American slaves into the southwestern frontier.

Slaves were forced westward in two basic ways. One way was for an eastern planter to move to the frontier and take his slaves in tow. In effect, some slaveholders sold their old plantations and created new ones in the more fertile West—often switching crops, from tobacco to cotton, for instance. Then there was the internal slave trade, in which eastern planters sold slaves to traders, who transported and marketed those slaves in the frontier region. The agricultural fortunes of eastern planters had been waning as their soil eroded and their commodity markets faltered. When the demand for slaves in the West soared after 1815, the price of slaves soared as well, and eastern slaveholders were quick to cash in by selling their slaves for top dollar. Thomas Jefferson, for example, sold nearly 80 slaves to stave off his mounting economic troubles. The movement of slaves westward was so monumental it might well be viewed as a separate stage of the African diaspora in the Americas.

Whether slaves were shipped west by traders or transported there by masters, they were easily spotted. Because movement suggested an opportunity for escape, groups of slaves were chained together in long coffles—in a manner reminiscent of the African slave trade. Some were transported

African American slaves operating one of the first cotton gins in the Carolinas. (Library of Congress)

overland; others on riverboats. Still others were taken from Atlantic sea-ports by ship and then deposited in the west's foremost slave market: New Orleans. The image of slaves being hauled westward in chains became all too common, and many, including a young Abraham Lincoln, found it disturbing. The trade called into question the so-called paternalism of southern planters, who had long defended themselves from critics by saying they treated their slaves as "part of the family." But, as critics pointed out, real family members were not sold to traders during economic down-turns or forced westward in chains.

But the movement was not stopped. Indeed, the frontier plantation system gained another boost in the 1830s, when the remaining lands of the Creek, Cherokee, Choctaw, and Chickasaw fell into the possession of Georgia, Alabama, and Mississippi. This prompted a second surge of migration from the East Coast into the southern interior. In one newly opened county from the Chocktaw Cession of 1830—the Mississippi River county of Bolivar, Mississippi—the white population grew to about

400 by 1850, and the slave population soared to more than 2,100. This frontier explosion included thousands of small farmers (the rugged yeomen families of fact and fiction), but, as the Bolivar County statistics suggest, it also included a core of planters and a huge number of slaves.

To get a sense of how large the movement of slaves really was, it is useful to compare it with the slave trade from Africa to England's 13 colonies. Between 1619 and 1808 (nearly 200 years), the African slave trade brought about a half a million Africans to Britain's mainland colonies and later to the United States. The number of slaves taken into the Old Southwest was far greater. Between 1790 and 1860 (only 70 years), the number of slaves shipped from the East to the West equaled roughly one million—double the number sold into slavery on the East Coast!

The trans-Appalachian frontier saw the rise of two distinctive agrarian sections in the United States. In the Northwest (Ohio, Indiana, and Illinois) slavery had been banned by the Northwest Ordinance. By contrast, slavery dominated life in the Southwest, even for the white yeoman majority that did not own slaves. In the Northwest, agriculture came to be tied to urban growth, as farmers produced foodstuffs for the North's expanding network of towns and cities. In the Southwest, agriculture was not geared toward urban markets; for upcountry yeoman, who owned small farms and no slaves, self-sufficiency was the primary goal, while plantations (large and small) forced their slaves to produce cotton for the textile mills of England and the New England industrial states. In the Northwest, canals and railroad lines aplenty linked rural producers to urban consumers in an expanding, and almost exclusively east to west, web of transportation networks. In Dixie, railroad lines were fewer and less important to agriculture. Rail lines seldom penetrated yeoman areas, and planters did not use them to market their cotton crops, which were floated downriver to be sold in the Southern seaports—New Orleans, Mobile, Charleston—whose fortunes in turn were tied to cotton exports. And so the frontier regions of the North and South reflected the direction of their own section.

Had the West stopped at the Mississippi, these divergent frontier regions might have coexisted for a very long time, for both were prosperous for the white majority and neither frontier was reliant on the other. But what might have occurred cannot be known, for the fact was that the West did not stop at the Mississippi. The Jefferson administration had purchased the massive expanse of French Louisiana in 1803, long before the nation had even begun to settle the trans-Appalachian frontier. In 1820, Missouri became the first state established west of the Mississippi, and only 30 years later, California attained statehood. This relentless expansion of the United States westward across the continent steered North and South inexorably toward Civil War.

THE COMMUNITY IMPULSE

The traditional African American sense of community evolved from African cultural traditions and the peculiarities of American slavery—including slavery on the frontier. Many Africanisms survived the Middle Passage and the plantation system, but, by necessity, they were shaped by the melting pot nature of American slavery and by the parameters of slavery itself. The color-bound structure of bondage in the United States—white owners, black slaves—guaranteed a strong sense of group identity on both sides. Common oppression and everyday life in the slave quarters wrought a collective spirit among those in bondage. And many blacks who escaped slavery continued to feel that connection to "their people"—as evidenced through Harriet Tubman's Underground Railroad, Frederick Douglass's abolitionism, and Mary Ellen Pleasant's support for John Brown's raid.

An aspect of American slavery that contributed to this community ethos was the emphasis placed on slave families—and the development of black community bonds as an extended or substitute family. In part because the United States enforced the law of "chattel slavery" (any children born to a slave became property of the slave's owner) and in part because the Constitution prohibited the importation of slaves after 1808, slave owners encouraged slave women to reproduce as often as possible. Slave-owning men fathered all too many children by slave women, but most children born into slavery were the offspring of black men. Some slave owners encouraged informal marriage among their slaves, and more often, slaves themselves created their own marriage bonds—in both cases, the famous broomstick jump signified the union. So, in its way, American slavery fostered the creation of slave families.

But that said, slave sales obviously ripped black families apart, and this process engendered an ethic that, in effect, made the entire slave community the family of slave children. Owners had no legal obligation to keep slave families together, and the rapid expansion of the cotton frontier made it especially difficult for slave families to remain in a single unit. Thus, the slave family was often broadly defined to include fellow slaves who were not blood relatives. If this type of family-community system had roots in West African traditions, it also stemmed from the cruel soil of a slave system that encouraged black reproduction but regularly put individual slaves up for sale. By choice or necessity, all slaves living in the same place might be said to have been extended families.

Slave community also developed in the slave quarters, apart from white scrutiny. There, slaves created traditions that reflected their own separate culture. Slave religion was a good example. The antebellum South was saturated with evangelical Christianity. Although some masters thought the message of liberation and spiritual freedom a bit too risky for congregants living in bondage, most thought otherwise. Many masters believed they had a Christian duty to save the souls of their slaves, and others simply believed the gospel would help "domesticate" their slaves. Whatever the masters' motivation, slaves heard the Christian message. Some were taken to church by their masters, and many converted. Hannah, who was introduced at the beginning of this chapter, was baptized in South Carolina, in the same Baptist church as her owners. Yet the message slaves heard was not always the message white evangelists intended. And the God slaves worshipped was not quite the same God their owners' worshipped.

The real religion of the slaves was the religion of the slave quarters—out of sight and out of earshot of the masters. Some masters kept an eye on the quarters, in which case slaves would steal away to the woods when they could to worship as they saw fit. Here, in isolation, the African traditions of dance, drumming, song, and praise held sway. Christian beliefs were grafted onto these traditional practices. Special emphasis was placed on the Old Testament, especially the story of the Hebrew slaves' liberation from Egyptian bondage. The field songs, or "Negro spirituals," that slaves sang in the cotton fields contained obvious references to a God of liberation. "Let My People Go!" sang the slaves. "Didn't My Lord Deliver Daniel?" one song asked rhetorically, before asking the follow-up question: "Then Why Not Every Man?" When, after the Civil War, southern freedmen quickly formed their own separate churches and Christian organizations, they were acting upon this longstanding African American tradition of independent worship, as well as their own tradition of a Christian message focused partly on liberation on earth.

One final aspect of slave culture contributed strongly to the tradition of black community: grapevine communication. Over the centuries, slaves in the United States developed a remarkable and mostly secret ability to spread news over vast distances, one black person to another. The grapevine method of delivering and receiving news operated out of sight of whites, and it gave African Americans an important sense of shared identity and interests—of being part of a people. In effect, the grapevine was fast-moving news or gossip. Slaves would go to great lengths (often literally) to pass along the news of the day. This informal information network brought news of the larger world, including the world of sectional politics.

White people sometimes discussed vitally important news within earshot of their house servants or field slaves, apparently thinking they were not smart enough to understand the implications of what was being said, or perhaps assuming there was nothing slaves could do with such information. When this happened, slaves often acted like they were not listening or that they did not care about white folks' business. But peoples from Africa were people with strong oral traditions, and because most slaves in America could not read or write (indeed were not allowed to read or write) listening carefully and recalling conversations were vital aspects of black culture. As the cotton frontier expanded, the grapevine expanded with it—as did the slaves' efforts to sustain a cohesive African American community.

BLACK INDIVIDUALISM

By definition, "community" required collective effort, of course, but slaves and free blacks were also individuals in 19th-century America—which was almost surely the most individualistic society in the world at that time. Not surprisingly, perhaps, some blacks were less interested than others in being part of the black community. Some tried to carve out lives of their own apart from other African Americans. Perhaps the best known was James Beckwourth.

James Beckwourth was born in the final years of the 18th century. Whether he was ever a slave is not so clear, but as a young man he was a free apprentice to a blacksmith in St. Louis. Soon, however, he bolted into the wilds across the Mississippi. Over the years, he was known to be

James Beckwourth, the legendary western explorer. (Courtesy Mercaldo Archives)

an explorer, a trapper, a prospector, and a scout. On occasion he was also a member of an Indian tribe. He was, in short, a classic mountain man in the 19th-century West. And like all mountain men, he was staunchly independent and reluctant to put down roots.

His life was a bundle of contradictions, with the kind of erratic twists and turns that befitted a mountain man. As a young man, he was adopted by the Crow Indians. After distinguishing himself through his ability to fight and slaughter the rival Blackfoot tribe, he was made a chief and married a Crow woman. Not long after that, however, he could be found serving as a scout for the U.S. Army during its efforts to drive the Seminole out of Florida. Like all mountain men of that era, he possessed an almost overpowering sense of independence, self-sufficiency, and a desire to keep moving. After the Florida wars, he went back to the Great Plains, where he operated with the Utes and Shawnees, stealing horses from Mexican dons. Later, he traveled with the famed U.S. explorer John Fremont and aided the U.S. Army during the Mexican War. When gold was discovered in California, he naturally tried his hand at panning.

His main claim to fame in California, however, was the discovery of a passageway through the rugged Sierra Nevada. During the gold rush, overland travelers from the East invariably bumped into the Sierra Nevada—and there was no convenient way through. Travelers were so close, and yet so far. Many people searched for a pass, but it was Beckwourth who discovered it in 1850. He led a wagon train through, and then set up a hotel and supply business to capitalize not on the gold, but on the new route to gold. Always restless, he soon moved on again.

During the Civil War, he seems to have served as a scout for the U.S. Army in its campaigns against Confederates and Indians in the Great Plains region. One of his last public acts was to testify before the United States Congress during the investigation of the Sand Creek Massacre of 1864. The massacre was a brutal and senseless slaughter of defenseless Indians who were supposedly living under the protection of the U.S. government. Beckwourth was no stranger to the slaughter of Indians, but in 1864 he stood before Congress and condemned the massacre and the officer who orchestrated it.

Perhaps because he was black, Beckwourth was mostly left out of the early histories of America's western pioneers. He is no longer forgotten, of course, and has been tramping across the pages of standard history books for some time now—sometimes portrayed as a kind of black pioneering hero, sometimes as a boasting curiosity, sometimes as a bit of both. For the purposes of this discussion, however, he serves as a reminder that, for some African Americans in the West, racial identity and connection to a larger community were matters of only passing interest.

TEXAS AND SLAVERY

In 1821, Mexico won its independence from Spain and abolished slavery. In its sparsely settled province of *Tejas*, however, Mexican officials wanted population growth and agricultural development. Southern slaveholders were willing to settle and develop the rich farmland in East Texas, land and climate suited to cotton, so Americans began to immigrate to Mexican Texas, and before long there were too many for Mexico's comfort. When Mexico officially closed the border to Americans, the southerners kept coming illegally, bringing large numbers of slaves. By the 1830s, the American-Mexicans greatly outnumbered their Mexican neighbors, and,

Slaves picking cotton in East Texas. (Hulton Archive/Getty Images)

along with some Tejanos who were disgruntled with affairs in Mexico City, the Americans soon declared themselves politically independent.

The Mexican leader General Antonio López de Santa Anna decided to crush this rebellion with the stated aim of freeing the slaves in Texas. His large army marched northward to meet the Texans, the main force of which had dug in at the Alamo mission in San Antonio. Santa Anna easily wiped out the Texans, leaving only one man alive—a black slave. Then, while mopping up the remaining rebel forces, Santa Anna let his guard down. He and his army got caught napping, literally, and he was forced to accept independence in return for his life. Officially, neither he nor Mexico recognized an independent Texas, but the Texans in fact controlled their land and proclaimed the birth of the Republic of Texas.

Texas quickly legalized slavery, which became entrenched as the dominant economic force—and still was when Texas became a state in 1845. In many of the rural counties around Houston, slaves constituted more than 50 percent of the population. Whites poured in to the newly opened land, bringing slaves with them—or looking to buy some. It was not all cotton. Rice could be grown along some of the rivers near the Gulf of Mexico, and some slave owners were already using black slaves to round up and control large herds of cattle. But, as elsewhere in the slave South, short-staple cotton was the main crop, and it was raised in most areas of East Texas.

Slavery in Texas was basically restricted to East Texas—in the counties east of the 98th meridian. Actually, there were not many Texans of any race or ethnicity living west of that line. For African Americans, the restriction of settlement in Texas provided slaves with several avenues of escape. None were easy, by any means, but the chances of successfully running away from bondage were considerably better than for slaves in the Deep South. The most dangerous option also offered the least chance of being followed: running straight west into the vast and violently controlled lands of the Plains Indians. One widely spread rumor was that the Indian warriors would adopt blacks into their tribes—seeing in them a kind of antiwhite population and, in any event, as useful allies in their struggle against white settlement. A second option was northward into Indian Territory, which was itself an area of slavery but one that offered unique possibilities for hiding and blending in.

The most obvious escape route was also the best: Mexico (see the sidebar on page 36). Generally, the Mexican government tacitly supported

EL PASO, TEXAS, IN 1859: DID MEXICO MEAN FREEDOM?

In 1859, Albert Deane Richardson, a white American journalist, traveled westward on the recently opened Butterfield Stage Line, which ran across Texas and the nation's newly acquired southwestern lands. After the Civil War his observations were published in a book titled *West of Mississippi: From the Great River to the Great Ocean* (New York: Bliss, 1867).

A passage from that book is quoted here. Richardson is recalling his view of El Paso, the westernmost town in Texas, located on the Rio Grande, with Mexico on the other side. This passage deals directly with racial conditions in the New West. As you read his words, keep in mind how African American views of the West were changing in the 1850s—and why they were changing.

> [El Paso's] four hundred inhabitants [were] chiefly Mexican. Its business men are Americans, but Spanish was the prevailing language. . . . There are only two or three American ladies; and most of the whites keep Mexican mistresses. Slavery is only nominal in western Texas, as [N]egroes could easily cross the Rio Grande into Mexico, where the natives sheltered them. . . . The American residents believed in the inalienable right of the white man to bully the inferior race (Richardson quoted in Green, *900 Miles*, 2 and 117).

runaway communities south of the Rio Grande, believing a populated area south of the border could act as a barrier to further expansion by the Americans. Former slaves developed one community just south of the border near the coast, in Matamoros. Other runaways moved farther into the interior, into the mountains of Mexico, where isolated groups of African Americans, Mexicans, and Plains Indians lived together. Texas slaveholders could and did cross the river to chase runaways, but in doing so they were outside the jurisdiction of their own government and faced resistance from the people of Mexico.

INDIAN TERRITORY AND SLAVERY

The Indian tribes that were forced into Indian Territory brought their own brands of slavery to the edge of the southern landscape. When it was clear that Indians in the South would have to leave their land, federal officials considered places to put them. Indian Territory seemed to be a solution for the government. It lay between the 94th meridian and the 100th meridian—between Arkansas and the High Plains. This transitional zone, as officials called it, would be a safe haven for the Indians. For one thing, Americans would not want the land because their traditional agricultural practices would not really work well on this semiarid land. In particular, the southern planters would not care for it. Then, too, the Plains Indians would not want it either, so they would not be constantly invading this land held predominately by the Five Civilized Tribes.

The Five Civilized Tribes of the Indian Territory had all enslaved blacks before their arrival, and they continued to do so. The four tribes from the Deep South—the Cherokee, Creek, Choctaw, and Chickasaw—had embraced slavery, southern-style, long before they were forced westward. The Cherokee government had strict and detailed slave codes that regulated slave behavior and established regular patrols for enforcement. President Andrew Jackson's removal of the Cherokee from Georgia was so brutal, and the resultant Trail of Tears so horrific, that it is easy to overlook

The Cherokees owned black slaves, who suffered with them on the infamous Trail of Tears, the forced march to Indian Territory, 1838–1839. (Woolaroc Museum, Bartlesville, Oklahoma)

the African American victims among the Cherokee victims. Nearly 200 of the Cherokees who died while on the Trail of Tears were black slaves. Very few individuals in Indian Territory actually owned slaves, and they made up the ruling elite within their own tribes.

The Seminole Indians, the other member of the Five Civilized Tribes, were forced out of Florida in the early 1840s and were the last to arrive in the territory. The Seminoles had a system of slavery that was noticeably different from that of the Cherokees. Spain held Florida until 1819, and from the colonial era onward, runaway slaves from the Carolinas and Georgia had been escaping across the border. In Spanish Florida, the Seminole Indians actually had most of the power, and they welcomed escaped slaves even as they reenslaved them. In a complicated system, Seminole slaves were allowed to live in their own separate communities; theirs was a family-oriented slave community in which no one was at risk for being sold on the market. The Seminole slaves did their own work and managed their own crops, giving an annual tribute payment to their masters, the Seminole. What emerged out of this system was nothing less than a unique racial-ethnic group: the Seminole Maroons. They were not merely black slaves in the traditional southern way, but neither were they Seminole Indians. The Seminole Maroons were unlike any other slave community in the American South. A close and mutually beneficial relationship developed between the Seminole Indians and the Seminole Maroons, and this relationship made it difficult for the U.S. Army to defeat the Seminole-Maroon coalition.

Different as they were, the community of Cherokee slaves and the Seminole Maroons both engaged in mass exodus from Indian Territory. Both were bound for Mexico. The Cherokee slaves had revolted against the Cherokee masters sporadically, but in 1842, a well-planned group escape took place. Bolting the Cherokee area, the fugitives crossed over the Creek and Chickasaw land en route to the Red River, the boundary between the Indian Territory and Texas. The Cherokee band was clearly pushing for Mexico; it was still a very long way from the Red River, but further speculation was moot, for a large detachment of Cherokee troops had been dispatched. These overwhelmed the fugitives, who were forced to return to Cherokee land. One group of Seminole Maroons made a more successful flight to Mexico, eventually establishing towns on both sides of the Rio

Grande. Living at the edges of so many borders had its advantages: Opportunities for gaining freedom were sounding more and more realistic.

THE MEXICAN WAR

The U.S. war with Mexico, which began in 1846, was a land grab under the guise of national protection. More than that, it was a land grab in the interest of the slave South. The official reason for the war was to secure the Texas border from Mexican depredations. The claim was that Mexicans had attacked Americans and spilled blood within the boundaries of Texas. No one with even a casual eye on national politics took that as the real cause of the war—Abraham Lincoln, a young antislavery congressman from Illinois, ridiculed the idea on the House floor—but everyone knew that this war and its outcome would be a gravely serious matter in America. The likely outcome was a massive addition of land to the United States, and that would bring the issue of slavery's westward expansion to a head.

The Wilmot Proviso made that point clear immediately. The war had scarcely been declared when a congressman from Pennsylvania moved that a military appropriations bill for the war include the provision that slavery could not be established in any of the Mexican lands acquired by the United States as a result of the war. Southerners of both major parties—Democrats and Whigs—raged against this Yankee attack on slavery. Northerners of both major parties joined forces to support the proviso. The northern majority in the House pushed it through; the southern bloc in the Senate killed it. Sectional loyalties were ripping apart the old party system.

The war itself lasted only a brief time and led to a massive acquisition of land for the United States. The Treaty of Guadalupe Hidalgo, ratified by the U.S. Senate in 1848, included a basic payout of $15 million to Mexico for its lands, as well as U.S. assumption of the Mexican government's debts to private American citizens. In return, the United States gained all of the present-day states of California, Nevada, and Utah. All but the southern end of present-day Arizona was included (the rest was added a few years later), as was most of present-day New Mexico and portions of Colorado and Wyoming. After the Texas Revolution, Mexico, Texas, and the United States had made overlapping claims to what are now the states of Oklahoma, Kansas, Colorado, and New Mexico.

The Treaty of Guadalupe Hidalgo resolved all of those boundary disputes in the favor of the United States, including establishing the Rio Grande as the southern border of Texas.

But the Mexican lands were not all: In the same year the war began—1846—the United States peacefully gained most of what it wanted from Great Britain in the far Northwest. The newly secured Oregon Territory included the present-day states of Oregon, Washington, and Idaho, along with portions of western Montana and Wyoming. So the land that would become the lower 48 states was all on the books. The United States now truly ran from sea to shining sea—or, to recall the geographical reference points highlighted in the introduction of this book, from Yorktown to Los Angeles.

In the brief time span of three years, Americans witnessed the acquisition of a vast new West. Americans no longer spoke of Mississippi and Alabama as the Southwest, or Indiana and Illinois as the Northwest. Those areas had become more starkly defined—economically, culturally, politically—as the South and the North. Much divided the North from the South, but the essence of their differences boiled down to slavery. So the winning of this new West between 1845 and 1848 had the effect of opening Pandora's box: Would these lands be opened to human bondage?

The discovery of gold in California in 1848 placed the nation on a fast-track toward disunion. Before the war with Mexico was over gold nuggets were found near Sutter's mill, but the secret held for a bit and then was put down as bunk. When the first large chest of gold reached the nation's capital in mid-1849, however, the rush was on. By early fall, forty-niners were pouring into California—by ship and by land, straight across the continent by the long and hazardous Overland Trail. By 1850, California Territory had a larger population than some of the smaller East Coast states. West of the 98th meridian there were, at the outset of 1850, no states at all, save the western half of Texas, which had few Texans living in it. So the status of California, with its gold and its seemingly limitless future, was a pivotal issue.

California gained its statehood—and its status as a free state—by virtue of the famous Compromise of 1850. In its original form, as a true compromise between North and South, the proposal found too few representatives in Congress willing to compromise, so it was voted down.

Ultimately, however, the original all-in-one plan (the so-called "omnibus bill") was parsed into separate bills, each favoring one section or the other, and each also having the support of a unity-first middle group, which supported all of them. Thus, each bill limped into law virtually without compromise from the staunch supporters of the North and South.

Each bill directly related to slavery in the West and their provisions were as follows. California entered the union as a free state. Texas gave up some of the territory it claimed (which went mostly to New Mexico) in return for the U.S. government's taking on the state's debts that were left over from the Republic of Texas era. New Mexico Territory and Utah Territory could become either free or slave at the point they petitioned for statehood. In Washington, D.C., slavery remained legal, but slave trading was abolished. And the South got one of the most powerful federal laws yet: the Fugitive Slave Act. This legislation gave overwhelming power to southern slaveholders to seek and seize runaway slaves in nonslave states and created a situation in which slave runners could apprehend free blacks and claim them as slaves. White northerners who aided runaways, or merely refused to help slave hunters, were subject to arrest.

For the history of African Americans in the West the key provision was adding California to the Union as a free state. This was a significant victory for antislavery forces and the first major setback for the slave power in Congress in more than half a century. The clause banning slave labor in California had been unanimously approved by the state's constitutional convention delegates. Perhaps America's New West would prove less hospitable to slavery than the Old Southwest after all. Perhaps the North was finally willing and able to successfully oppose the spread of slavery in the West.

THE CALIFORNIA GOLD RUSH

In 1847, when San Francisco was on the cusp of becoming an American town, it had a total population of 459—10 of whom were African American. Then, at almost the same time, the United States took over California and gold was discovered. The gold rush of 1849 transformed the nation as a whole, and it marked the beginning of a permanent black community in northern California—the first such community in the New West—in which San Francisco would play the dominant role.

During the gold rush, the African American population grew rapidly, along with the population as a whole. By 1850, black residents in California numbered nearly 1,000. Two years later, the figure reached nearly 2,000, almost all blacks in California then living in the gold rush counties between the Sierra Nevada and the San Francisco Bay. Blacks who arrived in the boom included both free blacks and slaves—divided, in the beginning, about evenly. Most of the free blacks were from northern states, especially New England, although a small number were Caribbean immigrants. Blacks migrants who were enslaved had been brought west by their southern white owners. Slave importations lagged after California came into the Union as a free state in 1850, but they continued nonetheless; indeed, the status of slaves within the free state would become a matter of intense controversy.

Black newcomers settled in the mining camps and in the towns and cities that served the camps. The rumor arose quickly in the gold rush that blacks were lucky in the mines, that they were somehow attuned to finding gold-rich claims. A few early big strikes by black miners apparently fueled this rumor, which spread back east when Frederick Douglass's abolitionist newspaper *The North Star* reported that blacks did indeed have a knack for finding gold and that free men who could go, should go. For blacks, working in association with white miners had its own benefits, namely that they were not likely to be robbed of their claim by other white men. Some slaves in the mines were able to purchase their own freedom and freedom for family enslaved back East. Hundreds of blacks in the California mines earned their freedom this way, collectively spending about $750,000 to buy freedom.

Most African Americans gravitated toward towns and cities, where wages for service work were unusually high—and steady—during the gold rush years. San Francisco was the essential port town, and African Americans could rely on wages from people coming to the mines and leaving the mines. Blacks worked as porters, shoe shiners, draymen, and—in high demand—cooks; they owned many small businesses: laundries, hotels, brothels, barbershops, restaurants, and the like. By the end of the 1850s, the black population of San Francisco had topped 1,000. The state capital of Sacramento, east of San Francisco, had nearly 500 African American residents by then. Marysville and Stockton, trading centers closer to the mines, each had about 100 black residents.

Mary Ellen "Mammy" Pleasant

One of the more influential African Americans in the antebellum West was also one of the most mysterious: Mary Ellen Pleasant of San Francisco, often known simply as "Mammy" Pleasant. She arrived in San Francisco—traveling alone, by ship, with some money—in the midst of the gold rush boom. Perhaps she had been a slave; perhaps not. Perhaps she was from Georgia; perhaps not. No one seemed to know, and Pleasant showed no inclination to clarify. Even her actions in San Francisco were hard to follow. She grew wealthy, but the sources of her wealth remained a matter of speculation, which seems to have been the way she wanted it. Fact and fiction blurred: she was a high-priced cook for a wealthy white man; she opened a string of laundry houses; she ran a boardinghouse hotel, which supplied other services; she was a voodoo priestess; she invested in mining ventures; she lived in a mansion. She did nothing to dispel rumors and may have fostered them to promote the image of herself as a person not to be messed with.

Pleasant believed in equal rights for African Americans and was willing to fight for those rights, but, not surprisingly perhaps, her civil rights activism sometimes became shrouded in mystery. It was claimed that she was involved in John Brown's raid on Harpers Ferry, that she traveled back East and delivered money to finance the rebellion. Later, during the Civil War, it was rumored that Pleasant made large donations to fund the Union Army. Closer to home, she was among a core of black activists who coalesced in San Francisco and Sacramento during the 1850s and 1860s. She financed defense lawyers for blacks—including Archy Lee (see the sidebar on page 48)—and joined other African Americans in petitioning the state legislature to pass civil rights laws.

Almost immediately, the question of black rights became a heated issue in California. Chinese miners, miners from Latin America, and Native American Indians all confronted their barriers to equal opportunity and suffered racial discrimination from white Americans, so issues of race and state law were front and center at almost every turn. Slaves brought to California had an advantage that few other blacks in the United States had: they lived in a place in which free blacks and abolitionist whites were numerous and actively engaged in spreading freedom to those enslaved. On the other hand, free blacks themselves had limited rights—no vote, no right to testify in court—so the range of black rights to be won ranged from basic freedom to complicated matters of citizenship. Setting a precedent that all subsequent generations of black westerners would follow, black Californians organized and fought for freedom and civil rights.

THE SLAVERY CASES AND COLORED CONVENTIONS

Building communities required leadership—a vision of what the free black community of the West should be, along with the will and the skill to make that vision a reality. San Francisco could boast the largest black community in the New West, and early on it developed an impressive group of black leaders, many of whom had migrated from the New England states, where traditions of community involvement and political activism were particularly strong.

There was good reason for blacks to be active in politics and civil rights. Shortly after California entered the Union as a free state in 1850, state legislators passed a number of laws that undercut the rights of African Americans. With these laws, blacks were denied the franchise and were excluded from the public schools. Another law forbade mixed-race marriages. Still another mandated that a black person could not testify against a white person in court or bring charges against a white person. Thus, California's early political leaders ensured that blacks in their state were free but not nearly equal.

Among whites, antislavery sentiment and antiblack racism could go hand in hand. After all, many white men joined the Free Soil Party (and later the Republican Party) in the 1850s in an effort to block the spread of slavery into the western territories. Their political slogan was "Free Soil, Free Labor, Free Men." Some of these Free Soilers opposed slavery on moral principle—all men were created equal and slavery was a sin. But most rank-and-file Free Soilers opposed slavery in the territories for more self-interested reasons. Slave labor would undercut their own economic opportunities.

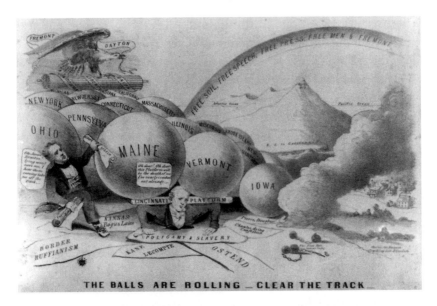

The Republican Party made its first run for the presidency in 1856, issuing this political cartoon that demonstrated their enthusiasm for Free Soil in the West and their disdain for pro-slavery Democrats, such as Buchanan. The Republicans lost in 1856 but elected Lincoln four years later. (Library of Congress)

In California Territory, some whites who supported an antislavery constitution did so in part out of their own calculations of self-interests. In a free state, California's ordinary white miners could not be squeezed out by slave labor. Even white Californians who opposed slavery on moral grounds were not necessarily in favor of equal rights for black residents. Not surprisingly, then, African Americans in California faced racial discrimination from the beginning of statehood. What's more, slave owners did in fact bring slaves to California, begging the question: Were slaves brought to the free state of California still slaves if their owner settled to live there?

During the 1850s, free blacks in northern California sought to free slaves who had been brought into the state, and they sought to obtain first-class citizenship for themselves. In these efforts they were not alone, for northern California had attracted its share of white abolitionists, mostly from New England, who provided essential support for California's anti-slavery and civil rights battles. White allies were essential, for state law effectively barred African Americans from using the court system. Blacks could not bring suit against a white person, serve on juries, or give evidence in court against a white person. The only way blacks could work the legal system was to have white allies fight for them in the courts.

In seeking to free slaves from bondage, this antislavery alliance had some success. California's slavery cases stemmed from two laws the United States Congress passed in 1850, both as essential components of the Compromise of 1850. One of these laws made California a free state. California had officially become a U.S. Territory after the war with Mexico officially ended in 1848. The discovery of gold soon thereafter and the population boom that resulted from it made California's territorial stage remarkably short. The territorial legislature drew up a state constitution in 1849 and applied immediately for statehood. That constitution made California a free state, but it did not answer a critical question: What about slaves already brought into the state (during the gold rush of 1849, for example) and those slaves brought into California after it became a state? Were those slaves now free?

The second legislation of note here—the Fugitive Slave Act—was one answer to that question. Demanded by southerners in Congress, the Fugitive Slave Act gave the federal government unprecedented power to help southern slaveholders recover runaway slaves in the free states of the North. California was covered by this legislation, but the focus of both southern supporters and northern opponents was the North, not the Far West. The law stated that southern slaveholders had the right to enter free states to seek runaway slaves and to take them back to the South—but that was not all. The law also made it a crime for anyone in a free state to assist escaped slaves or to impede their capture and recovery. The law caused a firestorm in the North, but it was soon tested in California as well.

A volatile and fascinating case erupted as early as the spring of 1851. The case involved a slave owner named Calloway who came to pan for gold in 1850, bringing a slave with him—a young man named Frank, who was able to make an escape in early 1851. That spring Calloway finally tracked down Frank and had him incarcerated, possibly until he could take Frank back to the South. But blacks in San Francisco learned that Frank was being held against his will. With legal assistance from antislavery whites, they received an affidavit demanding that Calloway release his slave. In the court case that followed, an antislavery judge ruled that Frank was a free man no longer subject to Calloway. The judge reasoned that the Fugitive Slave Act did *not* apply to Frank because he had not escaped across state lines. Frank escaped once he was *inside* California, so his escape was final.

The state's abolitionists were thrilled at this remarkable decision, but pro-slavery Californians fought back. They gained control of the state legislature in 1852 and passed California's own Fugitive Slave Law, under which Frank would have remained the property of Calloway. Even so, antislavery legislators got one compromise: the law was slated to be reviewed in 1855. When the state legislature met that year, the antislavery legislators had the advantage, and the law was not renewed.

It was in this larger context of state conflict over slavery that Hannah and Biddy Mason won their freedom in Los Angeles. At the time, Los Angeles was a long way from San Francisco and Sacramento in every respect. The 1856 decision to free Biddy and Hannah did not appear to have any link to the antislavery currents operating in northern California, but the timing is worth a second thought. Events happen in time for a reason. By the late 1850s, compromise over human bondage—in the United States and throughout the Western world—was becoming almost impossible.

For its part, the U.S. Supreme Court ended all hint of compromise in 1857, when its pro-slavery majority issued a ruling that fully empowered the South over any and all antislavery opponents. In its infamous *Dred Scott* decision, the court ruled that Scott had no right to sue for his freedom; a black person (even a free black person) could not be a citizen of the United States. But this was not all. Chief Justice Roger B. Taney's written opinion stated that, in accordance with the views of the Founding Fathers, black Americans "had no rights which the white man was bound to respect." And there was more: Congress, Taney wrote, had no constitutional right to ban slavery from any American territory. Potentially, this ruling invalidated the Northwest Ordinance of 1787—and all subsequent restrictions on slavery in the northern states and territories. As a legal triumph for the slave South, the *Dred Scott* decision had no equal, but Dixie's celebration was short lived, for the decision infuriated white northerners and helped to galvanize their opposition against southern planters and all efforts to extend slavery into the West.

The *Dred Scott* decision would have invalidated California's anti-slavery decisions of 1851 and 1856, and one might suppose that it rendered any future cases moot, but black leaders in California and their white abolitionist allies would not give up so easily. In 1858, the issue once again exploded in the California courts in a case involving Archy Lee, a slave brought to California before statehood. After a decade in California, Lee escaped from his owner. After he was captured by his owner,

---

ARCHY LEE AND CALIFORNIA FREEDOM

In 1847, Charles Stovall moved to California and brought his slave, Archy Lee. Stovall opened a school and received income from hiring out Lee. In 1858, Stovall decided to return to the South and to take Lee back with him. Not surrendering to this fate, Lee escaped and hid out in a hotel owned by a free black. Stovall found Lee and had him arrested under the federal Fugitive Slave Act. But Lee had abolitionist supporters—including Mary Ellen Pleasant—in northern California who sought to prevent this. The case went to court, sparking racial tensions and bringing to a head the question of slave status in California. In a way, the Archy Lee case was a replay of the recent Biddy Mason and Hannah Smith case in Los Angeles, but the Lee case went in different directions.

There were actually three separate and conflicting Archy Lee decisions in 1858. In the first, a court in San Francisco ruled in Lee's favor: in California, Lee was free. But Stovall appealed, and the California Supreme Court overturned the previous decision. It ruled that Stovall owned Lee, because the U.S. Supreme Court had upheld Stovall's ownership rights in its recent *Dred Scott* ruling. Lee was therefore forced back into Stovall's custody. That might have sealed it, but Stovall's response was to give Lee a cruel beating. Antislavery forces then had Stovall arrested on charges of assault and the third phase of the trial commenced. This time, the California Supreme Court ruled that Archy Lee was free. Lee's road to freedom, however winding and difficult, added to California's reputation as a free place. More broadly, it enhanced the notion that the West was a place of unique possibilities for African Americans *(Lapp, Archy Lee)*.

the question of his status—slave or free—went to the California Supreme Court. Free blacks and white abolitionists worked hard to win Lee's freedom. After a curious series of court rulings and events, Archy Lee went free, the *Dred Scott* decision notwithstanding.

The black communities of northern California were able to respond quickly in the Archy Lee cases because they had organized "Colored Conventions" in the mid-1850s. These California Colored Conventions were the first significant civil rights organizations established in the American West. For all practical purposes, they were northern California conventions, because the few African Americans in Los Angeles and Southern California generally were not in contact with blacks in the northern part of the state. Most of California's black population in the 1850s was concentrated in San Francisco, Sacramento, and, to a lesser extent, in the gold mining towns of Marysville and Stockton.

The California Colored Convention movement of the mid-1850s marked the first substantial campaign to attain black civil rights in the Far West. Blacks from New England were often in the lead in these conventions, and indeed the issues free blacks faced in California were similar to those they had faced in New England: They could not vote, they could not testify in court, and their children were barred from the schools. Free blacks in New England had organized Colored Conventions to confront these problems, so the calling of conventions in California was a natural extension of that. The conventions were like a New England town meeting. Delegates had the opportunity to voice grievances, debate possible solutions, and (it was hoped) come to some kind of consensus about what to do about the problems facing black California.

The first Colored Convention was held in Sacramento in November 1855. Delegates hailed from most northern California counties (no Southern Californians were involved in these meetings.) A key issue in this first convention, and of the two that followed, was black testimony in courts of law. State law prohibited black testimony in the courts, meaning they had no legal recourse unless a sympathetic white person brought suit on their behalf and witnessed the crime in question. The convention delegates agreed to mount a petition campaign to change the law (a solution familiar to anyone from antebellum New England). The petition garnered considerable support and made it to the California statehouse, where a pro-southern judiciary committee snuffed it out.

The campaign for court testimony gained momentum in late 1856 when the second convention met in San Francisco. With 40 delegates attending, this meeting was larger than the first; it also sought new strategies beyond the petition, including the shaping of public opinion through the press. It began subsidizing a race paper for California: *The Mirror of the Times*, which would prove to be the only black-owned paper published in the state before the Civil War. Once again, the legislature refused to act, but the petition and press campaign continued through 1857, when the final prewar convention took place. The newly formed Republican Party began to rise in California and threw its support to black testimony (and looked for loopholes that would allow black testimony in courts regardless of state law). Finally, during the Civil War, the state legislature of 1863 removed the racial barrier to testimony.

BEYOND THE WEST OF BONDAGE?

When the Missouri Territory petitioned for statehood as a slave state in 1820, the people and political representatives of the northern states began to recognize the threat of frontier slavery to their free-labor way of life. If slavery expanded through all of the former Louisiana Territory, free-labor artisans and small farmers in the North would be squeezed out by planters and their slave labor. The western lands would no longer represent a land of opportunity if the southern slave power laid claim to it. Congressmen reached a compromise: beyond Missouri, no new state lying north of Missouri's southern boundary (extended all the way to the Pacific Ocean) would be opened to slavery.

The immediate crisis abated but never went away, and in the late 1840s it intensified. After Texas entered the Union as a slave state in 1845, southern Democrats quickly sought even more western land for slavery. As mentioned, the Mexican War gave them that land, even though some southerners, including President Polk, were disappointed in the spoils, angry that the United States did not win more of Mexico's land. Some southerners now claimed that the newly acquired Oregon Territory should also be open to slavery. By the end of the 1840s, then, it looked as if the American West would never be a place free from human bondage.

But in the 1850s, geography and sectional politics got in the way of the southern slaveholders' dreams. One basic question involved the climate and land of the New West. Could plantation slavery spread in this new arid territory, a land so unlike what existed back East? The answer was yes and no. Yes, Anglos took their slaves westward, as servants and as laborers of all sorts. But it was also true that the rapid western spread of plantation slavery that had occurred in the Old Southwest after 1815 could not be replicated after 1848. The southern plantation could not be transplanted to this new, arid West. Planters lacked modern irrigation technologies, so the geography and climate prevented the spread of large-scale cotton or sugarcane production.

Then, too, there were basic questions of power. The Indian tribes of the High Plains proved a more formidable opponent than eastern woodland Indians. For the time being, they ruled the plains, American claims to the land notwithstanding. Equally important, Americans in the northern states and territories increasingly recognized slavery's threat to their way of life—not so much in the North itself but in the unsettled West. In the North, the Free Soil Party was organized to protect the West against a takeover by the "slave power."

Under these conditions, the West began to take on a new and liberating image for African Americans. For American slaves, westward movement by force had always been tied to bondage: first from Africa to the Americas, then from the East Coast to the Southwest. Now, at mid-century, other possibilities for the West were coming into view. Northern sentiment against slavery in the West was on the rise. The West was becoming a battleground between free soil and slave soil.

THE WEST AND THE CIVIL WAR

Antislavery sentiment in the North was fueled by southerners' aggressive use of the Fugitive Slave Act. Some northern states had passed laws protecting runaways from reenslavement and shielding their state's citizenry from litigious southerners, but the Fugitive Slave Act bulldozed all state's rights arguments in the North and gave the lie to southern politicians who argued for slavery (and its expansion) on the principle of state's rights. Then, too, Harriet Beecher Stowe's emotionally charged best seller, *Uncle Tom's Cabin*, stirred antislavery sentiment in the North, even as it was bitterly denounced by the slaveholding South.

With sectional tensions escalating, Stephen Douglas, the Democrat senator from Illinois, introduced the Kansas-Nebraska Bill in 1854. Douglas had no qualms about slavery, was a friend of southern Democrats, and had his eye on the presidency. If he could boost his southern support, he believed he could win the White House. So, in 1854, he orchestrated a bill that opened the Kansas and Nebraska territories to slavery, a possibility that had long been prohibited by the Missouri Compromise of 1820. Residents of the territories would choose whether they wanted slavery when they petitioned for statehood; the same process of popular sovereignty that had been assigned to the newly won Mexican territories west of the Rocky Mountains—New Mexico and Utah.

The bill demonstrated that the slave power was determined to open virtually all of America's western territories to slavery and that it saw all compromises on the issue as a temporary and necessary stop along the way to that objective. The South's enthusiastic reception to his bill was just what Douglas hoped, but he was startled by the explosion of northern protest against his proposal. He nonetheless stuck to his bill, which soon became law over considerable northern protests.

The Kansas-Nebraska controversy destroyed one of the nation's major political parties. The Whig Party was a national coalition that had included northern industrialists, western expansionists, and a smaller but solid core of leading southern planters. They favored government support for economic development and, in some instances, moral reforms, such as prohibition. The Kansas issue fragmented the party along sectional lines. The "Conscience Whigs" were men from the northern frontier areas, men such as Abraham Lincoln, who opposed the expansion of slavery into the western lands; others were New England abolitionists. The "Cotton Whigs" were northeastern industrialists who prospered by selling manufactured goods to the plantation South; textile manufacturers who enjoyed cheap-labor cotton from the South were also Cotton Whigs. Whigs in the South, increasingly alarmed by the Conscience faction, began to leave the party altogether. They switched to the Democrats, a party dominated by the South and favorable to slavery. Divided among themselves in the North and lacking any southern wing, the Whig party fell apart.

In the political vacuum that developed in the North, a new political party was born in the Old Northwest: the Republican Party. The essential core of the Republican Party included those who had been Free Soilers and Conscience Whigs; some northwestern Democrats also abandoned the party of Douglas and joined the new champion of free-labor homesteaders. The party's key political goal was to block the expansion of slavery to the West. An Illinois antislavery man, a frontiersman by birth, and a forthright opponent of Douglas became the Republican's leading spokesman. That man was Abraham Lincoln, who, for southern slaves, would become a powerful symbol of the West and its potential for emancipation.

Conflict over Kansas turned into war. Not surprisingly, pro-slave forces from Missouri flocked to Kansas Territory, determined to claim it for slavery. But they met opposition. White northerners also moved en masse into Kansas. Southerners had usually been well-armed and ready to get their way at gunpoint. Now northerners who opposed slavery or slavery's expansion appeared ready to take up arms. Southerners formed a government in Kansas. Northerners formed a government in Kansas. Bullets began to fly in what soon became known as "Bleeding Kansas." In Kansas, the Civil War had begun.

This brief description of the coming of the war necessarily oversimplifies. Scholars have dug deeply into these matters and continue to have significant disagreements about them. But few historians would deny that a key issue in fostering America's Civil War was the question of whether slavery would be allowed to exist in the nation's western territories. It was not so much a conflict between North and South, as it was a conflict over which section would win the West.

For American slaves and free blacks, California and Kansas became vital ingredients in the dream of emancipation. The Old Southwest was not the last word on the American West. The New West included California, a free state, a golden place, a place now hated by slaveholders. The West included Kansas, a place where white people, whatever their motives, were willing to fight and die to prevent slavery's further expansion. Among slaves, the West was transformed. It had been a place of enslavement, but now it was becoming a place that offered the potential of freedom.

CONCLUSION

In the half century between 1815 and 1865, slavery in the United States expanded rapidly westward, ultimately sparking the Civil War, which in turn led to the outright abolition of human bondage in America. The

European slave trade had ensnared some 12 million black Africans, forcing them westward in chains. The rapid growth of the trans-Appalachian frontier after 1815 elongated and often deepened African American misery. In the short run, the cotton frontier of the Old Southwest strengthened the grip of slavery on America. In the long run, however, American expansion created a surge of northern opposition to slavery, especially slavery in the western half of the nation, beyond the 98th meridian. By the 1850s, Americans across the continent knew, as Lincoln would say, that the nation could not continue to exist half slave and half free—not because North and South could not coexist where they were, but because both sections wanted and demanded control of the New West.

In this changing environment, African Americans developed a new and positive view of the West and what it might hold for them. After emancipation, the freedmen could look back upon the nation's frontier expansion and appreciate what so unexpectedly came out of it—the death of slavery in America. Now the West, and especially California, would filter into the hopes and dreams of a newly freed people, but the obvious question remained: What would freedom mean for African Americans in this West? Could this really be the promised land? In the final decades of the 19th century, blacks ventured far and wide across the region, seeking their own place in the western sun.

BIBLIOGRAPHIC ESSAY

The opening vignette for this chapter is pieced together from information presented in various parts of DeEtta Demaratus, *The Force of a Feather: The Search for a Lost Story of Slavery and Freedom* (Salt Lake City: University of Utah Press, 2002).

On the southern frontier, see Donald R. Wright's *African Americans in the Early Republic, 1789–1831* (Arlington Heights, IL: Harlan Davidson, 1993); Malcolm Rorbaugh, *The Trans-Appalachian Frontier: People, Societies, and Institutions, 1775–1850* (New York: Oxford University Press, 1978); and Gregory Nobles, *American Frontiers: Cultural Encounters and Continental Conquest* (New York: Penguin Books, 1997), which also places the Texas revolution in the larger context of slavery's expansion beyond the Mississippi River. On the political culture of slaves, including the significance of grapevine information, see Steven Hahn, *A Nation Under Our Feet: Black Political Struggles in the Rural South from Slavery to the Great Migration* (Cambridge, MA: Harvard University Press, 2003).

On black trailblazers in the New West—the West beyond the 98th meridian—see William Loren Katz, *The Black West*, 3rd ed., rev. and expanded (Seattle: Open Hand Publishing, 1987); Quintard Taylor, *In Search of the Racial Frontier: African Americans in the American West, 1528–1990* (New York: W.W. Norton, 1998); Gary Mitchell Palgon, *William Alexander Leidesdorff: First Black Millionaire, American Consul and California Pioneer* (Atlanta: privately published by the author, 2005); Lynn Hudson, *The Making of "Mammy Pleasant": A Black Entrepreneur in Nineteenth-Century San Francisco* (Urbana: University of Illinois Press, 2003).

Rudolph Lapp's *Blacks in Gold Rush California* (New Haven, CT: Yale University Press, 1977) and his *Archy Lee: A California Fugitive Slave Case* (San Francisco: Book Club of California, 1969) tell the story of California, including the Colored Conventions.

See also Dedra S. McDonald, "To Be Black and Female in the Spanish Southwest: Toward a History of African Women on New Spain's Far Northern Frontier," and Barbara Y. Welke, "Rights of Passage: Gendered-Rights Consciousness and the Quest for Freedom, San Francisco, California, 1850–1870" which are both in Quintard Taylor and Shirley Ann Wilson Moore, eds., *African American Women Confront the West, 1600–2000* (Norman: University of Oklahoma Press, 2003); and the essays by Willi Coleman and Lonnie G. Bunch III in Lawrence B. de Graaf, et al., *Seeking El Dorado: African Americans in California* (Seattle: University of Washington Press, 2001).

On slavery in the western territories and the coming of the Civil War, see James M. McPherson's *Battle Cry of Freedom: The Civil War Era* (New York: Oxford University Press, 1988) and Daniel Walker Howe, *What Hath God Wrought: The Transformation of America, 1815–1848* (New York: Oxford University Press, 2007). Allen C. Guelzo, *Lincoln and Douglas: The Debates that Defined America* (New York: Simon and Schuster, 2008), recreates the famous 1858 debates over the question of slavery's expansion into the New West. Books on Lincoln never end (nor should they). Perhaps the best single volume is still Carl Sandberg's 1939 classic *Abraham Lincoln: The Prairie Years and the War Years*, one vol. ed. (San Diego: Harcourt, 1974).

On African Americans in Indian Territory, see, among others, Taylor's *In Search*; Kevin Mulroy's *Freedom on the Border: The Seminole Maroons in Florida, the Indian Territory, Coahuila, and Texas* (Lubbock: Texas Tech University Press, 1993); Theda Perdue, *Slavery and the Evolution of Cherokee Society, 1540–1866* (Knoxville: University of Tennessee Press, 1979), or her brief survey "Indians in Southern History" in Frederick E. Hoxie and Peter Iverson, eds., *Indians in American History: An Introduction*, 2nd ed., (Wheeling, IL: Harlan Davidson, 1998).

Chapter Three

TRAILBLAZERS
IN THE NEW WEST,
1866–1890

After gaining her freedom in January 1856, Biddy Mason remained in Los Angeles. She and her daughters moved in with Robert and Minnie Owens, the former slaves from Texas who had helped her during the trial. Biddy worked as a domestic and became known as a dependable midwife in town. Her daughter Ellen married Robert and Minnie Owens's son, and the young couple soon had a son of their own. In 1859, Biddy got an unusual opportunity: A successful and wealthy physician, who had received a county contract to provide medical services for those in jail or the poorhouse, hired Biddy to be his assistant—at $2.50 per day, an excellent wage at the time. The Civil War of the early 1860s aided African Americans in Los Angeles by drawing many southerners back to Dixie and the Confederacy. When the Confederacy surrendered in 1865, Mason found herself living in a town favorable toward the Union cause. Los Angeles entered the Reconstruction era as a Lincoln Republican town.

Just what did "Reconstruction" mean? In the most basic sense, it was the means by which the defeated Confederate states were once again rejoined with the Union in good standing. To do this, they had to approve the Thirteenth Amendment to the Constitution, which abolished slavery and involuntary servitude in the United States. For slaves, emancipation was a glorious moment, a moment of liberation unlike any other. Official notification of freedom came to different people at different times, depending on where they lived. In much of the Southeast, slaves heard conclusive word about their freedom shortly after Lee surrendered to Grant in April 1865. In Texas, however, most blacks did not receive word that they were free until June 19, 1865—a day that would be commemorated as a holiday for black Texans—"Juneteenth" (see the sidebar below).

In a larger sense, Reconstruction was an effort to determine the rightful place of former slaves in the reunified nation. What would be the legal status of the former slaves? Would the freedmen be given the rights of first-class citizens or would some kind of second-class status be imposed—a kind of American caste system? If blacks were granted citizenship rights, would they receive the right to vote—that is, the right of elective suffrage—a right

---

"JUNETEENTH"

Juneteenth is an unofficial holiday celebrating the day on which slaves in Texas were officially declared free. On June 19, 1865, General Gordon Granger of the U.S. Army, with nearly 2,000 Union troops under his command, took control of the port of Galveston, and effectively the Confederate state of Texas. Lee had surrendered to Grant more than a month earlier, but the news was slow to reach the western theater of war. At last, on June 19, General Granger issued the official proclamation of emancipation for all slaves in Texas. Known formally as General Order No. 3, Granger's order was then sent across Texas to every seat of government.

Among black Texans, the celebration of emancipation on June 19 became known as "Juneteenth," which evolved into a full-fledged holiday within the black community. Although never a holiday officially recognized by the state, Juneteenth was like a July 4 celebration for the state's African American communities. It was a day off from work that included parades, speeches, potluck suppers, and, in some locations, rodeo contests. Between 1865 and the present, its popularity has waxed and waned, but it survived and is currently running strong.

The holiday began in Texas but did not remain there. Over time, large numbers of Afro-Texans moved westward across the southwest, some stopping in New Mexico or Arizona but many more continuing on to California. And they carried the Juneteenth tradition with them. Juneteenth was usually celebrated in Los Angeles, for example, and among some it still is.

even the wealthiest white woman did not have. Would the separate states be able to set restrictions on black rights, or would the federal government grant and protect basic civil rights? Would the old plantation lands be redistributed, with lots given to the slaves who had toiled the soil for so long? Would there be schools for black people? Such were the issues confronting the nation.

Each region of the United States—North, South, and West—faced its own challenges in the Reconstruction Era. In the South, racial tensions were as basic as life and death, but in the North blacks had never enjoyed anything close to full equality. Then there was the West. It was still a region largely unformed by Americans, a place for some trailblazing.

Biddy Mason was among those trailblazers. During the Reconstruction era, she built her economic security through real estate investments. Having accumulated some savings, she bought several inexpensive lots on the outskirts of the town. One was on Spring Street, where she built a home. Her residence served as something of a community center for the several dozen African Americans who lived in Los Angeles. As fate would have it, Spring Street became the city's main business and financial thoroughfare, and the value of Mason's property soared. By selling off some of her property and investing in more, she began to build considerable wealth. She was cautious with her economic ventures, and she kept a modest public profile. Unlike Mary Ellen Pleasant of antebellum San Francisco, Mason was not a mysterious person—no shady engagements, no rumors of voodoo. She simply helped other family members with their investments and entrepreneurial activities and tried to help people in need.

Biddy became one of the town's notable humanitarians, and she emerged as a respected leader in the small African American community. She established a day-care center, visited prisoners in jail, and aided the homeless and the poor. In 1872, she hosted a meeting of black residents in her home. There, with her pledge of financial assistance, black Angelenos established the First African Methodist Episcopal church. That same year, another group of black Angelenos established the Second Baptist Church. By the end of the decade, about 100 African Americans called Los Angeles home, and they had the beginnings of a community in their churches and businesses—and their role model and local success story: Biddy Mason, a woman who had found her freedom and her prosperity in the West.

Biddy Mason, who won her freedom in Los Angeles and became a pioneer leader of the local African American community. (National Archives)

This was the way most black communities in the West were born. A few families, a few key individuals who knew the meaning of freedom became magnets for newcomers. Marriages tied families together. There were jobs—though seldom good ones. Real estate in the towns and growing cities of the region offered a relatively safe and accessible means to gain financial security, if not wealth. But individual gain was not the end. Black residents came together to form networks of family and faith. Beyond churches, black residents would establish fraternal clubs

The African Methodist Episcopal Church, whose 18th-century founders are shown here, became a major force for community development and civil rights activism in the urban West. (Library of Congress)

and women's clubs, political organizations, black-owned newspapers, and community centers. Throughout the late 19th century, these urban communities remained small, but they would be vitally important in shaping the black western experience. Of course, for young men not really ready to settle down yet, there were other options.

THE COWBOYS

Some men found a place in the West as cowboys riding the open range, driving large herds of cattle out of Texas. After the Civil War, hundreds of thousands of wild cattle were roaming in West Texas and south of the Rio Grande in northern Mexico. These were longhorn cattle, the feral descendants of long-ago Spanish cattle. Their meat was tough and stringy, but these cattle were extraordinarily strong and hearty. They were there for the taking, and in the second half of the 1860s Texas cattlemen saw good economic reasons to take them, for the residents in northern cities were eager and willing to pay high-end prices for any kind of beef.

The plan was simple enough: Round up the free cattle, drive them north to be sold, and repeat. But it was not so easy. Cattlemen could not drive the cattle eastward through East Texas and up through the South because of all the farmers and fences and forests. To go north through Indian Territory was costly; the tribes required payment to let the cattle pass through. The solution was to drive the cattle up the Great Plains to railhead towns: Abilene, Kansas; Dodge City, Kansas; and Ogallala, Nebraska. The open range of the Great Plains was literally a wide-open space, and the ocean of grass was free of charge. Texans who knew their way around a horse and could learn to use a rope and drive a herd had something going, but any aspiring cattleman needed a good crew of cowboys to make the drive.

Many black men in the post–Civil War South knew how to work horses. Horses were a vital part of Old South life and culture, and it was often the slave men who worked in the stables, raised the horses for plantations, and drove the teams. Some in Texas had worked cattle before the war, and these men were in demand among cattlemen. Then, too, there was cooking to be done on the trail, and a man who could manage a chuck wagon and keep the cowboys satisfied with the grub could find employment. Frequently, older black men were the cooks for the outfits.

Most cowboys were white men, and many were southern-born whites, but the crews were usually mixed. This in itself was, in the America of the 1860s, a rare phenomenon, and in a curious way, the white cowboys seemed almost proud of it. In memoirs or interviews published after the open range had closed, cattlemen almost invariably make some reference to a black cowboy who was part of their crew. Sometimes he is spoken of simply as "a Negro." Sometimes a first name or a nickname is recalled: Jim, Sam, Big John. Open-range cattle crews should not be thought of as being racially egalitarian. Race and color mattered; it always did. Yet there did seem to be less stock placed on race when men were riding the open range. A good cowboy was a good cowboy.

Black cowboys drove cattle up all of the major trails. Three cattle trails stood out in fact and in legend. The Chisholm Trail, which opened in 1867, ran from the southern tip of Texas, up through Austin and Fort Worth, then through central Oklahoma and into central Kansas, ending at the town of Abilene, which, for all practical purposes, was developed specifically as a marketing point for Texas cattle. The Western Trail ran slightly west of the

Chisholm and made its way to another famous cowtown: Dodge City, Kansas. The Goodnight-Loving Trail began by moving almost due westward before hitting the Pecos River, which the cattle then followed northward up eastern New Mexico; from there the trail ran just east of the Colorado Rocky Mountains (along the "front range" as it is called) and up to Ogallala, Nebraska. Beyond Nebraska, the Goodnight-Loving Trail took cattle even farther north, into Wyoming and Montana. Texas cowboys seldom remained at the end of the line. Most drew their pay and headed back to Texas for another drive.

Most cowboys rode the range a few years and vanished from history. Nonetheless, two black cowboys remain widely known to the public today. One of these, Nat Love, is famous because he could tell a good, far-fetched cowboy story and, more than that, was willing and able to write it all down in a book. The other, Bill Pickett, rose to fame as a rodeo performer, whose talent was too remarkable to be missed or forgotten.

Nat Love's cowboy photograph graces the cover of this book. It is easily the most famous photo ever taken of an African American cowboy, and has been reproduced numerous times in history books and journals and museum exhibits. Love's photo has become an iconic image in both western history and African American history—the ultimate representation of the black cowboy. It is, by any standard of photographic portraiture, a ripping good picture. It seems to capture in a single image all of the adventure, freedom, and fun (not to mention the give-em-hell bravado) of being a real open-range cowboy. The photo survived because Love published it in his memoir, which has become nearly as famous as his iconic photograph.

In 1907, Love published an action-packed autobiography of his cowboy days—*The Life and Adventures of Nat Love, Better Known in the Cattle Country as "Deadwood Dick": a True History of Slavery Days, Life on the Great Cattle Ranges and on the Plains of the "Wild and Wooly" West, based on facts, and personal experiences of the author.* Love's *Adventures* has all the feel of a classic western, whether a dime novel or a Hollywood film. It is, in many ways, all of the classic westerns woven into a single story. At least that is true of the core chapters of the book. It is quite *unlike* the classic western in that the narrator begins life as a slave (the first five chapters) and ends his adventures not as a cowboy on the open range but as a Pullman porter serving the train-riding public of America (four chapters), with a final chapter reminiscing about the old days and the lost age of the open-range trail drive.

Nat Love's now-famous photograph, taken, by his own account, in 1876, after he had won a rodeo contest in Deadwood, South Dakota. (Library of Congress)

Readers today might be more surprised by the earthy, insulting language Nat Love uses when discussing other racial and ethnic minorities. Although he once fell in love with a "Spanish sweetheart" in Mexico (Love, *Life and Adventures,* 126), he generally refers to Mexican men as "greasers." In one particularly spicy episode, Nat and the boys from Texas have traveled into Mexico to collect a herd of horses their boss has purchased. Just for the hell of it, as Love himself might say, Nat decides to have some fun at the expense of the "the staid old greasers on whom we of the northern cattle country looked with contempt." In this case, he rode his horse straight into a saloon firing his colts all around, and then demanded that the "fat wobbling greaser who was behind the bar" serve drinks to both him and his horse. That done, and seeing that a "crowd of Mexican bums" was assembling to kill him, he once again unloaded his colts into the crowd on his way out of the saloon, making a safe and satisfying getaway (all of these quotes are from Love, *Life and Adventures,* 75).

Love's description of Indians is harsh but not as harsh as that reserved for Mexican men. Although he often fights with Indians and kills them when he feels he has to, he sometimes writes with a kind of admiration for the warriors. At one point he is chased and nearly killed fighting warriors of "Yellow Dog's Tribe," which then proceeds to take him in, dress his wounds, and adopt him into the tribe. They do all this, he thinks, because his own warrior skills won their respect and, as he adds, the tribe "was composed largely of half breeds, and there was a large percentage of colored blood in the tribe, and as I was a colored man they wanted to keep me, as they thought I was too good a man to die" (99). Even so, and despite his good treatment, Love escapes as soon as he can. Admiration and connections of color aside, there is in his story no shortage of "savages" and, after the fall of General Custer, "blood thirsty red skins" (Love, *Life and Adventures,* 95).

Such language makes for odd and uncomfortable reading for today's readers, but it would probably not have bothered many of Love's contemporary readers, black or white. (It almost surely *would* have bothered Latino readers, however.) One of the many barriers to African American equality in 1907 was a dearth of respect from most white people. At the time, most people in the United States saw their conquest of the West in a positive light. For these Americans, westward expansion was as a reflection of America's Manifest Destiny to rule the continent in the name of freedom and civilization. Yes, there had been white Americans who championed the rights of ethnic Mexicans and the Indian tribes, but theirs was not the dominant voice in American culture. Instead, most Americans believed the demise of the Mexicans and the Indians was a positive if perhaps regrettable step in the march of liberty. And it is important to understand that few white Americans even thought of including black Americans in this grand narrative.

What African American leaders of that era wanted, understandably, was to be included in the American story, not excluded from it. The notion that oppressed blacks were being used to oppress other marginal groups was a notion that would have made little sense to blacks in the America of 1907. A more common view would have been this: Blacks had been essential in pioneering, winning, and settling the West, so blacks should get credit for their contributions. Love's language might have seemed a bit crude to some Americans, but he was, after all, a cowboy telling cowboy stories, in which case a bit of coarse language was practically required by the reading public.

The now-famous photograph of Nat Love was taken in Deadwood, South Dakota, on July 4, 1876, or so Love's memoir has it. He and his crew brought a herd into Deadwood on the eve of the July 4th holiday and found the town full of cowboys. Naturally, celebrations the following day involved a contest of skill among the boys. First, there was a bronc-busting challenge, in which each cowboy had to rope, saddle, and ride a wild mustang. The one who accomplished this feat in the shortest amount of time would win $200. Several Negro cowboys were in the contest that day, but Nat Love took the prize—and did so with a record time of nine minutes, a time unmatched in the West (at least as Nat remembered it).

Thus, the admiring people of the town gave Nat Love the nickname "Deadwood Dick," but the day wasn't over yet! With the roping and riding finished, arguments arose over which cowboy was the best shot. A second round of contests invariably followed, this one involving skill with a Winchester rifle and Colt 45 pistols. Nat Love won again! In an appropriate cowboy use of the prize money Nat enlivened the revelry of all the cowboys in town. Or, as he himself wrote: "For that day I was the hero of Deadwood, and the purse of $200 which I had won on the roping contest went toward keeping things moving, and they did move as only a large crowd of cattle men can move things" (95).

It was there in Deadwood that Love had his photo taken in his cowboy garb. At least that is what he claimed in a photo caption. Actually, there are two cowboy photos of him in the book, both taken at the same time with the same backdrop and the same bunch of cowboy stuff included: saddle, lariat, hat, neck scarf, chaps, bandolier filled with bullets, pistol stuck in his belt. One photo has Love holding a lasso, and the caption reads "The Roping Contest at Deadwood, S.D." The next one, placed in a later chapter, carries the caption: "In My Fighting Clothes." This second one is the photo that has become so famous—with Love's cocksure stance, casual smile, broad-rimmed hat, long (almost dreadlocked) hair, and large, strong hands.

Readers today, in the early 21st century, will be struck by how small a role Love's race plays in his story. When Nat's story moves out of the South and into the Great Plains—out onto the open range—then, it seems, a man is a man. He and some other cowboys are Negroes, as Love himself makes clear, but in the story as he tells it, no white racism existed in the cattle crews of the West. He himself expresses harsh and negative views of Mexicans, and he acts on those views more than once, but in Nat Love's West, white Americans did not appear to hold negative views about him or other black men. Odder still in Love's memoir is his raceless account of life as a Pullman porter. Only blacks were hired as Pullman porters, and above that station no black man could rise on a train line. He scarcely mentions any other Pullman porters and associates himself fully with the train men, be they engineers or company presidents.

And yet, despite the absence of racial dynamics in this autobiography, *Life and Adventures* is forthrightly the story of a black American man. The first five chapters are an overview of Nat Love's youth as a slave in Tennessee. No ordinary (that is, "white") cowboy narrative could begin there. And although he never says it in the book, a clear but silent message is that his move into the West gave him—a black man—a chance to be just like any other American man, in this case a tough, reckless, freedom-loving American man. And finally, no reader in 1907 could have missed the point about Nat Love's shift from open-range cowboy to Pullman porter. Love himself could not have missed it, of course, but in his telling of the tale, there are no racial implications to be seen in the Pullman job. Instead, Love urges his readers to take to the rails, to travel the country in a Pullman coach, to see America in all of its glory.

Consciously or not, Nat Love's *Life and Adventures* creates its own grand narrative of the black American West. Out of slavery and the South (and having made sure his mother was taken care of), a young man with pluck and courage works his way westward to cattle country. To get a job with an outfit in Kansas, he busts a tough-to-break bronco on the first try. Still a greenhorn but quick on the uptake, he develops skill on a horse and skill with a gun; afraid during his first fight with Indians, he soon leaves all fear in the past. Winning the respect of all men on the open range, he partakes of every adventure the Wild West has to offer. Then, just when the open range gets fenced in and the adventure is over, he discovers a new frontier. On an iron horse, with a new crew of jolly men, he discovers new trails of adventure—only these railroad lines prove more prosperous, less dangerous, and more permanent. Out of the South and into the Old West; out of the Old West and into the New West. Nat Love had found the trail into America.

A black cowboy known more for his actual skills than for his ability to tell a tall tale was William "Bill" Pickett. Bill Pickett rode the open range, but his rise to fame came later, after the trail drive was replaced by the fenced-in ranch. Once the open range had been closed, Americans soon missed the old national romance of it all and developed a hunger for displays of old-time cowboy skills—riding and roping—in a comfortable commercial setting. Rodeos and elaborate cowboy shows became popular, and it was in this arena that Bill Pickett was transformed into a nationally known figure. He had been a cowboy with an especially good reputation; now he became the heart and soul of a rodeo show. Pickett was by all accounts an exceptionally gifted cowhand, but he could also perform an act of astonishing skill, strength, and bravado: He could bulldog a steer by using his teeth!

It is perhaps not too surprising that white Americans had a difficult time working black cowboys such as Nat Love into the popular cowboy narrative. The early dime-novel westerns that became so popular were white cowboy stories. These works of popular fiction were not so much antiblack as they were pro-white, promoting the character and courage of the American Anglo-Saxon man. Today, Nat Love and his famous

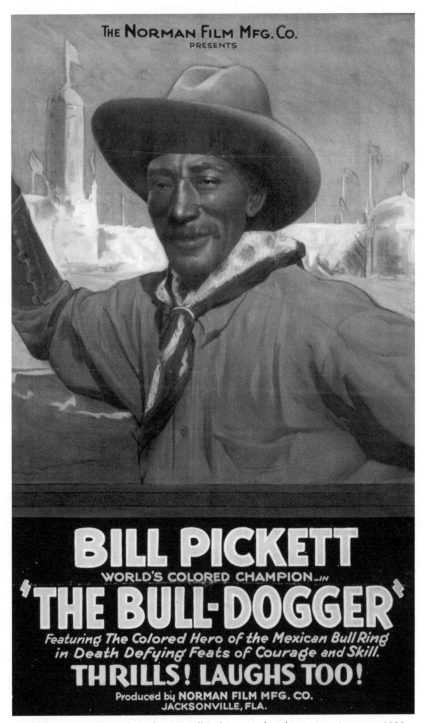

A real working cowboy and a rodeo star, Bill Pickett starred in this motion picture, ca. 1922. (Library of Congress)

photograph seem to be everywhere in the written history of America. There he is for everyone to see: Deadwood Dick in his full cowboy get up. Nat Love, black cowboy, has become a defining image of the American experience! He would, no doubt, love that.

But perhaps historians have overdone the emphasis on black cowboys. Based on loose evidence, a common estimate has been that 5,000 black cowboys worked in cattle country, perhaps 25 percent of the total. This number may be too high. There were black cowboys, to be sure, but probably not that many. In Texas, which had the largest number of cowboys, African Americans made up less than 5 percent of the cowboy workforce in 1880 and 1890. In any case, the open-range cattle kingdom did not last long, only a few decades after the Civil War. By the turn of the century it was over. Barbed wire, railroad expansion, the rise of high-plains farming, and the evolution the meat-processing industry put an end to the days of the free-range cowboy. By the 1890s, the healthy grasses of the free range had been mostly eaten away by the endless herds of cattle moving north from Texas. Soon, the open range had been bought up and fenced in. Cowboys could no longer drive their herds across it. Giant, fenced-in cattle ranches replaced the cattle trails.

SOLDIERING WEST

Another way to get to the West was to enlist in the U.S. Army. Making the west safe for Americans on the High Plains was largely the responsibility of the U.S. Army, and therein lay another western opportunity open to black men and their families. African Americans were first permitted to take up arms for the Union Army in Kansas, and it was in the West that they would make their mark in the postwar decades. Predictably, perhaps, black federal units used in the Reconstruction South sparked intense discontent among former Confederates; the federal solution was to establish all-black units out West, which would be used to defend American settlers from High Plains Indians and to take aggressive military action against the Indians when necessary.

In 1866, the U.S. Congress authorized the establishment of four all-black army regiments. Two of these, which were organized almost immediately with soldiers who had served during the Civil War, were cavalry regiments—the Ninth and Tenth Cavalries. The other two, delayed a bit in their organization, were infantry units—the 24th and 25th Infantry Regiments. Between 1866 and 1917, roughly 25,000 African Americans served as part of these army outfits. They manned more than two dozen forts in the western region and were heavily involved in the Indian wars and in policing the conflicts among the Mexicans, Americans, and Indians that sparked frequent violence in the Southwest borderlands.

War between Americans and the Plains Indians had been raging during the Civil War. Both Union and Confederate troops confronted various Indian tribes, which saw an opportunity to exploit the white man's conflict. The infamous Sand Creek Massacre, for instance, took place in 1864, well before the Civil War had come to its conclusion. The end of the war brought no peace at all to the Great Plains; indeed, the postwar American expansion into and through the Plains (railroads, towns, land rushes, homesteaders, cattle drives) created more violence than there had been before. The result was a collision with the Plains Indians, especially the Sioux in the northern plains and the Apache and Comanche in the southern plains and the Southwest. The U.S. Army in the West (black and white units) was charged with a difficult and deadly job. They were to protect white settlers from Indian attack and to deal militarily with Indians who would not otherwise be subdued.

At some point, these black soldiers in the West came to be called the "Buffalo Soldiers." The nickname remains to this day, but its origin is still uncertain and a matter of debate and speculation. The most common idea is that the name "Buffalo Soldiers" was coined by the Plains Indians themselves, a reference to the close, curly hair of the black soldiers. The official military insignia of these all-black units featured the figure of a buffalo, but whether that gave rise to the nickname or was the result of it is not altogether clear. The soldiers themselves, at least those in the late 19th century, did not call themselves Buffalo Soldiers, but the term "Buffalo Soldiers" nonetheless became widely known and widely used—with pride—by black Americans.

Why did black men join the army out West? Some of the motivations were basic: the army offered a steady job, if not exactly a well-paying one, and some young men were just looking for adventure. These motives were no different from those of most white soldiers. But for blacks in post–Civil War America, there were special reasons to wear the uniform. Men who had been slaves in 1860 had been allowed, in the later years of the war, to fight for the Union, to fight for the emancipation of their people. Black men donning the Blue therefore held a special kind of status among African Americans. Then, too, there was a strong element of patriotism involved. Here was a chance for African Americans to serve their country. Payment for that service might include more than army wages and thin rations. It might also include the gratitude, respect, and equal rights that the country could bestow. Such were the dreams of black soldiers who patrolled the open, often hostile West after the war.

A BUFFALO SOLDIER'S POETRY

The Buffalo Soldiers were patriotic defenders of U.S. interests in the Indian Wars, as is clear in their surviving letters, essays, and poems. Although again, like many whites, they often spoke of high regard for some Indians and occasionally expressed some guilt over U.S. treatment of them, they nonetheless saw and described Plains Indians as "savages" who were a threat to American civilization.

One Buffalo Soldier who wrote poetry, Private W. H. Prather of the 9th Cavalry, expressed the standard American view of the time in his account of the 1890 massacre at Wounded Knee, which marked the decisive end of Sioux independence. Part of stanzas one and four of "The Indian Ghost Dance and War" are reproduced here (the "7th" is the all-white 7th Cavalry). Later that winter, as Prather and his fellow Buffalo Soldiers suffered hunger and extreme cold near Wounded Knee, having been ordered to guard the Sioux survivors, Prather wrote an untitled poem with a different feel, two verses of which are reproduced.

"The Indian Ghost Dance and War"
The Red Skins left their Agency, the Soldiers left their Post,
All on the strength of an Indian tale about Messiah's ghost
Got up by savage chieftains to lead their tribes astray;
But Uncle Sam wouldn't have it so, for he ain't built that way.
....

A fight took place, 'twas hand to hand, unwarned by trumpet call,
While the Sioux were dropping man by man—the 7th killed them all,

And to that regiment be said "Ye noble braves, well done,
Although you lost some gallant men a glorious fight you've won."

[Untitled]
The rest have gone home,
To meet the blizzard's wintry blast.
The Ninth, the willing Ninth,
Is camped here till the last.

....

In warm barracks
Our recent comrades take their ease,
While we poor devils,
And the Sioux are left to freeze.

Source: Both poems are introduced and reproduced in Frank N. Schubert, *Voices of the Buffalo Soldier: Records, Reports, and Recollections of Military Life and Service in the West* (Albuquerque: University of New Mexico Press, 2003).

The Buffalo Soldiers lived in and around the West's rough-hewn forts, most of which were isolated on the High Plains. It would be difficult to classify army life for these men as either rural or urban. They lived in very isolated areas on the Great Plains, at least for the most part; but that did not mean they enjoyed freedom, for their living conditions were usually frontier-like, and their lives were tightly organized by military command. In the first few decades after the Civil War, army life in the West was difficult for everyone involved. Amenities were few, even for high-ranking officers, and were nonexistent for the rank-and-file soldiers. Food was bad and sometimes scarce. High Plains weather meant high winds, baking sun, monstrous thunderstorms, and killing blizzards, and if the weather did not get you, there was, especially in the 1860s and 1870s, the chance that a fight with hostile Indians or a band of rustlers could get you killed. On the other hand, the boredom of ceaseless drills and regimental routine could be deadening, making any danger—real or imagined—a welcome change.

Most of the enlisted men were young and single and lived in rough, crowded barracks. Pay was steady, but low, and opportunities for promotion or heroism few and far between. Like soldiers of any era, they developed a strong sense of unity, a loyalty to the group that was further enhanced by the army's strict patterns of racial separation and black sub-ordination. The Buffalo Soldiers were tough men who did not lightly suffer insult, which sometimes led to conflict among themselves. More problematically, it could lead to conflict with white citizens who insulted them or, all too often, attacked them.

The rank-and-file enlisted men usually lived in quarters outside the forts. Although many men were single or had wives and children back home, only a few brought wives and children to live with them near the fort. In the beginning, living conditions for black military families amounted to shanties, but as the 19th century advanced, living conditions for black soldiers generally improved. Then, too, the declining Indian threat and the spreading network of western railroads and cities made army life in the West a little more stable and comfortable. Isolated log forts evolved into military installations, some of which offered recreational facilities for the soldiers. New posts were established near growing cities, or larger towns evolved near established forts, making for living conditions that were more "normal" than in the earlier decades. More wives and children now accompanied their husbands.

The quality of life for black soldiers was partly a matter of luck, a matter of where one's company got stationed. One fortunate company of the 24th Infantry was assigned to Fort Douglas in Utah, a military post on the outskirts of Salt Lake City. They were fortunate because in this outfit, soldiers and their families could live in the city itself, taking advantage of city schools, churches, and entertainment opportunities. They could ride public transportation to work at the fort. Counting family members along with the soldiers themselves, this military community had a population of about 600. Naturally, they became a vital part of Salt Lake's small black community. Soldiers stationed at a fort in the middle of nowhere obviously had fewer urban amenities and fewer chances to connect with a larger black community. Such communities were developing in the postbellum era, in the towns and cities and in the countryside.

To Kansas!

Emancipation brought no sudden rush of former slaves to the West, or to the North. Instead, the freedmen sought to redeem the South they knew, even as their Republican Party allies in the North sought to "reconstruct" the old Confederacy. For African Americans in the South, Reconstruction did not go far enough—in particular, the freedmen were not given allotments of land—but they supported it for all they were worth, fighting to maintain the political rights they had gained.

Nonetheless, there was a trend toward western migration *within* the South itself. The black population of Texas soared in the final decades of the century, as freedmen from eastern states moved west. They were lured by the rich cotton-growing lands in East Texas—which were more fertile and less crowded than old plantation areas in the Deep South. Others moved to the growing cities of Texas, especially Dallas and Houston. The black population of the Lone Star State increased by roughly 70,000 between 1860 and 1870. This migration did not reflect a decisive move into the West (the region), but it did have something of the feel of an old-style, antebellum frontier movement, although this time without the slavery and chains. The rush to East Texas indicated a restiveness among former slaves in the South.

If East Texas was the westernmost "southern" place, Kansas was the easternmost "western" place, and it was the first western state to receive large numbers of black migrants after the Civil War. Why? First, it had a strong abolitionist heritage; Kansas Territory was the place where northern white abolitionists finally took up arms against the slave South and its efforts to open all of the West to slavery. John Brown had massacred southern slaveholders there. During the war, Kansas had taken in blacks who were fleeing slavery, and it had armed them to fight for the Union. After the war, Kansas developed a strong Republican government, one that tilted in favor of black civil rights more than most northern states.

That black southerners had a clear sense of racial conditions and how they differed from state to state was made obvious in the black rush to Kansas between 1860 and 1880. Almost no African Americans lived in Kansas when the war broke out, but by 1870, the black population of Kansas had topped 17,000. Ten years later, it exceeded 43,000. The vast majority of blacks who moved to Kansas migrated as individuals, as families, or in small groups, but perhaps 10,000 arrived as members of highly visible mass movements. Viewing their journey as an Exodus from the South to the West, these migrants became known as "Exodusters." Their stories made national news and even prompted a congressional hearing into the causes and consequences of their migration.

An early group movement to Kansas originated in Tennessee and was led by the Moses-like figure of Benjamin "Pap" Singleton. A former slave who had escaped to the North but returned to Tennessee after the war, Singleton traveled to Kansas in the early 1870s and came away convinced that homesteading lands could be the salvation of southern blacks. Beginning in 1878 and continuing for several more years, he helped lead several hundred Tennesseans to the plains of western Kansas. In short order, other black leaders back East boosted the trend by establishing the all-black town of Nicodemus not far from Singleton's colonists.

Both of these efforts were small and well-planned compared with the great Exodus to Kansas that occurred in 1879. In the rich cotton lands along the lower Mississippi River, especially in northeastern Louisiana and western Mississippi, white violence against blacks had reached a level of savagery that bordered on a pogrom. The state governments had been recaptured by former Confederates, and all federal troops had left the South in 1877, so African Americans had no protection at all. Economically and politically, they had no chance. If they complained or protested conditions, they were as good as dead. If they sought to leave, white planters sought to detain their labor. In this context, rumors flew among blacks that the federal government would send boats up the Mississippi to remove them to Kansas, to freedom.

Thousands of these Exodusters began to congregate and make camp on the banks of the Mississippi, awaiting ships to St. Louis, where they would embark for new lives in Kansas, their promised land. Eventually, riverboats *did* begin to take on the impoverished riverbank crowds, and as many as 6,000 Exodusters made their way to Kansas. Some East Texans also caught the Kansas fever, making their way to Kansas by rail or road. The large numbers of people gathered on the Mississippi riverbanks, the fact that they appeared to have no identifiable leaders, and the fact that they shared an unshakeable faith that boats would come and that they would be welcomed in Kansas—everything about the movement astonished Americans and their leaders, black and white alike. And rightly so, for nothing quite like it had ever happened in America before, and nothing like it has happened since.

Kansas proved no dream come true. Singleton's homesteaders struggled, as did all High Plains homesteaders, finding their eastern agricultural experiences ill-suited to the arid grasslands. The town of Nicodemus had its ups and downs. Those Exodusters who made it to Topeka were for a time given refuge by the local and state governments, but those public resources were inadequate to meet the needs of the Exodusters. Worse, there was too little land available for those who arrived. Inflated expectations soon felt the pin.

On the other hand, blacks didn't leave Kansas and return to the South. Kansas may have welcomed the 1879 wave of migrants with anxiety and with some reluctance, but it did not turn them away either, and authorities at both the state and local levels did make efforts to meet the migrants' needs. Without too much trouble, the state's growing urban economy absorbed the black migrants, who gave up their dreams of land for service jobs in Topeka and other towns and cities that were rising along the railways. And perhaps for many of these Exodusters, being safely out of deepest Deep South was, for a while at least, reward enough.

After 1880, black migration to Kansas stalled, but this rising western state maintained its image as a good state for African Americans. In the

Nicodemus, Kansas, ca. 1885, a black town created in the wake of the southern "exoduster" movement to Kansas. (Library of Congress)

final two decades of the century, Oklahoma and California would become stronger draws for blacks who were intent on moving west. Kansas, however, had played a key role in highlighting the opportunities the West held for African Americans in the post-Reconstruction era.

OKLAHOMA

Indian Territory—what is today the state of Oklahoma—was supposed to belong, forever, to the Indian tribes (called the "Five Civilized Tribes" or "Five Tribes") who had been forced to move there in the 1830s and 1840s: the Creek, Cherokee, Choctaw, Chickasaw, and Seminole. The agreement between the United States government and the Five Tribes did not last, of course, and given the long saga of treaty violations that characterized U.S. Indian policy throughout the 19th century, the eradication of Indian Territory does not in retrospect seem very surprising. It was part of a much larger trend in American history.

But the demise of Indian Territory and its rebirth as Oklahoma (which became a state in 1907) is of special interest in this book, because the tribes in Indian Territory imported black slavery from the Southeast and ultimately sided with the Confederacy during the Civil War. For their part, slaves in Indian Territory quickly fled to Kansas once the Civil War broke out, and they became the first African Americans to take up arms for the Union Army. For their part, the Five Tribes paid for their slaveholding and their support for the Confederacy. After the war, the United States nullified all previous treaties made with the tribes in Indian Territory. The new agreement forced all of the Five Tribes to free their slaves. The 1866 treaty also cut Indian Territory in half: the eastern half remained under tribal authority, and the western half became property of the U.S. government.

Reconstruction in Indian Territory was filled with conflict between the tribes and their former slaves. The depth of Indian hostility to the freedmen varied considerably from tribe to tribe. The treaty of 1866 gave each tribe the choice to grant, or not grant, tribal citizenship rights to their former slaves. The Seminoles and Creeks chose to give full citizenship and parcels of land to their former slaves. The other tribes proved less generous and sought to keep blacks in a subordinate position within their jurisdiction. The Chickasaw and Choctaw, in particular, exerted violent force to keep blacks down. But in this situation, blacks were not without a strong ally—the U.S. government.

As conflicts between the Five Tribes and their former slaves increased during the late 1860s and early 1870s, blacks brought their grievances to federal officials, and they began to get positive results. By the late 1870s, the federal government had ruled that U.S. authorities, and not the tribal governments in the territory, would have the final say in disputes between Indian leaders and their former slaves. Here was yet another federal wedge in the door of Indian Territory. Blacks who lived among the Five Tribes were beginning to see that their interests were connected more closely to the United States than their own tribal governments. Some tribal leaders warned that their former slaves made them vulnerable to increased federal intrusion.

To say that the Indian freedmen were responsible for opening Indian Territory to Americans is an overstatement, but there is a grain of truth to it. Without any blacks in the picture, the U.S. government would still have put the squeeze to the Indians and would have eventually allowed whites access to the land. The western part of Indian Territory, claimed by the federal government in the treaty of 1866, became Oklahoma Territory, and slices of it were initially granted as reservations to various Plains Indian tribes who succumbed to American power. The Dawes Act of 1887 abolished the communal land holdings of all Indian tribes in America, parceled homesteads out to individual Indians, and then opened the "surplus" land to American buyers—black and white alike. Shortly thereafter, in 1889, the United States opened Oklahoma Territory to American homesteaders, leading to one of the more famous incidents in western history, the Oklahoma land rush. Several more rushes took place during the first half of the 1890s, first in Oklahoma Territory and eventually in Indian Territory itself. By the turn of the century, Americans had gobbled up what would become, in 1907, the state of Oklahoma.

For African Americans, Oklahoma seemed to hold a special promise; it became the new Kansas. No, it was bigger than that. The Exoduster fever took the nation by surprise, but black desires for Oklahoma land—and perhaps even a specially designated "black state"—were clear early on. The presence of the freedmen in Indian Territory and the

Reconstruction Republicans' interest in their welfare there sparked the notion that the land taken by the federal government in 1866 might be set aside as a safe haven for African Americans to settle. Black leaders in Kansas, such as Edwin McCabe, turned to Oklahoma as the ultimate promised land for blacks. Sarah McCabe joined her husband in establishing the all-black Langston City. As African American leaders throughout the South boosted the idea of black immigration to Oklahoma, other all-black towns popped up in the territory. Black homesteaders took part in every land rush. They sometimes made the rush in groups, to protect themselves from white (and Indian) violence.

There were even rumors, denounced by virtually all whites, that McCabe would be named governor of Oklahoma Territory and that the state would become, in effect, a state reserved for African Americans. Utah, after all, was effectively a Mormon state. Why not a state for African Americans? That was not to be, and in truth there was never really any chance it would have been. But it was true that in the final years of the 19th century, Oklahoma was still a very western place and that the possibilities for the black advancement there appeared to be exceptional, especially compared with the South and even, for a time, Kansas.

Oklahoma became a state in 1907, after which its politics and race relations tilted more toward the South than the West, its cowboy boots notwithstanding. But for a critically important time, it represented western opportunities for blacks who were facing deteriorating racial conditions in the South. And long after statehood, many thousands of black Texans left the Lone Star State to find new homes in Oklahoma.

THE BLACK TOWNS

The all-black towns of the West were another obvious source of community cohesion among black westerners in the late 19th century—and into the 20th. Black towns sprang up in the West after the Civil War, offering homes, farms, and security for African Americans only. These settlements were almost always established by blacks themselves, although whites were sometimes involved in purchasing or financing the real estate involved. Black towns were small towns, usually located in the countryside, with farm lots scattered around a front-street business district. Nicodemus, Kansas—established during the Exoduster days—was a good example;

it could have been seen as a rural settlement or a hopeful western town, or both. Most black towns were established between 1880 and 1915, the decades between the Exoduster movement and the First Great Migration, during which time black life in the South reached its nadir.

Black towns did have a bit of antebellum history, however, especially among the blacks owned by or associated with the Seminole Indians of Spanish Florida. In the early years of the 19th century, the Seminoles encouraged the creation of separate black communities near their own tribal settlements. They viewed the people of these black towns as both subjects and military allies—"subjects" because many of the Negroes were in fact Seminole slaves and "allies" because the black settlements had considerable autonomy and willingly joined the Seminoles to fight off the U.S. Army and southern slave hunters. When the Seminoles were forced out of Florida and sent to Indian Territory, blacks who went with them reestablished separate communities in the new Seminole lands.

After the Civil War, more separate black settlements popped up in Indian Territory, because the 1866 treaty with the U.S. government demanded that former slaves be given land on which to settle and farm independently. Blacks in the now-tiny Seminole Nation established the town of Lima, but almost all of the new black towns in Indian Territory were established in the Creek Nation, which accepted the idea that freed blacks ought to become full-fledged citizens with land of their own to work. Virtually no black towns were established in the Chickasaw, Choctaw, and Cherokee nations, those groups being hostile to equal rights and land distribution. As of 1905, there were 12 black towns in Indian Territory; of these, 10 had been established in the Creek Nation.

The most famous of these was Boley, which was *not* established by Creek freedmen but by white northerners in conjunction with black developers. Boley was a railroad town that boomed like a Hollywood stereotype, with more than its share of shoot-'em-ups. In this case, though, the rough crowd consisted largely of Creek Indians, Creek freedmen, and white bandits, and the embattled minority of respectable town builders and farmers were African Americans buying into a good farming area and a town with promise.

To the west, in the Oklahoma Territory taken away from the Five Nations in 1866, the major black town was Langston, an offshoot from the

Kansas exodus and, perhaps more famously, the birthplace of Langston Hughes (who was, in fact, related to the town's namesake). But Oklahoma statehood in 1907 would hurt towns like Boley, partly because the eastern part of the state took on a Jim Crow political order that undermined the prospects of black progress. But all-black towns continued to emerge in Oklahoma after statehood, most of them small and destined to stay that way.

Throughout the West, black towns and homesteading settlements were established. Dearfield, Colorado, drew its population primarily from poor blacks in Denver. After a few difficult years, it stabilized; then, during the World War I agricultural boom, it prospered—only to decline after the war, a victim of a general homesteading crisis that swept the High Plains, and of loss of population to Denver, which was offering increasingly good economic opportunities by comparison. New Mexico Territory attracted some black town builders; the hardscrabble lands of southern and eastern New Mexico gave rise to El Vado, Blackdom, and Dora.

In 1908, in rural California, Allen Allensworth, an African American and a retired U.S. Army chaplain of high rank, established a rural township and agricultural colony that took his name and lasted more than half a century. The town of Allensworth was located in the San Joaquin Valley, a sun scorched stretch of earth that, given massive irrigation and large-scale farming, could be an astonishingly productive agricultural region. For small farms with marginal soil and uncertain water supply, it was almost impossible to turn profit and survive. That the Allensworth settlement did survive was testament to the passion and commitment many residents and community leaders brought to the enterprise. That it never generated much enthusiasm or support among African Americans flocking to the cities of Los Angeles and Oakland was testament to the fact that, for most blacks moving West, racial separatism and rural life were not high on the list of aspirations.

Colonel Allensworth himself did not actually live in Allensworth. He lived in Los Angeles and promoted the colony to blacks who were less affluent and needed an opportunity—and therein lay a conundrum. The African Americans who developed black towns were, by and large, middle-class promoters. They were boosters who saw their towns in both ideological and economic terms. Ideologically, a black town was an exercise in black uplift and opportunity; it was a way to give ordinary blacks an even chance—or something like it—in the business of making a living. Without having to fear white prejudice or retribution, black families in black towns could focus on their lives and livelihoods, like most ordinary Americans. More than that, black towns were a way to give the lie to white critics who claimed that dark-skinned people were incapable of self-government or wealth accumulation. At the same time, there was no dodging the fact that black towns were developmental promotions. The owners were boosters who had profits to consider, and they themselves did not always live in the colony, a fact that lent some tension to the social fabric.

It is difficult to say with any certainty how many black towns were established. There was sometimes a fine line between a carefully planned black township and an informally planned black village or agricultural settlement. Plus, some of the black towns proved short lived. The word "colony" has also caused confusion. African American boosters and real estate developers used the term inconsistently. In the black press, a colored "colony" could refer to a wide variety of community types: a real black town, such as Boley; a black neighborhood on the edge of a mostly white city; or even just a few home sites to be sold to black buyers, such as the "colony" in Abila, California. This has made it difficult for historians to provide an exact number. Estimates of how many existed inevitably vary. One recent and thorough study placed the number of black towns in the West at nearly 50.

There is an interesting parallel between cowboys and black towns. Few African Americans actually lived in black towns, or even knew anyone who had. Yet the black towns retain a strong hold on the historical imagination of African Americans and are often overly romanticized. What they symbolized for African Americans—independence, self-determination, prosperity—was more important than their impact on the pattern of black settlement in the West. Overwhelmingly, blacks who moved to the western states settled in the larger cities and became part of the black communities in those urban areas.

THE RISE OF THE URBAN WEST

When the Civil War ended in 1865, there were few cities of any size west of the 98th meridian. San Francisco, the gold rush city, was the great exception. San Antonio, Santa Fe, and Los Angeles were old towns but not large towns—all of them retained the feel of Mexico and lacked any noticeable dynamism. Denver was still raw, a product of the 1859 gold rush to Colorado, which had of course been curtailed by war. Salt Lake was an isolated Mormon outpost. Seattle was a logging camp. The cowtowns of the Great Plains had yet to be envisioned. The towns of America's western region were still small, and they were separated by vast stretches of open, arid, and sparsely populated land.

But by the end of the century, the West had become a region of large and rapidly growing cities. The cowboys, the cavalry units, and the sturdy homesteaders—for Americans back East, those rugged westerners symbolized the *real* West. But it was the urban West that really took off in the late 19th century. Breakthroughs in western transportation and communication made this possible. Railroads spread quickly, bringing telegraph lines and rail towns with them. At the same time, steamship travel across the Pacific and an underwater telegraph cable connecting the United States to Asia brought the West's cities into the full flow of a truly national and international economy. The timing mattered. Before western rural areas could build up economic momentum, the western cities grabbed the market share of the economy. Paradoxically, too, the vast and arid spaces of the western region promoted concentrated urban development. This was no place for the family farm or the little mill town. People moved to places where daily survival could actually happen. The dream of the Great Plains homestead died hard among the American people, but gradually it did begin to die. The West would soon be filled with ghost towns—but not ghost cities.

By 1900, the region's scrappy antebellum towns had grown into big cities. San Francisco had nearly 350,000 residents. Denver could boast a population of 130,000. Omaha and Los Angeles had both roared to 100,000, and Portland and Seattle were not far behind. These cities were growing fast, too. True, the West seemed to offer settlers unlimited amounts of open land, but this land was largely unsuitable for family farming. Within the Great Wide Open, larger cities became magnets for population and economic development, so that the West became, despite all appearances, a very "urban" region, with rapidly growing cities separated by vast distances.

In the West's burgeoning cities, small black communities slowly began to develop. Between 1880 and 1900, the number of African Americans living in Denver grew from 1,046 to 3,923. Omaha and Topeka, both of which became home to several thousand Exodusters, counted some 3,500 black residents each by the turn of the century. Black Los Angeles grew from scarcely 100 to more than 2,000 in this 20-year span. In the Northwest, black communities were still quite small, but they were growing. By 1900, Portland counted 775 African American residents, and Seattle and Spokane had about 400 each.

San Francisco had the largest black population in 1865, but that community ceased growing and leveled off at about 1,600 residents throughout the late 19th century. Black San Francisco stopped growing for several reasons. Geography played a role, for in this landlocked, increasingly crowded city, real estate prices were often prohibitive. What's more, the white's-only labor unions were a powerful force in postbellum San Francisco, and white workers were not keen to have black neighbors or black competitors in the job market. It was not that whites in the city became outright hostile to African Americans—as they were to the Chinese in the infamous anti-Chinese movement ("The Chinese Must Go!" was the slogan of the all-white Workingmen's Party of California that was organized in San Francisco in 1877.) But the opportunities available to blacks during San Francisco's gold rush boom constricted noticeably in the late 19th century.

As it turned out, however, African Americans kept settling in the Bay Area—mostly in Oakland, a railroad town across the bay from San Francisco. Oakland became the terminus of the first transcontinental railroad and so became a major railroad center; there were plenty of railroad-related jobs for blacks at the bottom of the labor ladder, and more than that, there were plenty of Pullman car porters headquartered there. The Pullman men had status within the black community; they made comparatively good wages and tips and often bought homes in Oakland. East Bay real estate was less crowded and less expensive. The relative decline of black San Francisco, then, was Oakland's gain. Oakland's African American community numbered more than 1,000 by 1900, and it would soon be larger than that in San Francisco.

These communities would prove important far beyond their limited numbers. By establishing churches and newspapers, they created the essential ingredients to building a sense of community cohesiveness. By establishing businesses, political connections, and civil rights organizations, they made a claim on the new urban West, showing a firm resolve to be permanent residents of the region, with an equal chance to share in its bounty. By creating local fraternal orders and women's clubs, and by tying those local organizations to their state, regional, and national organizations, black communities began to sink roots out West and simultaneously to spread the news about the opportunities that existed there.

BUILDING "COMMUNITY"

As the number of black residents increased in western cities, African American leaders took steps to foster a sense of community and a tradition of mutual aid among their city's black residents, most of whom were newcomers. The black population of a city was not equivalent to the black "community" of a city. Community meant a sense of belonging, of safety, of power in numbers, of values, of common struggles. The ideal of black community solidarity took shape in the form of black churches, black-owned newspapers, and civil rights organizations. Historians call these "institutions," and the institutions that black westerners began to build in the late 19th century bear close observation. They would create the foundation for black urban life in the 20th-century West.

Churches usually came first, and the black population of any place did not have to be large in order for churches to come to life. The gold rush was still in a rush when the first black churches in California were established—St. Andrews African Methodist Episcopal (AME) in Sacramento (1851) and the Zion AME of San Francisco (1852). These would be followed by the impressive Powell Street AME and Third Baptist Church in San Francisco. During the Civil War, as slaves fled bondage and flocked to Kansas, a series of churches popped up there, including two in Topeka. Omaha would soon have a black Baptist church and a black Methodist church.

During the postwar decades, the pace of black church development quickened. In Los Angeles, Biddy Mason and the local black Methodists met in her home in 1872 to establish the First AME Church. The Second Baptist Church of Los Angeles was established at about that same time. (Both First AME and Second Baptist remain vital congregations in Los

Angeles in the 21st century.) In a different kind of setting—Ft. Douglas, just outside Salt Lake City—Buffalo Soldiers established both an AME church and a Baptist church. By 1900, Denver, with a black population of fewer than 5,000, had nine black churches. And so it went.

Black churches were houses of worship, but they were also something more. They were also community centers. Negro churches hosted all manner of neighborhood meetings and special events. Job openings were announced at Sunday morning services. Sometimes churches even functioned as de facto banks for black entrepreneurs, who often found white banks unwilling to loan money to African Americans. Civil rights organizations almost always met in the black churches, as did many women's clubs and men's fraternal groups. Political rallies were held in the church sanctuaries. Newcomers knew they could find a welcome and a social network in the black churches. As the largest and most prominent manifestations of the community, the church buildings themselves offered physical testimony of the organization, ambition, and faith of African Americans in the West. As such they gave the lie to any white assertions of black inferiority, while also providing black residents—old-timers and newcomers alike—with a powerful sense of identity and belonging.

In every western town and city, the black-owned newspapers followed the establishment of the churches by about 5 to 10 years, after the population had grown enough to support a small, weekly publication. Why would black residents need a newspaper of their own? Racial and ethnic minorities throughout the United States had them. The Germans, Italians, and Jews had their own weekly newspapers that effectively acted as small-town newspapers within large cities. In Los Angeles, there was a weekly for people of Mexican descent, published in both Spanish and English. The Japanese had their own newspaper as well. So it was not unusual for blacks to have their own news outlets. Black weeklies—which blacks called "race papers"—developed primarily because the white-owned, daily newspapers seldom printed news (at least positive or meaningful news) about African Americans.

The arrival of race papers in western towns and cities naturally paralleled population growth. San Francisco's black residents enjoyed two race papers—the *Pacific Appeal* and the *Elevator*—as early as the 1860s; however, Salt Lake did not see any until the 1890s. Dozens of race papers were

---

RACE PAPERS

African Americans used the term "race papers" to mean black-owned newspapers. Race papers appeared weekly and were published by little storefront operations. Each issue was only four to eight pages long, and the quality was sometimes slapdash, but even small black communities usually had at least one race paper, and larger communities usually supported several.

The newspapers existed partly because the coverage blacks received in the white daily newspapers left much to be desired. News about blacks was seldom featured in the mainstream papers at all, unless it was negative. On a basic level, then, Race papers filled a community need: They presented news by and about African Americans.

In a larger sense, race papers were also an important part of black politics and culture. Politically, they rallied the community, pointing out injustices, identifying supportive white candidates, and promoting campaigns and causes for civil rights. All of the race papers around the country swapped news, so black residents of, say, Oakland, probably knew more about what was happening in black Chicago than did the white people of Chicago. The papers were thus an important part of what might be called the black national network, which was the railroad-era equivalent of the slave-era grapevine. Race papers often blurred the line between local news and gossip; they were informative *and* entertaining, heavy with church news, and loaded with advertisements for black-owned business. Because they were storefront operations, and because the editors were viewed as community leaders, the newspaper offices often doubled as community centers.

established in the West during the late 19th century, but few had staying power. In most places, a stable, long-lived newspaper would be lacking until the 20th century. Usually, a black community had more than one race paper at a time, and in the 19th century, there were some nasty power struggles between rival editors—all the more ugly, perhaps, because the black communities of that era had so little power to struggle over. Still, if early race papers in the West were usually short-lived and sometimes divisive, they were a sure sign that people were putting down roots and trying to build homes in the cities of the region. A quiet turning point toward staying power and regional consciousness occurred in 1899, when a group of African Americans from western cities met in Salt Lake to organize the Western Negro Press Association.

Civil rights organizations were another important building block for black communities. Local and short-lived organizations could be found in most of the West's black urban communities during the Reconstruction era. In the 1870s, for example, Denver saw the establishment of a Central Political Equal Rights League. In northern California, the leaders of San Francisco, Oakland, and Sacramento held meetings reminiscent of the antebellum colored conventions. Most of these organizations were organized to meet a specific local crisis and existed only briefly.

The main civil rights organization in the late 19th century was the Afro-American Council (AAC—sometimes referred to as the Afro-American League). The AAC was established in the 1890s by urban leaders back East, who sought to create a national organization. At the national level, the AAC quickly faded, but out West the AAC caught on at the state and local levels and proved more robust. In some communities, local councils survived until the early 1910s. The councils ensured that black communities were organized, that black-owned businesses were advertised, and that African American economic successes were announced to white America. They also called for fair political opportunities in local and state politics, investigated charges of police brutality, and urged state action against antiblack violence. At the turn of the century, local councils could be found throughout the urban West. Along the Pacific Coast, there were chapters in Los Angeles, San Francisco, and Seattle. In the Rockies, councils were organized in Denver and Helena. On the High Plains, Topeka had its chapter of the AAC. These organizations, like black newspapers, fostered more than group consciousness; they also fostered regional consciousness.

Thus, the small but active black communities in the urban West built the institutions necessary for their future growth. And whereas the number of black homesteaders would dwindle and the population of the all-black towns would decline, the African American communities that arose in western cities between Reconstruction and the turn of the century would survive and sometimes thrive. They were the future of the black West.

BIBLIOGRAPHIC ESSAY

The opening vignette for this chapter is from DeEtta Demaratus, *The Force of a Feather: The Search for a Lost Story of Slavery and Freedom* (Salt Lake City: University of Utah Press, 2002). Population figures throughout this chapter are easily found in Quintard Taylor's *In Search of the Racial Frontier: African Americans in the American West, 1528–1990* (New York: W.W. Norton, 1998) and Walter Nugent's *Into the West: The Story of Its People* (New York: Alfred Knopf, 1999).

Philip Durham and Everett L. Jones's *The Negro Cowboys* (New York: Dodd, Mead, and Co., 1965) was the first major book on the subject and still makes for a fun and illuminating read. Nat Love, *The Life and Adventures of Nat Love* (first published in 1907) is an easy and eye-popping read; of the many editions available, the one with Brackette F. Williams's insightful introduction (Lincoln: University of Nebraska Press, 1995) is especially useful. John W. Ravage's *Black Pioneers: Images of the Black Experience on the North American Frontier* (Salt Lake City: University of Utah Press, 1997) contains photos of black cowboys in real working conditions (that is, not photos posed in studios, such as that of Nat Love). Ravage's book also contains a two-photograph sequence of Bill Pickett bulldogging a steer with his teeth.

The first history of the Buffalo Soldiers was written by one of those soldiers— Chaplain T. G. Steward, a minister who had earned his doctorate in divinity in the early 1880s and then later served many years with the 25th Infantry. In 1904, Steward published *The Colored Regulars in the United States Army*, which has now been republished (with a helpful foreword by Frank N. Schubert) under the title *Buffalo Soldiers: The Colored Regulars in the United States Army* (Amherst, NY: Humanity Books, 2004). Schubert provides an insider's look into the lives of the Buffalo Soldiers in his collection of documents by and about the soldiers: *Voices of the Buffalo Soldier: Records, Reports, and Recollections of Military Life and Service in the West* (Albuquerque: University of New Mexico Press, 2003). Though now dated, the classic work on the subject is worth reading: William H. Leckie, *The Buffalo Soldiers: A Narrative of the Negro Cavalry in the West* (Norman: University of Oklahoma Press, 1967). Taylor's *In Search*, chapter 6, offers an overview of the Buffalo Soldiers with an eye toward community formation in and around the forts.

On the rural experience during this period, see Nell Irvine Painter, *Exodusters: Black Migrations to Kansas after Reconstruction* (originally published 1977; reprint, New York: W.W. Norton, 1992), and Taylor's *In Search*, which provides a broader sweep of the rural experience of blacks in postwar Texas, Oklahoma, the Great Plains, and elsewhere.

On black towns, see Kenneth M. Hamilton, *Black Towns and Profit: Promotion and Development in the Trans-Appalachian West, 1877–1915* (Urbana: University of Illinois Press, 1991). The black experience in western cities during the postwar decades is described, region-wide, in Taylor's *In Search*.

SEEKING FREEDOM IN THE WEST, 1890–1920

In 1906, Paul and Maria Bontemps were living in Alexandria, a small town in the center of Louisiana. Their life there was generally good and prosperous. They had two healthy and precocious children: a son named Arna, who was four years old, and a daughter named Ruby, who was a bit younger. They lived in a large two-story house, and Paul was in the process of building a new home in town. Both Paul and Maria had deep family roots in central Louisiana; they were Louisiana Creoles—descendants of the French-African-Indian unions that had emerged in Louisiana Territory during the French-colonial era. Before the Civil War, many Creole men had been landowning farmers and craftsmen—the Bontemps men among them. They had not been slaves. By Louisiana tradition and law, Creoles had been neither white nor black. Instead, they occupied a narrow middle range between the dominant racial categories.

Maria's family (the Pembrookes) was Creole as well. They, too, had roots in central Louisiana, where they had built a reputation for being well-educated and prosperous. Before her marriage, Maria herself had been a teacher. After her children were born, she turned her attention to their upbringing and education. Paul provided for the family through skilled construction jobs, especially the laying of brick, a traditional Creole craft. He also played trumpet on the side, filling ragtime gigs in New Orleans. In short, Paul and Maria Bontemps seemed to be doing well in the New South.

But ill winds were beginning to blow in their direction. At the outset of the 20th century, white people in Louisiana increasingly viewed Creoles as black people and, therefore, as second-class citizens who did not have the civil rights enjoyed by whites only. What's more, Louisiana whites viewed Creole prosperity with deepening resentment. The middling status formerly held by Creole families was beginning to disappear. So far as whites were concerned, Creoles were now "blacks." That translated into trouble for Paul and Maria Bontemps. Maria Bontemps felt the changing wind first. She began to worry about the safety of her proud and prosperous husband—and their children.

Paul's own epiphany came in 1906, after the Atlanta riot, in which a white mob tore through black Atlanta, spread fears of racial violence across the black South. One evening after the riot, Paul was walking home and was accosted by two drunken white men, one of whom yelled "Let's run over the nigger!" Bontemps escaped unharmed that night but realized that his life in the South had come to a close and that the family should leave Louisiana, and soon. Within days he was on a train heading for the West Coast, and the rest of the family came shortly afterward.

Friends had sent word: Los Angeles was wonderful—plenty of work, good homes, good schools, and better racial conditions. The Bontemps family purchased a home in Watts, a little town south of Los Angeles that had a diverse population and a nice streetcar connection to the big city. Young Arna Bontemps would soon lose his mother, Maria, to sudden illness, and much later still he would become a major figure in African American literature. He would develop conflicting feelings about Watts and Los Angeles, but he recalled those earliest days with a kind of enduring wonder—sun-drenched days, white neighbors who were kindly, and his mother—happy as could be. He also recalled his parents' motivation for leaving Alexandria. He grew up in a household devoted to the idea that leaving the South and moving to the West were the key to black freedom.

A DIFFERENT KIND OF BLACK EXPERIENCE

Between the early 1890s and the early 1920s, a steady stream of African Americans—primarily families like the Bontempses—left the American South for the cities and towns of the West. The word "steady" is important here. There was no major surge from the South to the West. That fact set the West apart from the North. In African American history, this 30-year period is famous as the opening period of the First Great Migration, which began in earnest during World War I, when large waves of southern blacks left Dixie for the industrial cities of the North. Perhaps as many as half a million African Americans moved out of the South between roughly 1915 and 1920. During this same period, black migrants to the western region numbered fewer than 100,000. During the first phase of the Great Migration, the West experienced only what might be called a "Modest Migration."

It might also be called a "Selective Migration," because few black southerners had the West in mind when they left the South. Those who did were usually those who had experienced some economic success—or at least economic stability—in the New South. They could afford the expensive train fare. They could arrive in the growing West with some cash savings. They could take advantage of the generally low price of homes and real estate. They were more interested in the overall quality of racial conditions and schools than they were for industrial jobs. And, like Paul and Maria Bontemps, they had a great deal to lose if they stayed in the South; and, among proud and successful blacks such as Paul Bontemps,

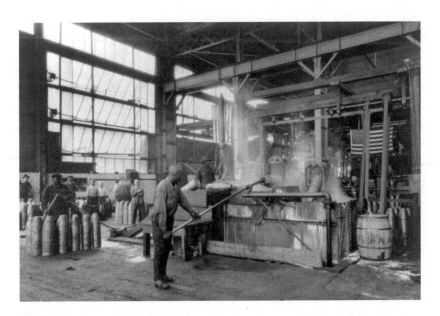

Men working in the Oakley Chemical Company, New York City, making munitions during World War I, 1917. Many African Americans fled the South in the early 20th century to pursue opportunities for a better life provided by industrial jobs in the North. (Library of Congress)

there had emerged a growing realization that black prosperity and black pride were not going to be tolerated within Dixie.

The West, then, emerged as a different kind of place for African Americans in large part because the Great Migration bypassed the region and the Selective Migration created smaller, more affluent black communities than existed anywhere else in the nation. The South remained home to the vast number of African Americans, and most lived in rural poverty. Blacks in the urban South remained rigidly segregated. By 1920, the black population of the urban North had skyrocketed upward, a white backlash had erupted, and black ghettos had taken shape. The black population of western cities, by comparison, was quite small and was not, during this period, densely packed into any residential area. And, in the homes around western blacks, there resided a diverse population of Asians, Mexicans and other Latinos, and American Indians, all of whom added another distinctive feature to African American life in the West.

This chapter examines the decades during which black communities in the urban West diverged from their counterparts back East. First, it will survey the racial crisis that swept the South beginning in the 1890s. Then, it will turn to migration out of the South, comparing different phases of migration, as well as the differences between migration to the North and the West. Next, this chapter will examine the racial conditions blacks found—and helped create—in their new western homes. Finally, it will examine black westerners in World War I and the violent racial crises they experienced during and after the war era. Those crises caused blacks in the West to wonder whether they really could put the South behind them.

THE SOUTH IN CRISIS

The gains of Reconstruction were not trivial in the least. The Thirteenth Amendment to the Constitution (ratified in 1865) outlawed slavery and involuntary servitude. The Fourteenth Amendment (1868) defined former slaves as full citizens of the United States and placed some restrictions on the political power of former Confederate leaders and Confederate states. The amendment also codified the equality of all citizens before the law and each citizen's right of due process before the law. The Fifteenth Amendment (1870) stated that the right to vote could not be denied on account of a man's race, color, or former condition of enslavement.

(The word "man" in the previous sentence is used intentionally, for the Fifteenth Amendment excluded all women, regardless of race.) These Reconstruction amendments altered the law of the land with startling rapidity. In addition, the Reconstruction governments of the South established systems of public education that offered former slaves one of the things they hungered for most: education.

But the gains of Reconstruction did not last. Southern white Democrats—the former Confederates—were outraged beyond reason and committed themselves and their region to the subjugation of all blacks. If they could not retain formal slavery, they insisted on creating a strict system of racial caste, one in which even the wealthiest black remained lower on the social scale than even the poorest whites. They called this system "white supremacy" and insisted that the South must be a "white man's country."

Southern Republicans fought the spread of white supremacy, but by the end of the 1890s, they had been defeated. Northern Republicans, who were virtually all white, grew tired of the southern conflict and withdrew the last of the federal troops from the South in 1877, officially ending the Reconstruction process. Gradually, the conservative southern Democrats destroyed the Republican Party in the South. They used several tactics to do this. The most blatant was to murder Republican leaders (which Democrats referred to as "bulldozing") or run them out of the South. Republican voters were threatened, beaten, and killed. Democrats also rigged the elections; they stuffed ballot boxes with fake Democratic votes or destroyed ballots of Republican voters. Northern Republicans knew this and fumed about it, but they did not send troops to restore democracy to the South. That gave southern Democrats the freedom to push black voters (and poor whites who voted Republican) out of the political system and to establish an ironclad system of white supremacy—the Jim Crow system, in which African Americans had no vote and in which strict racial segregation and subordination were the law of the land.

To have the right to vote in America is to have the "franchise." Those who lose the right to vote are said to be "disfranchised." After Reconstruction ended, the southern Democrats disfranchised black voters. One method was the poll tax, which required citizens to pay an annual tax in order to register to vote and to stay registered. This took many blacks and poor whites out of the political system; they simply did not have the cash to pay or were not willing to spend it on a vote that might not be counted anyway. Another method of disfranchisement was the literacy test, which required registrants to read and successfully interpret the Constitution—interpret it to the satisfaction of the Democratic registrar!—before being allowed to vote. Southern Republicans, black and white, fought against such measures, of course, and they were able to prevent their disfranchisement for a while.

In 1890, few southern states had actually implemented disfranchisement laws, but that soon changed. The 1890s brought a series of disasters to the nation and the South, including an economic depression, massive political conflict with the rise of the Populist Party, bitter conflict between capital and labor, and, most disastrous for southern blacks, a wave of mob lynchings that swept the South. Thousands of black men, and some black women, were lynched by white mobs in the 1890s. And the federal government, controlled at the time by northern Republicans, did nothing to stop the bloodbath. This was the ultimate form of disfranchisement, the ultimate means to subordinate another race of people: the unchecked lynch mob.

The number of African Americans who were lynched increased with sickening speed in the 1890s. Hundreds of lynchings were recorded each year during the decade. White southerners alleged that blacks were lynched as punishment for crimes, especially murder and the rape of white women, but southerners knew better. Crime and punishment was not the issue; the issue was the white people's power to kill black people—anytime, anywhere, for any reason—without themselves being charged with criminal activity. African Americans who were lynched were sometimes hanged; but all too often, they were tortured, then hanged, then shot, then burned, then mutilated. Enterprising photographers took photographs and sold souvenir postcards to commemorate the event. Not a single white southerner was convicted of any crime in relation to any black lynching; very few were even charged, even though, in the vast majority of cases, law enforcement knew who did the lynching. Indeed, all too often southern sheriffs were implicated in the lynchings.

With disfranchisement complete, Jim Crow segregation laws spread across the lawbooks of the South. At the state, county, and local levels, formal segregation statutes were passed into law. Virtually all public places and all public services were segregated—African Americans were not excluded from public life but were emphatically subordinated within it. And beyond de jure segregation was a powerful culture of white supremacy and black subordination. This de facto segregation, not written into law, was treated seriously, as Paul Bontemps's experience on the Alexandria sidewalk attested. Southern whites expected and insisted that blacks look at the ground when they talked to a white person and hold their tongue when insulted by a white person. Blacks could not approach or enter a white person's house by the front door. Whites of all ages called black men "boy," and by custom, white folks never called blacks by their last name— a privilege granted to whites only. And so it went, through all walks of life in the South. From place to place, the customs might be a bit different, but the customs of Jim Crow were overwhelming throughout the region.

Thus, by the end of the century, African Americans in the South had no legal or political protection from hostile whites. The dream of Reconstruction was over. Blacks had sought to transform the land of their enslavement into a land of equal rights. For a while they had strong allies

This 1913 cartoon satirizes the white South's obsessive devotion to Jim Crow segregation, the technological progress of the era notwithstanding. (Library of Congress)

in the North. Within five years, they saw the Reconstruction amendments become the law of the land, but the gains did not last. Southern Democrats "redeemed" their region for white supremacy, and, in the North, the party of Lincoln morphed into the party of business. In the 1890s, disfranchisement, Jim Crow, and lynching swept across the southern states. It was in this violent context that large numbers of African Americans first began to abandon Dixie and the dream of reconstructing the South.

THE "TALENTED TENTH" MIGRATION

The first to leave were those with the most to lose if they stayed. Paul and Maria Bontemps may have been better off than most, but in this inaugural phase of outmigration they were not exceptional. A small but significant number of southern blacks had prospered in the New South, against all odds. They had purchased land, built homes, obtained education, and established successful businesses. Most of these had found their success in the region's towns and cities. Urban places seemed safer for blacks, and often they were. But after 1890 no place in Dixie seemed safe. The Atlanta race riot of 1906 confirmed that black concerns were well founded. More affluent blacks in the South—let us call them the black middle class—had access to information about life outside the South. They could travel, scout out other places to live, and explore options. They had high hopes for their children; they wanted good schools. Many decided their best option was to leave the South before all they had gained had been lost.

The following statistics give an indication of the scope and scale of this early migration. In 1900, the number of southern-born blacks living outside the South stood at about 335,000. This was a rather small number. It included all African Americans living in northern or western states who had been born in the South, even if they had been born in, say, 1840, and found their way out of the South in, say, 1863. Without doubt, however, that number—335,000—included tens of thousands who had abandoned the South after 1890. Then, in the first decade of the 20th century, the era of the Great Migration reached something of a takeoff point. During that decade (1900–1910), as the best scholarly estimates show, about 205,000 African Americans moved out of their southern homes and into the North and West. Compared with later decades,

200,000 outmigrants would not seem like much, but at the time it rep-resented a significant departure in demographic trends.

In the cities of the West, this demographic shift could be seen in the rise of small but steadily growing black communities. By 1910, nearly 5,000 blacks lived in California's Bay Area, most of them in Oakland. More than 5,000 lived in Denver. Even Seattle, about as far from the South as one could move within the United States, could claim some 2,300 African American residents. By 1910, though, Los Angeles had clearly emerged as the western city with the largest and fastest-growing black community. In that year, about 7,600 blacks called Los Angeles home. That was a larger black population than Detroit had at the time and only slightly smaller a community than Cleveland. All black communities in the West, however, including Los Angeles, were tiny compared with Chicago (44,000 black residents) and the long-standing communities of Philadelphia (134,000) and New York City (152,000).

Why do scholars call this phase of outmigration the migration of the "Talented Tenth"? What did "Talented Tenth" mean? The term was actually coined in about 1900 by W. E. B. Du Bois, the black educator and civil rights activist. Du Bois was northern born and bred, but he had spent his years as an undergraduate student at Fisk University in Nashville and, after receiving his PhD from Harvard, took a faculty position in sociology at Atlanta University. There he watched with anger and despair the hor-rors of the 1890s. He also became an opponent of Booker T. Washington, the southern born and bred educator who had founded Tuskegee Institute in Alabama. Tuskegee was essentially a vocational school, and Washington emphasized that black education should be centered around practical trade skills. Du Bois disagreed. He believed in classical education and ongoing political action to obtain full civil rights for African Americans in the South and elsewhere. Of course, not everyone could obtain a true university edu-cation. It was up to a smaller group of blacks to get college degrees and lead the race toward equality in America. This smaller group Du Bois labeled the "Talented Tenth"—the one in ten among African Americans who could and would become leaders. He offered this idea to a national readership in his pathbreaking book *The Souls of Black Folk*, which appeared in 1903.

The term was problematic even then. It had an aristocratic tone to it, one that the aristocratic-minded Du Bois identified with. It was also,

W. E. B. Du Bois, a founding member of the NAACP, helped spread the organization in the West. (Library of Congress)

mathematically speaking, way off the mark. Nothing close to 10 percent of the black American population could afford to go to college. And yet the term caught on among the black middle class, who embraced both the ideal and responsibilities of leadership. No one understood the 10 percent figure to be exact; it was instead an ideal, an essential value for living. For educated blacks, themselves facing a mountain of racial prejudice from whites and often the ridicule of blacks themselves, the notion of a Talented Tenth also served as ongoing motivation and inspiration.

Because the black middle class was heavily represented in the early phase of the Great Migration, this quiet exodus is often referred to as the Talented Tenth Migration. Of course, poor blacks left the South during this period, too, but the best evidence suggests that Deep South sharecroppers were not yet leaving in large numbers. In the West, the middle-class trend was even more pronounced because of sheer distance. In 1903, a single train ticket from Atlanta to the West Coast cost about $40. No sharecropper could even imagine paying that, much less taking along an entire family. And if hopping freight cars for the North was in fact possible for poor but ambitious blacks, distance and deserts rendered impossible that kind of journey to the Far West.

When W. E. B. Du Bois visited the West Coast in 1913, he made note of the middle-class character of the black urban communities he found there. Praising African Americans in Seattle for their ambition, political activism, and intelligence, he added, "they have push, for their very coming so far westward proves it" (Taylor, *Forging*, 79). In writing about blacks in Los Angeles, he took a moment to note that the "color line" was apparent, but the essence of his report in *The Crisis* was his wonder and delight at the affluence of the community. Black westerners themselves had a similar sense that they were a group set apart, that their journey to the Far West and their successes there reflected something special—about themselves and about their western home.

For black migrants to Seattle, Los Angeles, and other western cities, the West was more than just another place on the map. The very idea of the West had long had a palpable power within white America. African Americans, as seen in Chapter 2, had different visions of what the West had been and could be—and their point of view stemmed from the expansion and destruction of southern slavery in the 19th century. By the 20th century, blacks had come to view the West as an exceptional land of opportunity, as the great hope for racial equality in America. Blacks in the West embraced, and openly espoused, what might be called the "Western ideal." The idea was not that the western region actually provided equal opportunity for blacks; rather, it was that racial conditions were better

---

THE PULLMAN PORTERS

In the age of transcontinental train travel, virtually all major lines provided sleeping cars made by the Pullman Palace Car Company of Chicago, organized by George Pullman in 1867. Pullman did not merely build cars and sell them to railroads; he leased the sleeping cars to the rail lines on the basis of a full-service package: the cars came with stewards included (as well as dining car cooks and waiters), and these became known as Pullman porters. Certain major cities were designated as Pullman hubs, and in these places the Pullman company hired and organized its porters for any given rail line. Most important, George Pullman ordered that black men, and only black men, would be employed as Pullman porters.

So it was that African American men in Pullman uniforms became a deeply engrained symbol of train travel. Pullman porters made decent wages for the time and enjoyed a high status within the black community. The work was difficult and exhausting, for the porters were always on call, had a long list of responsibilities, and were away from home for long periods of time. Still, it made for a good living if a man could take it.

In the West, there was a strong relationship between Pullman jobs and urban black communities. As the urban West grew rapidly after 1890, Pullman jobs pulled many men and families westward. Western cities that served as Pullman hubs—Oakland, Los Angeles, and Denver—developed solid and sizable black communities. American rail travel and the black urban West emerged as part of the same process of national expansion.

---

there than elsewhere and that equality of opportunity was within the realm of possibility. Here, amidst the constant refrains about western egalitarianism, the walls of antiblack racism might be dismantled. That, at least, was the Western ideal in its fullest sense.

THE GREAT MIGRATION

The Great Migration was sparked by World War I, which began in Europe in 1914. This war sparked a remarkable chain of events that drew together northern industry and southern blacks. When Europe went to war, the people of the United States, along with President Woodrow Wilson, remained mostly interested in staying out of the conflict—out of the conflict, but not out of the international trade the war necessitated. European nations soon became desperate for American industrial products, everything from bullets to beef. As a result, American factories boomed. Greater demand fueled greater production. Quite suddenly, the factories ran short on labor. For the American North, this was a new problem, because poor immigrants from Europe had always filled the factories, meeting the need for cheap labor in the mills. On the eve of World War I, the numbers of European immigrants arriving each year was stunningly high; then, almost overnight, the European labor supply was completely cut off. That changed everything.

Unprecedented industrial demand plus a limited supply of workers equaled an unprecedented labor shortage in the nation's industrial heartland. Those trends, coupled with the push of Jim Crow down South, resulted in the Great Migration. From the meat-packing plants of Chicago to the steel mills of Pittsburgh, northern mills looked to black southerners to fill their low-wage, big-muscle jobs. Some companies sent hiring agents into the south to recruit, and some southern blacks took the free train ticket and headed north for a job. Initially, southern whites observing this process said "good riddance," but it soon dawned on southern planters and small-town business owners that their cheap, powerless labor supply was being drained away. The South soon began to crack down on recruiters and made it difficult for African Americans to leave Dixie, but by then it was too late. The black information network had kicked into high gear: letters flew among family and friends; Pullman porters brought fresh information to every railroad hamlet in the South; black newspapers—most notably the *Chicago Defender*—urged their southern brethren to come up North; and southern ministers inquired about conditions and brought word to their congregations. Company recruiters were no longer necessary, and blacks who wanted out found a way out—taking the back roads and hopping freight cars for a better job, a better life. By mid-1916, the Great Migration was in full swing, even though the United States had not yet entered the war.

The rapid influx of black southerners jolted the North's industrial cities. Previously, black communities in the North had been rather small, rather middle-class, and relatively integrated into the social fabric of their cities. American-born whites had been more concerned with the massive influx of new immigrant groups from southern and eastern Europe—the Poles, the Hungarians, the Italians, the Russian Jews, the Slavs—whose languages, religious customs, and cultural traditions seemed so alien to people whose roots stemmed from northern and western Europe. Yes, industry needed their labor, but would these seemingly "un-American" newcomers ruin their cities? That had been the nagging question for white northern leaders and their communities. For them, the "Negro problem" had been a "Southern problem." But no more. As the black population of many northern cities quickly skyrocketed, the response among white residents was something akin to panic. There were calls to stem the flow, but they never had a chance of stopping the Great Migration. The industrialists held power, the economic boom was undeniable, and, once the United States entered the war in 1917, resisting black migration to defense plants had an uncomfortably unpatriotic ring to it. So the migration continued and gained momentum.

If northern whites could not stop the influx of southern blacks, however, they nonetheless took aggressive and hostile action to control the migrants and their impact. The less obvious forms of race prejudice in northern cities gave way to the open posting of Jim Crow signs. Police kept an especially sharp eye on the newcomers. White northerners— especially old-stock whites—mostly took action on the housing front. They desperately wanted to keep black people out of white-only neighborhoods. Their principal weapon in this battle was the racially restrictive real-estate covenant or, as it was usually called, the "restrictive covenant." Restrictive covenants were legal clauses written into property deeds. They mandated that a particular piece of property or home could be sold only to white people—"Caucasians only." Sometimes restrictive covenants excluded Jews as well. Older neighborhoods formed voluntary associations that made sure all their housing deeds were officially revised to include restrictive covenants. New housing developments could simply blanket their properties with restrictive covenants and use that protection against black intrusion as a selling point for white buyers.

The result was the black ghetto—an area of the city in which African Americans had no choice but to live. They were legally barred from moving outside of it. To be sure, the boundaries of black sections did expand into areas supposedly off-limits to African Americans, but never without resistance and usually into less desirable working-class areas. Black migrants were hemmed in. The inevitable result was overcrowding and, eventually, the deterioration of housing conditions and city services. Sections of northern cities that had been partly black became virtually all black; what had been working-class housing became overcrowded ghettos.

No Rush Westward

If the Great Migration from South to North sometimes resembled a kind of demographic stampede, the migration from South to West resembled a kind of carefully planned trot to greener pastures. In 1910, the Talented Tenth Migration had been under way for more than a decade, and there was not much difference between the flow North and West; by 1920, the Great Migration of World War I had transformed many northern cities while transforming virtually no western cities. Some numbers will help. In 1910, both Los Angeles and Detroit had roughly 8,000 black residents; by 1920, Detroit's black population had soared and was well on its way to 120,000 by 1930; in contrast, black Los Angeles had grown to nearly 16,000. For the black West, the increase in Los Angeles was far and away the most substantial gain of any community in the region. From 1910 to 1920, the number of African American residents in Oakland grew from roughly 3,000 to 5,500; in Denver, from 5,400 to 6,000; in Seattle, from 2,300 to 2,900; in San Francisco, from 1,600 to 2,400; and in Portland, from 1,000 to 1,600. The region's small communities remained small. The First Great Migration had bypassed the West.

The obvious exception was Los Angeles, which emerged as the undisputed center of the black West. But even here the usual Great Migration narrative did not apply. Los Angeles had plenty of industrial development—in food processing, petroleum, iron, and steel—but these industries did not rely on the labor of new immigrants or fling their doors open for black southern workers during the war. Blacks who already lived in Los Angeles did get a foot in the door of the factories during the war, but local industry did not need to target outsiders. Enough local whites and ethnic Mexicans and blacks were available to fill the positions. A similar situation emerged in Seattle. During the war, for example, local blacks were allowed to work in the shipyards when the manufacturers ran a bit short on labor, but there was no rush of African Americans—from the South or anywhere else—to the Seattle shipyards. Local labor supply filled the bill on the West Coast.

Why did black Los Angeles grow so much faster than the black communities in other western cities? There were several reasons. One was the growth of the city itself. Other western cities were growing fast, but the population of Los Angeles rose at a phenomenal rate. Urban growth fueled its own strong economy. Simply meeting the needs of the expanding population required construction, services, retail, and transportation. On top of that, large industries developed, including the citrus and food-processing industries and, eventually, the motion picture industry. But Los Angeles was not the kind of town people came to for specific jobs. People came to Los Angeles for the whole package: sunshine, warm winters, inexpensive real estate, strong economy, bunches of jobs—just a nice place to live. Black migrants often came for the readily available real estate. There was a lot of open and undeveloped land in and around Los Angeles, and that mattered greatly to a people who were systematically excluded from well-paying jobs. A nice little home did not cost much, and inexpensive lots were available to build on.

For blacks moving West, Los Angeles's climate was important, but it was not as important as the *racial* climate. The racial conditions of the urban West were better than they were in the South and, beginning in World War I, the North. There was more social freedom and less overt racial tension, in part because there were other "colored" races—the Chinese, the Japanese, the Mexicans—to draw away the prejudice of whites. By today's standards, blacks in the urban West were hardly free at all. By the standards of the early 20th century, the urban West was a breath of fresh air for America's black citizens.

Personal migration stories told by African Americans who moved to the West during this Great Migration do not reflect the employment pull normally associated with this demographic epoch. The Hawkins family of Shreveport, Louisiana, to give one example, was prospering in Shreveport. They had a family business, but toward the end of the war, racial tensions in Shreveport seemed to intensify, and black prosperity did not sit well with local whites. Some of the Hawkins's friends had moved out

West, and the family decided to leave Dixie. They tried Denver, which they thought too cold. They knew people in Los Angeles, who highly recommended it, so they moved there. Mr. Hawkins set up a newsstand on Central Avenue, bought a home for the family, and eventually sent one of his sons to Berkeley and another to UCLA. The Hawkins family may have been better off financially than most southern black migrants, but the evidence suggests that their motivations in moving to Los Angeles were more the rule than the exception: good homes, inexpensive real estate, nice climate, good schools, and generally good racial conditions. Theirs was no farm to factory migration.

COMMUNITY LIFE IN THE BLACK WEST

The four key aspects of black community life in the urban West were homes, churches, newspapers, and institutions. The ability to buy a home—sometimes a nice, new home—set the West apart from the South and the North. Home ownership rates in 1910 tell the story. Along the West Coast, black residents were far more likely to own a home than their counterparts back East. In Los Angeles, 36 percent of all black households owned their home. Other cities also had healthy home ownership rates: Seattle, 27 percent; Portland, 23 percent; and Oakland, 30 percent. San Francisco, surrounded by water and losing its black population to Oakland, came in low: 16 percent.

In major eastern cities, 16 percent would have been considered excellent. For example, a mere 2 percent of African Americans in New York City owned their homes. Those in Chicago (before the Great Migration, remember) scarcely beat that: 6 percent. Other Midwestern cities fared a little bit better: Cleveland, 11 percent; Detroit, 17 percent. Blacks in southern cities had as good or better chance of owning their homes as their northern counterparts. In the interior West, successful home ownership for African Americans was hit and miss. Omaha with 16 percent and Denver with 20 percent were not so strong—but it is worth noting that both were on the way up: African Americans in Denver would enjoy a home ownership rate of nearly 40 percent by 1930, and blacks in Omaha reached a rate of more than 30 percent. Black Topekans enjoyed a rate to rival Los Angeles.

It was not easy to move from the South all the way to the West Coast. To those who could get out of the South with some savings, the West looked especially enticing. A selective migration began. For the poorer blacks of the South—those looking for a start, for a break—the industrial North beckoned. For those who already had some money and could be more selective, the West looked more attractive, and so many of the South's black middle class headed West.

Beyond the pride and benefits of home ownership, western real estate was important for another important reason: Few good jobs were open to black workers in the West. On the whole, black men could land jobs as day laborers, porters, custodians, and chauffeurs. Black women were overwhelmingly domestics. For people with middle-class outlooks and poor job prospects, buying and selling real estate was a realistic and essential means to upward mobility. It was no accident that many blacks in the urban West sold real estate on the side. They could get a realtor's license from the state and get in on the action. The scope of their transactions were usually small, and they catered almost exclusively to black clients. Some merely guided buyers and sellers for the commission, but most African American realtors would also purchase inexpensive lots as they came available and then sell them for profit as the values increased— and the values were almost always increasing in western cities. Another way to earn money in real estate was as a landlord: renting out homes or small apartment buildings.

The main threat to black home ownership and real estate transactions was the racially restrictive real estate covenant. Similar to what occurred in northern cities in the wake of the Great Migration, restrictive covenants began to spread in the white neighborhoods of the West in the 1910s. In the older neighborhoods, whites formed associations that added racial covenants to all property deeds in their area. New housing developments wrote covenants into every deed of the subdivision. Generally, the wealthier the white neighborhood the more successfully they could exclude black residents, along with Asian, Latino, and sometimes Jewish residents as well. This did not mean blacks in the West lived in black ghettos; it meant they lived in sections of the city that were uniquely diverse and rather less prosperous. Blacks in Seattle, for instance, tended to live in the Central District, but they were a minority within that district, which was also white and Japanese. Blacks in Los Angeles tended to live in the Central Avenue district, but they too were a minority within that district, which included a diverse collection of white people, Asians, and Latinos.

Within these diverse nonwhite sections, what created a deeper sense of community among African Americans? For one, the Negro churches. These were all-black institutions of various denominations, mostly Baptist and Methodist, and they were vitally important to black residents. Los Angeles had a significant number of black Catholics, a reflection of its connection with heavily Catholic Louisiana, but most black Christians were Protestant. The principal denominations were the African Methodist Episcopal Church (AME), the AME-Zion, and the Baptist churches affiliated with the National Baptist Convention. By the dawn of the 20th century, there were many firmly established black churches in the towns and cities of the West, and the congregations had built large, sometimes elaborate, buildings in which to worship. The sanctuaries of the major churches were a common meeting place for political meetings, civil rights organizations, and community celebrations.

Similar black-only, black-owned institutions tied the community together. Small businesses were important, mostly restaurants, drug stores, beauty salons, and barber shops, which could be found near black homes in any western town or city. The black fraternal organizations—Masons, Elks, Shriners, and such—were an important part of community life, as were the sororities that paralleled them (but were not the same thing as the Colored Women's Clubs, discussed later). The major cities had colored branches of the Young Men's Christian Association (YMCA) and Young Women's Christian Association (YWCA), which, along with the church youth groups, were popular gathering places for children and teenagers. Some communities held regular meetings at which anyone could speak out on any subject of concern. Black Los Angeles, for example, established the Sunday Forum, which was open to all and became a common meeting ground.

All of these institutions were tied together by the black-owned newspapers, which blacks called "race papers." Many race papers appeared in the West between 1890 and 1920. Blacks in San Francisco developed some of the region's earliest weeklies, *The Pacific Appeal* and the *Elevator* emerging as rivals—which spiced up the grapevine and put a little extra heat into political campaigns. As the Bay Area community shifted to Oakland in the early 20th century, the *Oakland Sunshine* began its run.

Denver had the *Colorado Statesman* and the *African Advocate*, the latter of which, however, became less interested in the settlement of Colorado than in a Back to Africa movement. In Salt Lake, the *Utah Plain Dealer* won out in a scramble of half a dozen black weeklies that rose and fell. Farther north in the Rockies, blacks in the mining town (and state capital) of Helena, Montana, supported the *Plaindealer*, which put in a vigorous five-year run from 1906 to 1911. Kansas had the largest black population in

---

CHARLOTTA SPEAR AND JOE BASS

In 1910, Charlotta Spear arrived in Los Angeles from the Northeast. She came for her health—warm sun, dry air—but through a curious turn of events she became owner and editor of a local Race paper, *The Eagle*. The paper was about to fold, but Spear made it work and emerged as a leader within the community. Joseph Bass grew up in Kansas and had all the makings of a successful Race man. He worked for race papers and with the Republican Party, proving to be a forceful advocate for civil rights. In 1905, Bass moved to Helena, establishing the *Montana Plaindealer*, but in 1911, he went for a tour of the West and never returned. He loved Los Angeles and never left.

Naturally, Bass stopped by the *Eagle* and met Charlotta Spear, and that was the beginning of an influential partnership. They married in 1914 and split duties: Charlotta was managing editor; Joe was content editor. They became a force to be reckoned with in black Los Angeles, as the *Eagle* became a leading Race paper and both Joe and Charlotta remained widely engaged in civil rights efforts. In the early 1920s, Charlotta served as an officer for both the integrationist NAACP and the black nationalist Universal Negro Improvement Association.

Joe died in 1934, but Charlotta lived for 35 more years, a rising political star. After World War II, she emerged as one of the city's leading black radicals. In the 1952 presidential election, she was nominated for vice president on the left-leaning Progressive Party ticket. The ticket fared poorly, but Charlotta Spear Bass enjoyed her status as the "radical matron of LA," continually tailed by the Federal Bureau of Investigation (FBI), until her death in 1969.

the West, and the *Topeka Plaindealer* and *Topeka Colored Citizen* emerged in the wake of the Exoduster movement. Black Los Angeles had a series of short-lived race papers in the late 19th and early 20th century, but two of particularly lasting importance emerged under new ownership in the 1910s: Frederick Roberts's *New Age* and the *California Eagle*, owned and operated by Charlotta and Joe Bass (see the sidebar on page 110).

Familiar neighborhoods, the Negro churches, black organizations and businesses, and the race papers—all of these fostered a collective sense of community in western cities. They ensured that African American residents came to think of themselves as a community. This sense of shared identity and commitment to place fed western civil rights activism between 1890 and 1920. Three key groups for black civil rights were the Afro-American Council, the Colored Women's Clubs, and the National Association for the Advancement of Colored People.

THE AFRO-AMERICAN COUNCIL

In the 1890s, a new national organization emerged to foster racial equality in America: the Afro-American Council (AAC). The AAC was an all-black organization, a loose confederation of state and local branches whose goals varied from place to place. The principal aims fell under the basic categories of economic independence and political rights. The national organization was short lived and fizzled before the decade was out, but in some western states and cities—Topeka, Kansas, for example—AAC chapters survived and kept fighting the good fight.

California's African Americans were especially devoted to the AAC as an agent of change. The AAC was the first statewide civil rights organization in California and, although its members did not think of it this way, it provided a kind of testing ground for the civil rights organizations that came later. Although it was never particularly powerful, the California AAC was active on many fronts, was visible to state and local political leaders, and brought important issues to light. When a black man was lynched near an obscure railroad yard in the Mojave Desert, the state AAC demanded (unsuccessfully, as it turned out) that the governor make a strong public statement against lynching. The AAC also kept an eye on the prisons and courts and worked actively to free prisoners held on false charges; in this they were often successful.

The AAC held annual conventions where racial conditions were discussed and economic gains for blacks in the state were highlighted—as an inspiration to blacks and as a message to whites: equal opportunity for Afro-Americans would result in mounting prosperity and productive citizenship. While trumpeting entrepreneurship, the AAC also took stands for black labor—most of the early leaders were blue-collar workers with middle-class aspirations—and persistently sought patronage jobs from the Republican Party. Many of the AAC leaders in the early 20th century were in fact employed as custodians by city, county, and state governments, and at the time these jobs were some of the best available to black wage earners in the state.

The California AAC was divided into two sections: Northern California and Southern California. When the group was organized in the mid-1890s, the Northern California group dominated the organization, because the black population of San Francisco and Oakland (the Bay Area) was a larger than the Southern California group emerging in Los Angeles and, to a lesser extent, Pasadena and other scattered towns. But around 1900, the black population of Los Angeles began to grow more rapidly than that in the Bay Area, and it was not long before the Southern California section became dominant in the state AAC. This bruised Bay Area egos, but the trend was clear; by virtue of its greater numbers of members within the AAC, the men from Los Angeles and Pasadena were able to control virtually all of the state-level offices. The solution was to create two functioning branches within the state—northern and southern—which would elect their own officers and pursue their own aims under the larger state organization.

The California AAC's greatest success may have been its mere survival. By 1910, more than a decade after the national movement had collapsed, the California AAC was still in operation, still a visible presence in local and state politics. And the organizational division into northern and southern branches would effectively be copied by the race organizations that organized in the wake of the AAC, most notably, the Colored Women's Clubs and the NAACP. The AAC in California was the vanguard of organized civil rights activism in the urban West.

THE COLORED WOMEN'S CLUBS

Although women were involved in the California AAC, the organization was dominated by men. Through most of its history, the AAC allowed women to serve in auxiliaries, whose main function was to put on the annual conventions for the men. Not that this was a trivial job; on the contrary, the AAC's image rested largely on the style and efficiency of its annual meetings, which were held in larger cities and which were sometimes reported in the white newspapers. After 1910, the California AAC opened its membership to women, perhaps because it was the spirit of the times (California gave women the right to vote in 1911) or perhaps because membership was declining. In any case, women played a marginal role in the AAC.

The colored women's clubs were a different matter. These organizations were, as the name indicates, for women only, and they played a major role in the lives of African American women (and of the larger black community) throughout the nation and the West. Colored women's clubs were not the same thing as the "societies," or social clubs, which were the female equivalent of the men's fraternities (the Elks Club and such); the societies and fraternities sometimes engaged in charity work as part of their club activities, but mostly they were purely for fun. The women's clubs, by contrast, had a more serious tilt. They were dedicated to community service, especially to activities and institutions that would assist black women and children who needed a helping hand in a difficult world.

The California Association of Colored Women's Clubs (CWC) was organized in 1896, which was about the same time the California AAC developed its state-level organization. Many of the leaders of the CWC were in fact the wives of AAC leaders. There was no formal connection between the two state organizations, but things happen in time for a reason, and the 1890s was the time when African Americans began to establish permanent groups for civil rights and race work at the state and national level. Like the California AAC, the California CWC formally divided itself between a northern group and a southern group (they later added a central California division). Also, like the men's council, the women's clubs aimed at political and economic issues. They supported woman suffrage in California, debated candidates at election time, took public stands on issues involving race, established training schools for young women, and promoted economic progress for both the individual and the community. Not all club women were middle class, but the clubs and the women who joined them vigorously espoused middle-class values, which in the black community included Christian values.

In Los Angeles, the CWC established two key institutions during the early 20th century. One was the Sojourner Truth Industrial Home, established in the early years of the century. It was a home for single women and single mothers who arrived in Los Angeles without family or money. It was, literally, a home for women who had no home. The women who lived there took classes that taught them a trade (hence the "industrial" in the name of the home), classes in homemaking skills, and classes that taught the Bible and Christianity. The home started small, but in the early years of the century, the women's clubs in Southern California began to raise funds to build a large and beautiful Spanish-style home. With donations from the black community, especially the churches, they achieved that goal. The second institution was the Women's Day Nursery, a day care center for children of working women. A very high percentage of black women worked outside the home, so the center was much needed among women who did not have an extended family or support network to care for their children. Like the Sojourner Truth Industrial Home, the Women's Day Nursery received strong support from the Negro churches. By 1920, the Women's Day Nursery was caring for hundreds of children.

Women's clubs sprang up everywhere throughout the West. They were far more common than AACs, and far larger as well. And unlike the AAC, they grew ever stronger as the century progressed. Perhaps most important, the colored women's clubs gave black women a place in western society in which they could pursue their own personal aspirations even as they served the community. They could become leaders and make things happen. As a group within America that was constantly attacked and maligned by white mainstream society, black women fought back in part with their women's clubs, which they themselves created and sustained.

THE RISE OF THE NAACP

The National Association for the Advancement of Colored People (NAACP) was organized back East in 1911 and became the most important civil rights organization of the 20th century. It included both women and men in its membership and in leadership roles. It was emphatically a biracial organization—black and white together—and indeed its preeminent founders and early leaders in the Northeast were white, many of them the children and grandchildren of the old abolitionist families. These white racial liberals were sometimes called—and sometimes called themselves—the neoabolitionists. That said, almost all members and leaders at the local level were African Americans, and the essential national figure for the organization was W. E. B. Du Bois. The aim of the NAACP was full equal rights for African Americans. Du Bois's task was to create a nationally recognized journal or magazine to highlight and promote the work of the NAACP. The result was *The Crisis*, a monthly illustrated magazine, which became the leading publication for black civil rights in the United States and was essential reading material in the homes of middle-class blacks.

The NAACP headquarters was in New York City, but Du Bois's *Crisis* spread quickly from coast to coast, and by 1913, black westerners were looking to organize their own local chapters. That summer, Du Bois journeyed to the West Coast for a grand tour, starting in Seattle and moving southward to Los Angeles. Du Bois loved the West Coast and sent enthusiastic articles to the *Crisis*, lauding the beauty of the region and the spirit of the black communities he found there. He described them as prosperous, fearless, and independent; he liked their spunk, their race enterprises, and, especially in Los Angeles, he liked their automobiles. On the civil rights front he found that blacks had greater freedom out West, but they were still faced with a sharply drawn color line. Not long after Du Bois's visit, the NAACP began to be organized in West Coast cities.

In Los Angeles, the black attorney E. Burton Ceruti wrote to the national office in late 1913, inquiring about the possibility of starting a chapter in the city. Not long after that, in early 1914, Dr. John Somerville, a local dentist and young leader in black Los Angeles (and friend of Du Bois), helped establish the Los Angeles chapter of the NAACP. Membership was small at first, but it had the support of the middle-class leadership and the major churches; plus, the California AAC had expired and the NAACP was on the rise nationally, so the chapter survived and grew. The other center of the California NAACP was, of course, the San Francisco and Oakland region, where the national office chartered a group that included most of the Bay Area. But NAACP chapters were not restricted to the larger cities. They popped up everywhere. California alone had dozens of chapters, and by the end of World War I, virtually all of the urban West was organized. In towns large and small, blacks confronted race prejudice in ways that were typical of America at the time but utterly contrary to what black westerners thought the West should be.

One of the things that put the NAACP in the national limelight— that is, beyond the interest of African Americans and neoabolitionists— was the first blockbuster movie to come out of Hollywood. This film was *The Birth of a Nation*, and it appeared to national acclaim in 1915. The film marked the birth of Hollywood as a motion picture empire, but it was also an aggressively antiblack film. The director of the film, D. W. Griffith, broke all kinds of technological barriers in filmmaking. He also broke African American hearts with his depiction of blacks in the South, especially the Reconstruction South. Griffith took his story and his white-supremacy message from an ardent evangelist of white supremacy: Thomas Dixon, an unreconstructed novelist and playwright whose work was dedicated to the cause of subordinating black people to the lowest level of society (he favored reenslavement) and to ensuring that white people would reign supreme. Dixon was especially determined to make white northerners and westerners feel guilty about abolishing slavery and giving civil rights to blacks.

Dixon distilled his message in a play titled *The Clansman*, which proved most popular outside of the South. It portrayed the Ku Klux Klan as the heroes of the Reconstruction era, saving a prostrate South from corrupt Yankees and savage Negroes. When Dixon's theater production reached Los Angeles in 1908, black leaders moved to shut it down before it sparked race riots. They were rebuffed by city officials, but when a race riot nearly did break out during the *Clansman*'s run in Los Angeles, white leaders began to take things more seriously. One person who saw only opportunity in the *Clansman* was D. W. Griffith, who purchased the movie rights to the play and had Dixon help him write the screenplay for the film version of *The Clansman*. The film begins at the end of the Civil War as black soldiers in Union Army uniforms begin to plunder a southern city. These men are white men in blackface, and their movements mimic rather closely the movement of apes. They are hunting white women.

Representations of blacks did not get better. A later scene set in a state legislature during Reconstruction shows black politicians in the

The first Hollywood blockbuster, The Birth of a Nation *(1915), was also a vicious attack on the character of African Americans and, as this scene from the film indicates, a glorification of the Ku Klux Klan.*

worst possible light. One ravishes a piece of chicken while they pass a bill making miscegenation legal. The black men cheer passage of the bill as they eye white women standing in the gallery above. Eventually, the black antagonist—explicitly made arrogant by his promotion in the U.S. Army—makes advances on the white woman protagonist. She flees, reaches the edge of a cliff, and, seeing him coming, jumps to her death. The film shows her body hitting a small boulder at the bottom of the cliff. Her brother arrives before she dies, she tells him what happened, and, to avenge his sister and protect the rest of the white women of the South from black men, he forms the Ku Klux Klan, which rides forth as heroes at the end of the movie. New Yorkers were wild for it on opening night, with both Dixon and Griffith in attendance, and the triumphant pair changed the title to *The Birth of a Nation*, apparently celebrating the awakening of an America fully committed to southern-style white supremacy.

Blacks in Los Angeles were actually divided over the film. Griffith hired many African American actors to play minor roles, and he paid good money. The key "black" roles were played by white actors in blackface, but many background players were in fact African American, and in the face of criticism from the race papers and black leaders, they defended their work and for the most part defended Griffith himself, whose shockingly negative portrayals of blacks in his film did not seem to transfer to his personal relationships with black actors. Leaders of the local NAACP and publishers of the local race papers, such as Charlotta Bass of the *Eagle*, could not accept this point of view. Honest work in theater or films was one thing; supporting *The Birth of a Nation* and its maker quite another.

Across the nation, as in Los Angeles, local chapters of the NAACP tried to stop the screening of the film. Almost everywhere, chapter leaders met directly with city officials—mayors, city councils, police chiefs—who often shared their concerns over public safety and racial violence. The national office of the NAACP made a concerted campaign of it and was in contact with officials throughout the nation. Results of the NAACP's efforts were mixed but usually not successful in the end. Mayors and city councils were more open to injunctions to stop the film from showing than were judges, who generally claimed they could find no legal basis for issuing or upholding such injunctions. That, basically, is what happened in Los Angeles. And the film played on. But the NAACP was on the map, and, although results varied, most city administrations came away with a favorable opinion of the new group and its leaders.

WORLD WAR I

In the spring of 1917, President Woodrow Wilson finally took the United States into the world war, and he did so with a spirit of high idealism. America would "make the world safe for Democracy." The phrase immediately became part of everyday American vocabulary and, for African Americans, sparked the hope that this war in Europe might bring greater democracy to blacks within the United States itself. This was not a new dream. From the original American Revolution on through the still fresh war against Spain, black Americans hoped that wars fought for freedom and liberty would create conditions for greater freedom and liberty for African Americans, especially if they forthrightly supported the cause and were willing to fight and die for America and the principles of democratic freedom. Not surprisingly, then, black Americans responded enthusiastically to the nation's call to arms.

Even before Wilson's war message, the Buffalo Soldiers stationed in the Southwest had been fighting along the U.S.–Mexican border. Pancho Villa and other Mexican "bandit" gangs were creating havoc on both sides of the border and were pursued by both the U.S. Army and Mexico's *federales* troops. Germany, hoping to keep America out of the war, was using spies and provocateurs to stir up conflict between the United States and Mexico throughout 1916. Ironically, the bloodiest battle occurred between the ostensible allies in this situation—the U.S. troops and the Mexican *federales*. Both were trailing Pancho Villa when they ran into each other in the town of Carrizal, south of the border. Although they were allies, there was no love lost when these groups fell to blows. The *federales* resented the presence of U.S. soldiers on Mexican soil, and the Buffalo Soldiers were convinced the Mexican troops were in cahoots with Villa and were blocking U.S. efforts to capture him.

At Carrizal, the tensions snapped, and a shooting war erupted between the Buffalo Soldiers and the *federales*. Dozens were killed and wounded. Both sides sustained losses, and the much larger Mexican company took a dozen Buffalo Soldiers as prisoners. The result was nearly war between the two countries, but cooler heads prevailed and the U.S. soldiers were released near El Paso. The city was mostly white and ethnic Mexican with a small black population, and whites in Texas had a long tradition of brutalizing the Buffalo Soldiers charged to protect them. But in 1916, the city's white citizenry turned out to cheer the African American men in a hero's parade. Yes, they were black men, one local editorial stated, but they were serving the nation in uniform and deserved the honor they received. That was unusual praise from white El Paso, and it was exactly the kind of respect blacks were hoping to win across the United States when they fervently joined the American war effort in 1917.

Almost from the start, that hope began to unravel. Southern leaders in Congress insisted that Negroes not be allowed to fight for the army, for they would become arrogant, forget their place, and demand their rights.

P.O.   *7th U.S. Corps*

To the colored soldiers of the U. S. Army.

Hallo boys, what are you doing over here? Fighting the Germans? Why? Have they ever done you any harm? Of course, some white folks and the lying English-American papers told you that the Germans ought to be wiped out for the sake of humanity and democracy. What is Democracy? Personal Freedom, all citizens enjoying the same rights socially and before the law! Do you enjoy the same rights as the white people do in America, the land of Freedom and Democracy? Or aren't you rather treated over there as second class citizens? Can you go into a rest urant where white people dine, can you get a seat in a theater where white people sit, can you get a Pullman seat or berth in a rail roadcar or can you even ride, in the South, in the same street car with white people? And how about the law? Is lynching and the most horrible cruelties connected therewith a lawful proceeding in a democratic country?

Now, all this is entirely different in Germany, where they do like colored people, where they treat them as Gentlemen and not as second class citizens. They enjoy exactly the same social privileges as every white man, and quite a number of colored people have migthy fine positions in business in Berlin and other big German cities.

Why then fight the Germans only for the benefit of the Wallstreet robbers to protect the millions they have lent to the English, French and Italians? You have been made the tool of the egotistic and rapacious rich in England and in America, and there is nothing in the whole game for you but broken bones, horrible wounds spoiled health or — death. No satisfaction whatever will you get out of this unjust war. You have never seen Germany, so you are fools if you allow ▮▮▮ to teach you to hate it. Come over to see for yourself, do ▮▮▮ the fighting who make profit out of this war; do ▮▮▮ em to use you as cannon food. To carry the gun in th ▮▮▮ ce is not an honor but a shame. Throw it away and come over to the German lines You will find friends who help you along.

The German government printed this leaflet for distribution among African American Army units fighting in France. There is not evidence the propaganda had any effect, but African Americans both in the United States and France were asking many of the same questions. (National Archives)

They raised the specter of black soldiers in Union blue during Reconstruction, an image recently etched into white American minds through *The Birth of a Nation*. Blacks did get to serve in the army, but the indignities continued. All young men had to register for the military draft—Mexican,

American Indian, Asian, U.S. citizen or not—and all had to fill out a draft card that had a line drawn across one corner, within which there were these words: "Tear off if of African Decent." But indignities were one thing, antiblack race riots were quite another.

Buffalo Soldiers who had been patrolling the U.S.–Mexican border were posted temporarily near Houston, with its deeply southern sensibilities. White Houston was not about to quietly respect black men in uniforms with guns, and the black soldiers were not about to quietly accept racist abuse from white citizens and white law-enforcement personnel. Tensions escalated, and eventually a shooting war broke out in Houston—white residents and law-enforcement officers against a group of Buffalo Soldiers. Once that bloody altercation was over, white Houston stormed the all-black district of the city, attacking blacks and destroying their property. In the military trials that followed, two dozen Buffalo Soldiers were sentenced to death by hanging; another large group received sentences of life in prison. No whites in Houston faced charges of any kind. The Buffalo Soldiers who did not take part in the shooting incident were sent back to Fort Huachuca on the southern border of Arizona and were barred from any service in France during the war.

Through enlistment and the draft, African Americans did serve in France. Because they were not allowed to fight alongside white Americans in this war for democracy, they fought in their own units and with the French Army. The French treated the black soldiers as heroic liberators, with respect and, more than that, as social equals. This was an eye-opening experience for African Americans—and for many white southerners in the U.S. Army, who often reacted with shock and hostility to the way black men were treated in France. On the home front, African Americans adopted the role of super patriots and supported war bond campaigns and other forms of support with enthusiasm. Even W. E. B. Du Bois used his *Crisis* to encourage black Americans to support the war effort full tilt and save their civil rights protests for later.

Generally, African Americans did just that, but it would be difficult, for the war seemed to bring on more, not less, race prejudice in America. Houston turned out to be the tip of the iceberg. Throughout the nation, especially in areas where the East was beginning to run into the West, race riots broke out. In 1917, the black community in East St. Louis went up in flames, and local whites ran virtually the entire population of blacks out

These African American soldiers in France—along with 162 other black infantrymen in World War I—were awarded the Croix de Guerre medal for gallantry by the French government. (National Archives)

of town in what amounted to a pogrom. The war ended in late 1918, and the troops came home from France as triumphant victors. Black veterans evinced a new spirit of pride and self-confidence. Early the next year, the national economy tanked, an anticommunist red scare began (making all activism suspect, including civil rights activism), and Wilson's campaign for a just and lasting postwar peace fell apart quickly: labor unions and capitalists became locked in fierce conflict, and the carnage of the world war among so-called civilized nations began to sink in. In general, a spirit of intolerance swept across the nation.

Then came the race riots of 1919. Chicago exploded first. The African American population of the city had grown rapidly during the Great Migration, and the postwar economic downturn created an unwelcome competition for factory jobs—pitting African Americans against the European immigrants who had arrived before the war (people from

Czechoslovakia and Poland, for example). At a deeper cultural level, race prejudice was the heart of the matter. As the summer grew very hot, the spark on all this tinder was a racial incident at the city's swimming beach on Lake Michigan, which had a section of water marked off for colored. A young black man in the water crossed the line and all hell broke loose on the Chicago beach and then in the city itself—mainly on the South Side, where most African Americans lived. Whites attacked blacks in the black section—the usual pattern in American race riots at the time—but the pattern changed when black residents fought back, World War I veterans among them. Farther south, in the rural area of Elaine, Arkansas, which lay along the Mississippi River, a race riot erupted that, as in Chicago, saw blacks fight back without hesitation and with every weapon at their disposal. Out on the Great Plains, Omaha was engulfed in a race riot. Most other western communities escaped major riots, but racial tensions were high everywhere, and black westerners recognized with despair and bitterness that their wartime support for democracy in Europe had not resulted in greater democracy within America. Far from it.

In 1920, Americans drew a collective breath and tried to move beyond their postwar nightmare. That was more difficult for black Americans, who had so much invested in the war and who had been the main target of wartime and postwar violence. But as subsequent decades would show, African Americans did not give up the fight. In the West, blacks could and did still believe in the western ideal—that this was a place where racial equality might finally become a reality. Frederick Madison Roberts, a leading race man in Los Angeles who had become the first African American elected to the California state legislature, won reelection in 1920 with a solid biracial coalition of white and black voters (see the sidebar on page 124). After his political victory he wrote an editorial in the *New Age*, his weekly race paper. In it one can almost sense Roberts's disappointment about what the war had wrought and his determination to keep fighting for equal rights. "Suppose we all pull together now," he wrote, "and help make the country safe for Democracy" (Flamming, *Bound for Freedom*, 187).

BIBLIOGRAPHIC ESSAY

The opening vignette is from Douglas Flamming, *Bound for Freedom: Black Los Angeles in Jim Crow America* (Berkeley: University of California Press, 2005),

THE ELECTION OF FRED ROBERTS, 1918

In 1918, Frederick Madison Roberts became the first African American elected to the California state legislature, when he won the race for the 74th Assembly District in south Los Angeles. Roberts was born in 1879 in Chillicothe, Ohio, a small black community anchored by the descendants of Sally Hemings, the now famous slave-mistress of Thomas Jefferson (Hemings's son Madison, freed in Jefferson's will, was Fred Roberts's grandfather.) Fred's parents, Andrew Jackson Roberts and Ellen Hemings Roberts, moved to Los Angeles in the mid-1880s. He grew up with the city, got a college education in Colorado, received training in mortuary science in Chicago, cut his teeth in Republican Party politics, and returned to Los Angeles to join his father's business—Roberts and Son's Funeral Home. Fred became the owner-editor of a Race paper, *The New Age*, and a leader in churches and social circles. All of this gave him an excellent background for success in black politics.

Among potential voters in the 74th District, only about 20 percent were African American. The rest were overwhelmingly white—and from very diverse backgrounds. Mostly, however, the whites were from the northern states and were Republicans who still saw Lincoln as the figurehead of their party. Roberts won a seat in the California statehouse by creating a political alliance between African Americans and white Lincoln Republicans in his district. In both 1918, and again in Roberts's reelection bid in 1920, an antiblack campaign was organized against him, but in both cases his biracial coalition triumphed. In office, he was able to strengthen California's civil rights laws and remained in office until 1934, still the only African American in the state assembly.

41–44. On Arna Bontemps generally, see Kirkland C. Jones, *Renaissance Man from Louisiana: A Biography of Arna Wendell Bontemps* (Westport, CT: Greenwood Press, 1992).

On the racial crisis of the New South, see Leon Litwack, *Trouble in Mind: Black Southerners in the Age of Jim Crow* (New York: Vintage Books, 1998); J. Morgan Kousser, *The Shaping of Southern Politics: Suffrage Restriction and the*

Establishment of the One-Party South (New Haven, CT: Yale University Press, 1974); Joel Williamson, *The Crucible of Race: Black-White Relations in the American South since Emancipation* (New York: Oxford University Press, 1984); and C. Vann Woodward, *Origins of the New South, 1877–1913* (Baton Rouge: Louisiana State University Press, 1971).

On the Talented Tenth generally, see David Levering Lewis, *W. E. B. Du Bois: Biography of a Race, 1868–1919* (New York: Henry Holt, 1993); W. E. B. Du Bois's 1903 classic, *The Souls of Black Folk* (New York: Vintage Books, 1990, with an introduction by John Edgar Wideman); Cynthia Neverdon-Morton, *Afro-American Women of the South and the Advancement of the Race, 1895–1925* (Knoxville: University of Tennessee Press, 1989); William B. Gatewood's *Aristocrats of Color: The Black Elite, 1880–1920* (Bloomington: Indiana University Press, 1990); and Albert S. Broussard, *African American Odyssey: The Stewarts, 1853–1963* (Lawrence: University Press of Kansas, 1998).

The Great Migration from South to North is covered in many books, including James Grossman, *Land of Hope: Chicago, Black Southerners, and the Great Migration* (Chicago: University of Chicago Press, 1989); Peter Gottlieb, *Making Their Own Way: Southern Blacks' Migration to Pittsburgh, 1916–1930* (Urbana: University of Illinois Press, 1987); Kenneth L. Kusmer, *A Ghetto Takes Shape: Black Cleveland, 1870–1930* (Urbana: University of Illinois Press, 1978); and Joe Trotter, ed., *The Great Migration in Historical Perspective: New Dimensions of Race, Class, and Gender* (Bloomington: Indiana University Press, 1991).

Black migration to Western cities from 1890 to 1920 has been treated in several case studies. Douglas Daniels's *Pioneer Urbanites: A Social and Cultural History of Black San Francisco* (Berkeley: University of California Press, 1990) marked an early contribution, as did Thomas C. Cox, *Blacks in Topeka, Kansas, 1865–1915* (Baton Rouge: Louisiana State University Press, 1982). Flamming's *Bound for Freedom* covers Los Angeles for this period, and Quintard Taylor's *In Search of the Racial Frontier* provides a regional survey. Books that focus on the period after 1940 but also cover the decades for this chapter include Albert S. Broussard, *Black San Francisco*; Quintard Taylor, *The Forging of a Black Community: Seattle's Central District from 1870 through the Civil Rights Era* (Seattle: University of Washington Press, 1994); Shirley Ann Wilson Moore, *To Place Our Deeds: The African American Community in Richmond, California, 1910–1963* (Berkeley: University of California Press, 2001).

On the film *The Birth of a Nation* and the larger story of blacks in Hollywood, see Thomas Cripps, *Slow Fade to Black* (New York: Oxford University Press, 1977); and Donald Bogle, *Bright Boulevards, Bold Dreams: The Story of Black Hollywood* (New York: One World/Ballantine, 2006).

CHAPTER FIVE

BETWEEN THE WORLD WARS, 1920–1940

In 1924, Verna Deckard drove into Los Angeles in a new Ford coupe. At least it had been new before she drove it all the way from East Texas to Los Angeles. Now as she drove down Central Avenue, the heart of black Los Angeles, her dusty car had a good many miles on it, but she was very happy. And why not? She was 16 years old and had just driven her car halfway across the continent. The car was a birthday present from her father, Jule Deckard, an auto mechanic who had made a good living in Terrell, Texas. Her father and mother were in a car just ahead, and her father had put a sign on it: Texas to Los Angeles. And as they drove down Central people on the street waved and yelled out "Hello, Texas!" The 1920s marked the automobile boom in America, and newcomers to Los Angeles increasingly arrived by car.

The Deckard family had actually come to Los Angeles just for a vacation and to see Verna's brother, who already live there. Her parents had arranged for another young man to ride with Verna along the way, in case she needed a break from driving. She never gave up the wheel. And, as it turned out, she never went back to Texas. She loved the city. Plus, she did not want to go back to "bad old Texas" because of the racial conditions there.

For the Deckards, East Texas had provided some economic opportunities but also the obvious Jim Crow restraints—and personal dangers. Only a few years before Verna's big trip, her father had been attacked by white men intent on killing him. A family friend had come to visit—an African American woman with a very light complexion. When Mr. Deckard escorted her to the train station for departure, white men mistook her for a white woman, and they aimed to take Deckard down. That night, Deckard took a sledgehammer to the head and a bullet through the arm, but he escaped and fled for a time to Los Angeles with his son. Soon the father was ready to return to Texas, but the son would not go back. Amazingly, Deckard revived his automobile business and continued to prosper—hence, Verna's new car. But Verna herself wanted out of Texas. She was tired of the burdens of Jim Crow, tired of the way white folks treated her.

So it was that as Verna Deckard's summer vacation in Los Angeles was coming to an end, Verna was determined to stay. Because she was not yet a legal adult, her parents could simply make her return with them to Texas, but she had a plan. While in Los Angeles, she acquired a boy-friend who was of legal age. Shortly before the Deckards were to return to Texas, Verna and her boyfriend showed up with their new marriage license! Mom and Dad graciously conceded to the inevitable and gave their blessing to the couple. Verna Deckard stayed out West. Mom and Dad returned to Texas, but not for long. Soon thereafter, they arranged for the sale of their home and business, and then they too moved to Los Angeles for good.

Los Angeles was a good place for an auto mechanic, as it was a city that had gone wild for cars. It was, for that matter, a city gone wild in many respects. The automobiles, the flappers, the Hollywood scene; the jazz clubs, the bootleg gin, the modern beach culture—all of these trends dis-tanced Los Angeles from its Spanish-Mexican past. Indeed, it was during the 1920s that the old Spanish name of Los Angeles was suddenly replaced by a new appellation: "L.A." In any event, the city of L.A. was exploding with growth and general prosperity when the Deckards settled in.

It was fortunate for the Deckards that they arrived in the mid-1920s. Only a few years earlier, racial tensions in L.A. had been intense: the Ku Klux Klan had made an explosive appearance in the city, and the black community feared an all-out attack by white Angelenos. But conditions were better by the middle of the decade. Verna Deckard's happy memo-ries of her early years in L.A. stemmed partly from the fact that she was a young woman with wheels—and a new, exciting life ahead of her. Those happy memories were also due, however, to the timing of her arrival. She arrived in L.A. when the black community was in full bloom.

A DESCRIPTION OF WATTS IN THE 1930S

Oral history interviews are an enjoyable way to conduct historical research for students and scholars alike. The following excerpt is from an oral history conducted by the Oral History Program at the University of California, Los Angeles (UCLA). The topic was jazz music, and the interviewee was jazz legend Cecil "Big Jay" McNeely, who offered interesting recollections of what childhood was like in Watts during the 1930s:

> I was born in Watts in 1927. There were three boys in the family: my brother Robert, who played saxophone with me, and Dillard, who later came in and played bass. We traveled together on the road for many years. We were born on 110th Street. It was a mixed community, all nationalities were there. It was complete peace at that time. Spanish kids, Orientals, and whites. We all went to school together, no problems.
>
> We used to go down all the time and watch Simon Rodia building the Watts Towers. Watts was a beautiful place. They used to deliver the milk in a little horse-and-buggy. We had the ice man—we had to buy ice. We had a lot of chickens and ducks and things in our place. We had a hundred feet by a hundred, and had a well on it, and grew all types of vegetables. See, my father [Dillard McNeely] was from the South, and, like a farmer, he knew how to grow all the vegetables. . . .
>
> Parents were concerned about the other parents' children. You'd get one whipping down the street, you'd get another whipping when you'd get home. The teachers had the authority to teach and punish, so there was a lot of respect for parents and for one another's property and for one another. No crime. We had all nationalities, Spanish, Chinese, Japanese, white, all living together, no problem (Bryant, et al., *Central Avenue South,* 179–180).

The two decades between the two world wars were in fact a roller coaster of ups and downs for blacks in the urban West. The Roaring Twenties, the Great Depression, the New Deal—these shaped the lives of all Americans. But for African Americans the interwar years were especially influential. In the 1920s, civil rights activists struggled to deal with new forms of white hostility and racial discrimination as well as a general public apathy toward all things serious. At the same time, African Americans experienced an exciting surge in black nationalism, as symbolized in Garveyism, the evolution of race enterprises, and the rise of jazz. The Great Depression that began in 1929 and continued through most of the 1930s hit the African American economy with full force. It also prompted a sea change in black politics, as African Americans abandoned the Republican Party and joined the liberal wing of the Democratic Party—leaving the party of Lincoln for the party of Roosevelt. The trauma, thrills, and general turmoil black Angelenos encountered during the interwar decades were common to blacks throughout the urban West. The worst of the traumas, however, was reserved for the black community of Tulsa, Oklahoma.

THE TULSA RACE RIOT

Oklahoma—formerly Indian Territory—became a state in 1907, and from that time through the end of World War I, the city of Tulsa grew at a rapid clip. Located in the northeastern part of the state, Tulsa was mostly white but had a sizable black population. The African American community there was generally a prosperous one, but with Oklahoma hugging the South, it was tightly segregated. The homes of the black middle class and their businesses were centered on Greenwood Avenue, and "Greenwood" became a shorthand reference for the black community in Tulsa. Much of Greenwood would be burned to the ground in the 1921 riot.

The spark of the riot was a false accusation by some white men that a black man had made advances on a white girl. The black man, Dick Rowland, would later be acquitted, but in keeping with the white South's way of racial justice, the guilt or innocence of a black person proved irrelevant to the punishment that would follow. After the sheriff locked Rowland in the courthouse jail, a white newspaper announced in its midafternoon edition, in bold headlines, that a lynching would be held that night.

Some men of Greenwood decided to intervene; they would not let Rowland be lynched. Among them were the leaders of black Tulsa, including, for example, John Williams, who had prospered nicely in Tulsa and was one of the leading property owners in Greenwood. As twilight gave way to darkness on the night of May 31, about two dozen men of

Victims of the Tulsa riot of 1921, their homes burned to the ground, line up to receive supplies after the riot. (Library of Congress)

black Tulsa got their guns, met near the center of the Greenwood district, and drove to the courthouse. The white mob around the courthouse already numbered several hundred. The sheriff had taken action to prevent Rowland's capture, and he also called for the mobilization of the National Guard. The Greenwood men offered the sheriff their services; he refused and convinced them, for a time, that he had the situation under control. They returned to Greenwood for a while.

The white crowd downtown grew, and another part of the mob tried to break into the National Guard Armory to take the guns and ammunition held there. The National Guard held off the mob at gunpoint but did not force it to disperse. When reports of this escalation reached Greenwood, the black men reassembled, now about 50 or 75 in number, and returned to the courthouse. As usual in such situations, the question of who fired first and why would never be clearly answered, but there was a shot, and from that came a race riot.

Bullets flew. The black men, outnumbered roughly 75 to 3,000—but all armed—fought their way out of downtown and back toward the Greenwood neighborhoods. Throughout the night and into the morning, a white mob fought its way into black Tulsa in what amounted to door-to-door combat. The burning of Greenwood began on June 1, in broad daylight, as city and county law enforcement rounded up African Americans and took them to internment centers. Perhaps as many as 6,000 blacks were force-marched to internment sites. White men involved in the violence were not stopped or disarmed until very late in the day, when the National Guard finally moved to stop the destruction of Greenwood. Until then, the whites were free to burn Greenwood as they chose. White photographers accompanied the mob into Greenwood and took action shots of the burning.

The damage—in human life and black property—was staggering, even when seen in the context of the 1919 riots. The riot was so chaotic that the number of deaths due to the violence could never be tallied with any accuracy. Estimates range from roughly 30 to 300 persons dead—and perhaps half of these were white men. More than 1,000 African American homes and businesses were destroyed. The very heart of a large and prosperous black community lay in ashes. Blacks in Tulsa would rebuild and rebuild well, but that took time, and many left the city for other western cities, including Los Angeles. For its part, white Tulsa's officials, along with state-level politicians, openly and emphatically blamed the riot on the blacks themselves, more particularly on the black men who had arrived downtown with guns and, as the white officials told it, opened fire on innocent men, women, and children.

Beyond Tulsa itself, the riot sent shock waves through the nation and more particularly blacks in the West. Was this the return of 1919? Tulsa had seemed like a good town for African Americans; if an attack like this could happen in Tulsa, it could happen anywhere. The violence in Tulsa created a riot scare in Los Angeles. The Ku Klux Klan was active and public in Los Angeles at the time, and rumors of a Klan riot ran through the black community in June 1921. A Klan membership list surfaced in L.A., valid or not, and the names included an uncomfortably high number of law-enforcement officials, judges, and elected representatives. One rumor that made its way down Central Avenue was that black Los Angeles would get the "Tulsa treatment" on July 4, and that the Klan and the local police had already established a secret signal for storming black neighborhoods. Local race papers, including the *Eagle*, tried to squash these rumors, but black attorney Hugh MacBeth wrote to the mayor, alerting him to the rumors and asking him to call for calm in the city, fearing that an isolated racial conflict might in fact spark a riot even if none had been planned.

One difference between black Tulsa and the black communities on the West Coast involved residential demographics. Greenwood was an all-black section of town. In that sense, it was a very southern-style place. No other major western city had these kind of fully black neighborhoods. Blacks lived interspersed with ethnic Mexicans, Japanese, Chinese, and many whites as well, both native-born and immigrant. Businesses were similarly interspersed. There would be no way to attack the "black district" of Los Angeles, San Francisco, or Seattle without also destroying the property of many people who were not blacks. On an individual level, diverse housing demographics would not help protect someone from a hate crime, but perhaps at the group level—one group attacking the neighborhood of another—it may have helped protect African Americans on the West Coast from white mobs.

The Tulsa race riot marked a terrible beginning to the 1920s. Perhaps it is best understood not as the opening of racial tension in the 1920s but rather as the final bloody episode of the white-on-black racial violence that exploded at the edge of the West during the late 1910s: Houston (1917); East St. Louis (1917); Chicago (1919); Elaine, Arkansas (1919); Omaha (1919); and Tulsa. For African Americans it was another painful reminder that a nation dedicated to making the world safe for democracy was still largely unwilling to provide basic human rights—life, liberty, and the pursuit of happiness—for its black citizens, even those in the American West.

THE SECOND KU KLUX KLAN

In the early 1920s, a second incarnation of the Ku Klux Klan (KKK) swept across the United States and was especially strong in the urban West. The original Klan of the 1870s had been officially destroyed by President Grant and the Republican Party during Reconstruction. Night riders, often called "whitecaps," and other vigilante groups continued to terrorize the South in the decades that followed, but not under the official Klan banner. In 1915, however, a "second" Klan was organized in Atlanta. The immediate cause was the local screening of D. W. Griffith's *The Birth of a Nation*, which denounced radical Reconstruction and black people generally, even as it promoted the ideal of white supremacy. It praised the Klan as a heroic organization that upheld white supremacy and protected white womanhood from black men. A group of whites, inspired by this message, met outside town on top of Stone Mountain, where they burned a cross and reestablished the Klan.

After World War I, the second manifestation of the Klan grew rapidly, primarily outside the South. The national headquarters in Atlanta sent missionaries into the North and West. The second Klan was antiblack, but it was also explicitly against Jews, Catholics, recent immigrants, and Latinos. In the early 1920s, the western Klan saw success at both the local

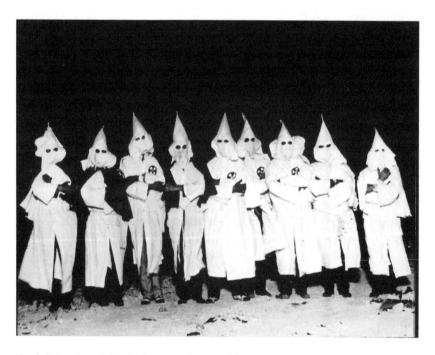

Symbolizing the racial and religious intolerance of the 1920s, the Second Ku Klux Klan grew strong in the urban West, targeting Catholics, Jews, and African Americans. (Hulton Archive/ Getty Images)

and state level. It emerged in cities such as El Paso and Los Angeles, where the Mexican and Catholic populations were especially strong.

The Klan headquarters in Atlanta was eager to create a strong organization in Los Angeles. It sent two officials to do the job: William Coburn, the grand goblin of the Klan's Pacific States Division; and G. W. Price, the imperial representative for the California empire. They arrived in the spring of 1921 and found plenty of interest, even as they kept a low profile. Events that summer brought them out into the open. First, a popular movie theater in L.A. brought *The Birth of a Nation* out of the vault and began to show it; the local NAACP and other black leaders protested to city officials, who agreed that local racial conditions might turn violent if the film continued to be shown. Quietly, the city convinced the theater to shelve the movie. This flushed the local Klan into the open, as Coburn personally threatened the Los Angeles city attorney for negotiating this move.

A torrent of public denunciation rained down on Coburn and the local Klan. The city government, city and county law enforcement officials, and the major daily newspapers all slammed the KKK. The *Los Angeles Times* even offered an editorial that essentially insisted on racial equality. The district attorney, Thomas Lee Woolwine, got a warrant to search the L.A. headquarters, where he found the official membership list.

The list was thick with the names of law-enforcement officials, some of whom had publicly denounced the Klan. Most denied affiliation or explained that they had joined under false pretenses. One public official, the president of the L.A. City Council, refused to deny his membership. But the discomfort of those white leaders on the KKK membership list was nothing compared with the discomfort felt within the black community. Some very important and influential leaders were listed on the Klan's membership rolls—including judges and many people who were leaders of, or employed by, city and county law-enforcement agencies. Black distrust of local law enforcement and the penal system was hardly new, but now it increased. Who, behind the badge and the bench, could they really trust?

Politically, the Klan was not able to gain control of the state government in California, but the same cannot be said for the state governments of Oregon and Colorado, where the KKK dominated politics, albeit briefly, in the early 1920s. Oregon's Klan, more than 10,000 strong, was centered in Portland but made itself felt in the halls of the state capitol. In the

1922 elections, the Oregon Klan supported the Democratic candidate for governor, Walter M. Pierce, who, like the Democratic Party progressives in El Paso, found in the Klan a useful and comfortable vehicle for control. The same election saw Klan-supported candidates win a majority of seats in the Oregon legislature, where, in order to eliminate Catholic schools, they passed legislation requiring all children to attend a *public* school. Later in the 1920s, the U.S. Supreme Court overturned the law, ruling it unconstitutional and allowing Catholics to attend their church-run schools. Colorado elected its Klan governor two years later, in 1924, when the "hooded empire" also claimed the state legislature. In both states, Klan-supported officials soon lost power, in part because of ineffective governance and in part because those who opposed them got better organized politically.

Scandals and internal divisions divided the Klan at all levels, and by the late 1920s most whites had more or less put the Klan itself out of mind. What worried black civil rights leaders was that many blacks in the city also seemed to have put the Klan out of mind, believing they were not a real threat. Perhaps they were not, yet the Klan continued to organize and rally on and off during the 1920s, and the larger question of KKK infiltration of law enforcement and the criminal justice system never went away.

GARVEYISM OUT WEST

Black nationalism rose to new heights during the early 1920s, as self-help and community cohesion seemed ever more appealing and essential in the wake of the race riots and the reemergence and spread of the KKK. Pan-Africa movements were apparent throughout the globe in the wake of World War I and the shake-up in European colonial regimes that accompanied the war. In the United States, it was a Caribbean immigrant—Marcus Garvey—who created the most influential nationalist organization, the Universal Negro Improvement Association (UNIA), which promoted cultural pride and economic self-sufficiency.

The UNIA's cultural power stemmed from its over-the-top pageantry and Garvey's unabashed embrace of all things flamboyant. He and his fellow UNIA officers wore ornate, full-dress military uniforms that seemed to outsiders to be almost an unintentional parody of the formal dress of English-style colonial rulers. In full dress, Garvey himself wore a Napoleon-style admiral's hat with a large feather as a plume. From a cultural point of view,

Marcus Garvey, the charismatic leader of the Universal Negro Improvement Association, the dominant black nationalist organization of the 1920s. (Library of Congress)

the UNIA sometimes appeared to be a national and extreme version of the traditional black social club. Garveyism's public displays of blackness were, in any case, emphatically *not* a mirror of white American culture, and that was part of its power.

Garvey's economic program was more specific and practical, although it had its own emotional power: the Black Star Line. This was to be a line of steamships that would establish lines of trade and commerce between black America and black Africa. UNIA dues were invested in the ships, and those with more money could invest more in the Black Star Line. Trans-Atlantic trade with Africa would deliver a strong return on investment. The promises made were grand—too grand, as it turned out—but after the violence and heartbreak of 1919, black America needed to feel that grand was possible. They needed to believe it was possible to unite black Africa with black America and to watch both grow strong and prosperous together. The UNIA spread like wildfire across the nation, to rural hamlets, small towns, and big cities.

Small-town chapters were an important part of Garveyism in the West. In the bigger cities of the region formal membership expanded into the hundreds, but it only took seven members to form a chapter, so the smallest of black communities could organize their own chapter and be part of the larger picture. African Americans in Ogden, Utah, had their chapter. Coffeyville, Kansas, and Mesa, Arizona, had chapters. And the list went on—in the central valley of California, where few African Americans lived, there were divisions in Bakersfield, Wasco, Fresno, and Durante. The larger cities of the region organized, too. On the Great Plains, chapters were formed in Omaha, Nebraska, and Tulsa, Oklahoma. Denver had its chapter in the mountains (as did Colorado Springs on the front range), and Phoenix had its following in the Southwest. The West Coast states were well covered, top to bottom: Seattle, Portland, San Francisco, Oakland, Los Angeles, and San Diego.

As the New York headquarters of the UNIA soon discovered, western chapters tended to go their own way and did not readily take orders from the East Coast. That was a lesson the NAACP was beginning to learn, and it was a lesson black civil rights groups and nationalist organizations in the East would continue to (re)learn for the rest of the 20th century. Westerners were independent folks, and that included black westerners! They had their own ideas about how to do things, and throughout the 20th century, black leaders from back East, especially New York City, were surprised and often frustrated by the independent spirit of their western brethren, who didn't hold for advice from New York.

The largest UNIA chapter in the West was also the most independent minded: UNIA Division 156 in Los Angeles. The city's middle-class leaders, and indeed a broad spectrum of black Angelenos, were swept up in the excitement of Garveyism. Noah Thompson, the journalist and realtor, was selected as the initial president; Charlotta Bass, owner of the *Eagle*, was elected as the "lady president." At its height in early 1921, Division 156 had about 1,000 members on the rolls. A popular minister in black Los Angeles, the Rev. John Dawson Gordon was summoned to New York to be a leader at headquarters.

With strong support from the local community, division president Noah Thompson traveled to New York that summer to represent the L.A. group at the national convention. Thompson kept black L.A. informed about the proceedings, and his reports were troubling. Two days of the convention were spent debating how many buttons should be on the coat of a particular officer. When Thompson asked national officials to discuss the finances of the Black Star Line, he received evasive answers. Thompson insisted that the delegates be shown the ships that had been purchased—the UNIA rank and file had invested $250,000 in the Black Star Line—but he got no satisfaction. Before long, it became clear that the only ships purchased by the UNIA were clunkers bought at high prices; they were only worth scrap. Thompson discovered that the UNIA was effectively broke, despite all of the money paid in from across the country.

This was just the sort of bad business that black Los Angeles could not tolerate. They felt duped. The L.A. division announced a declaration of independence and formed its own Garvey-like group—the Pacific Coast Universal Negro Improvement Association (PCUNIA). The New York office responded by decertifying Division 156 and barred the old officers from membership in a new and officially sanctioned division in L.A., which could only muster about 100 members.

Garvey nonetheless remained a popular figure for most black Angelenos, and when he first visited L.A. in the summer of 1922, he received what had become the standard greeting for visiting dignitaries—the automobile caravan parade down Central Avenue. Frederick Roberts, up for reelection to the legislature that fall, rode next to Garvey in the main car. The president of the reorganized UNIA of L.A. was Douglas Greer, a popular music teacher. The local UNIA survived under Greer's leadership, but the conflict between the pocketbook sensibilities of Central Avenue's black leaders and the vague accounting methods of New York's UNIA was never resolved. Later in the decade, an embattled Garvey formed a strange, unofficial alliance with the KKK, praising the Klan for supporting racial separatism. Before long, he was deported on charges of mail fraud, and Garveyism gradually faded. Even so, the wellspring of black nationalist sentiment in the West did not dry up, and as the century progressed new nationalist leaders and organizations would once again tap into that reservoir of emotion and pride.

THE NEW NEGRO RENAISSANCE

By the mid-1920s, African Americans were speaking confidently of "the New Negro," a phrase coined by blacks themselves. It referred especially to the younger generation—mainly those in college—who had a confident new spirit about them, a spirit of self-confidence and self-respect. The New Negroes were well educated, optimistic, assertive, and impatient for their rights. They were organized, creative, and possessed a sharp eye for opportunity. They wrote and performed music, wrote fiction and poetry, studied medicine and law, and made it clear that they were willing and able—immediately—to lead the race into a new era. Not all of the (suddenly) "Old" Negroes were always pleased with what they perceived as the unearned arrogance of the younger generation. There was some conflict between the two groups, but for the most part, the middle-aged race leaders were proud of this rising generation and did what they could to promote the New Negro youth.

Cultural production was an important part of the New Negro movement. Jazz was the most popular aspect of it, but young blacks also wrote fiction and poetry about all things black—Africa, slavery, juke joints, cotton fields, Negro churches, the Black Metropolis. Young black scholars, especially sociologists, wrote about the African American condition. Painters and sculptors and muralists also left their mark on the era. In short, there was a flowering of black culture and literature, and blacks in the West would be an important part of it.

The art and literature movement was centered in Harlem, which by the mid-1920s had become a large, virtually all-black district in Manhattan. There jazz clubs were hopping, Broadway was opening itself to black composers and musicians, and white publishing companies were suddenly looking for black authors. Harlem became a magnet for blacks throughout America and the Caribbean—the unofficial capital of the African diaspora. And because Harlem was so central to the New Negro arts movement, the movement would come to be known as the Harlem Renaissance.

The renaissance idea was coined by W. E. B. Du Bois, who lived and published *The Crisis* in Harlem, but oddly enough, his first major use of the term "renaissance" seems to have been in Los Angeles—and in the *Los Angeles Times* at that. Du Bois had come to L.A. in 1925 to stage his theatrical pageant, *The Star of Ethiopia*. The *Times* promoted the event and gave Du Bois nearly a full page to write about it, which he did in an article titled "The New Negro Renaissance." In antiquity, Du Bois explained, black Africans had created wealthy and powerful kingdoms that were filled with art and beautiful cultural and architectural representations. Then came slavery and the triumph of the Europeans over Africa, and with it came the virtual demise of high art by the Negro people. Like Greek and Roman culture in the Dark Ages of Europe, it had been all but lost, but now the revival of

Emblematic of the Harlem Renaissance of the 1920s was the glittering Cotton Club, which featured jazz greats such as Duke Ellington and Cab Calloway. Larger western cities had their own versions of the Cotton Club. (Michael Ochs Archives/Getty Images)

black art and culture—at the very highest levels—was being revived by a new generation, the New Negroes of America. The black arts movement that had captured urban America was not something completely new, nor did it owe its power to European influences. Instead, it should be understood as a renaissance of high African culture.

The black West had an unanticipated and underappreciated influence on the Harlem Renaissance. That influence resulted from the migration of black western writers and artists to Harlem itself, where their work served to alter the course of the Renaissance in the mid-1920s. The four leading figures in this process were Langston Hughes, Wallace Thurman, and Arna Bontemps, all of whom were writers, and Aaron Douglas, who was a painter. All were roughly the same age—in college during the early 1920s—all were brilliant, and all of them were "New Negroes" who were eager to get to Harlem once the renaissance took off. Indeed, they were the core of what historians sometimes call the "New Negro" phase of the Harlem Renaissance.

Du Bois and other middle-aged, middle-class leaders initially dominated the Harlem Renaissance. The historian David Levering Lewis, the leading scholar of the renaissance, has called this the "Talented Tenth" phase of the arts movement. The aim was, in keeping with Du Bois's article for the *L.A. Times* mentioned previously, for African Americans to produce high art—painting, sculpture, music, and literature—that would demonstrate to racially prejudiced whites that blacks were indeed equal to European-Americans in talent and artistic genius, and therefore deserving of equal political and social rights as well. Du Bois wanted to use high art as a tool for winning respect from white people; that, he thought, would be a stepping stone toward winning civil rights.

The younger generation embraced a different ideal and inaugurated the second phase of the movement, which Lewis has labeled the "New Negro Renaissance." These young adults wanted to stir things up. They wanted the freedom to express themselves artistically without having to conform to middle-class restraints. Some were also enamored of the 1920s ideal of "modernism," which held that industrial civilization was beyond help and that civilization could only survive if it sought and embraced what was still "real" in the world, what had not been corrupted by industrialization, what was still "primitive." And what was still primitive in America?

Langston Hughes, born in Oklahoma and raised in Kansas, was one of several young westerners who influenced the literary trends of the Harlem Renaissance. (Library of Congress)

In the modernist view, Negroes, especially Deep South Negroes, who had maintained a part of their African primitivism. Unlike Du Bois, who was celebrating the reawakening of Africa's ancient grandeur, the young people of the New Negro Renaissance were celebrating the persistence of ancient African primitivism. A return to bedrock human nature, to pure passion and emotion, was the modern world's only hope. That, in the loftiest sense, was the idea, and for those less interested in the loftier ideals of modernism, the New Negro arts movement was, at the very least, very cool.

Langston Hughes was born in 1903 in the all-black town of Langston, Oklahoma, and raised by his grandmother in Topeka, Kansas. His father left the United States for Mexico, where he became a substantial landowner. His mother traveled the entertainment circuits of the northern cities. Topeka had a strong black community, but Hughes's grandmother kept him at the margins of it. He visited his father in Mexico a time or two, finding him cold to literature and openly critical of American Negroes. In his teenage years, he moved to Cleveland to live with his mother. There was a large black community there, but, just like his grandmother in Topeka, his mother largely steered clear of the black community and raised Langston in a mostly white section of the city. Hughes, then, was raised on the margins of black American life. He did not know the cotton fields of the South; he knew the wheat fields of Kansas. He did not know black slang; he knew Spanish. But Langston Hughes longed to be a part of black America, to be immersed in its culture and heritage. As he saw it, he had been robbed of his racial birthright.

A precocious writer from a young age, and hungry for black culture, Hughes developed a unique ear for African American language and music and found a way to reproduce it in a seemingly simple and unerringly lyrical style of poetry that seemed a perfect fit for the 1920s. Earning a scholarship to Columbia University in New York brought him to Harlem early in the decade. Instead of plunging into his studies, he went down to the docks, hired on as a deckhand on a trade ship bound for Africa, and left New York on the spot, famously throwing his college books into the ocean as the ship put out to sea. He saw Africa. He saw Paris. He had poems published in *The Crisis* and other black journals. And by the time he returned to Harlem in mid-decade, he was already something of a legend in local literary circles.

Arna Bontemps of Los Angeles became one of Hughes's best friends in Harlem—and indeed for the rest of his life. They were roughly the same age, and they shared much in common. Bontemps's parents and grandparents were Louisiana Creoles who did not readily identify with or associate themselves with the black community in Los Angeles. Like Hughes, Bontemps knew Spanish. And Bontemps's own father had also made something of a break from black America and its culture. He sent Arna to an otherwise all-white boarding school in the virtually all-white San Fernando Valley, telling him "Now don't go up there acting colored." (Flamming, "A Westerner," 85). The school itself was excellent; Bontemps made friends and excelled in his studies, but he felt he was missing out on his heritage. The feeling increased when he attended a virtually all-white college in northern California. He developed a longing, quite akin to that of Langston Hughes, to connect with black culture. Back in L.A. he read the early poetry of the New Negro Renaissance, and it struck a chord; he went to the jazz clubs not for the party (he was a lifelong teetotaler) but for the jazz itself and for the crowd and the feeling of being somehow at home. He had a poem published in *The Crisis* and soon bought a train ticket to New York. He arrived in Harlem shortly before Hughes returned from Africa.

An artist from Nebraska, Aaron Douglas, joined Hughes and Bontemps in Harlem, where he quickly made a name by painting the iconic images of the renaissance. Douglas grew up in Omaha in a middle-class household, but his parents were more a part of the black community than the families of Bontemps or Hughes. He grew up with a copy of *Crisis* on the coffee table, and he grew up with artistic ambitions that took him to the University of Nebraska in Lincoln. There the art he studied was virtually all European, and that was the style he mastered in college; he produced some impressive paintings in the impressionist style, in which carefully placed (but seemingly casual) and colorful brush strokes produced a striking "impression" of an ordinary scene. Douglas had only been in Harlem for a week or so when a popular German artist insisted that Douglas forget the European styles and use his talents to represent African primitivism. Douglas, not long from Nebraska, made this move with enthusiasm. Almost overnight, it seemed, he created the essential look of the Harlem Renaissance, creating large, overlapping silhouettes of stylized Negro figures, some of which carried the connotation of ancient Africa, others that carried the connotation of blacks in the American South, and still others that reflected the Great Migration to northern cities. He gave up the power of color and relied on graduated shades of light pastels, often arranged in circular patterns that seemed, at a glance, independent from his human figures.

There was nothing else like his Afrocentric work at the time, and one wonders how he could have defined a style so quickly and effortlessly. Part of the answer is that his formal training and high level of talent gave him the expertise he needed to grab hold of and remake the black primitivist genre. Another answer—a related one—is that he, like Bontemps, was hungry to connect with "Negro-ness." After all, there were few African American students at the University of Nebraska, much less in the art department. He became the "father" of African art in the Renaissance, not because he had seen Africa or even the American South, and not because he had been immersed in the culture of the Black Metropolis. Instead, his Africanism was born on the Great Plains, where, surrounded by white folk and reading about Harlem, he aspired to be at the center of the New Negro arts movement.

Another major contributor to the New Negro phase of the renaissance was Wallace Thurman of Utah. Like the others, he came of age mostly isolated from other African Americans. After high school he went to Los Angeles, took some classes at the University of Southern California, started a short-lived literary journal on Central Avenue, worked in the post office for a bit, and got the Harlem bug. In New York, he quickly distinguished himself by his flamboyant Bohemian lifestyle and his intellectual genius. Naturally, he fell in with the young renaissance crowd of Harlem and became friends with Hughes, Bontemps, and Douglas.

One night in Harlem, these young intellectuals were gathered casually at Aaron Douglas's apartment when Thurman suggested they start their own literary journal. The black middle class had supported their work, but Thurman thought they had outgrown the old guard. It was time for the New Negroes to strike out on their own. They would call their journal *Fire!!* Most of the young Renaissance writers joined in the endeavor, and Douglas provided the artwork. The range of topics, the styles of presentation, the quality of the pieces—all varied considerably. But no one missed the intent of *Fire!!*, which amounted to a declaration of independence from the Talented Tenth leadership.

Edited by Thurman, *Fire!!* was published on a shoestring budget, and it survived for only one issue. And that issue, after selling poorly, did not actually survive, for the stacks of unsold copies accidentally went up in flames! But the break had been made, and the blacks from the West had been at the center of it. Those westerners had not emphasized their western-ness; that, indeed, was what they were trying to get away from. In all of the excitement, no one else saw *Fire!!* as a product of the West, but at the core that was what it was.

During the late 1920s, the literary works of Hughes, Bontemps, and Thurman increasingly referenced the West. Hughes's poetry made references to the western frontier and western migration, and his first novel, *Not Without Laughter*, was set in Topeka and opened with the coming of a tornado. Bontemps's first novel, *God Send Sunday*, began in the South but shifted to the West in the second part, as the protagonist moved to Los Angeles. The geography of Thurman's first novel, *The Blacker the Berry . . .* moved in the other direction: the story opened in Los Angeles and then moved east, to Harlem. In the end, Thurman's tragic protagonist considers moving back to her native West. An exile even in the Negro capital of the world, she is haunted by her very black skin and the preference of the black middle class for Negroes with light complexions. Defeated, she stands on the street staring at a blinking neon Western Union telegraph sign. But no, she decides not to return. If Harlem could not save her, neither could the West.

New York's readers of the 1920s, black and white alike, scarcely knew what to make of these western settings—they seemed out of place in the Harlem Renaissance—so readers mostly read past them, and so have most historians. But viewed in light of their western upbringings, the first novels of these young writers make much more sense. The West was still a different place for African Americans, a place where there was no Black Metropolis, where there was no Harlem, and where African Americans sometimes felt a long way removed from the rest of black America. Hughes, Bontemps, and Thurman were all trying to work through that feeling—to find Negro-ness not only in Harlem but also in the West itself.

The Harlem Renaissance died sometime in the early 1930s, and the three western writers returned to the West for at least part of the 1930s. The exact date the Renaissance expired became a matter of some disagreement, at least among the participants, but with the coming of the Great Depression in 1929–1930 the writing contracts dried up, and Harlem itself was hard hit by unemployment and distress. In 1935, the residents rioted and inaugurated a new definition of "race riot." In this case, and in most cases after 1935, a race riot was no longer a white mob descending on a black section of a city; it was, instead, a phrase used to indicate that the black residents of the ghetto had risen up within their own neighborhoods, burning and looting the white business establishments and institutions that, in their view, were getting rich off black poverty.

Langston Hughes spent some time in Los Angeles, where his experiences were largely negative. In California, he wrote a memoir in the 1930s, titled *The Big Sea*, a book that had not a single word about California in it. Arna Bontemps went South to Alabama to teach in the early 1930s, and then returned to L.A. to write one of the great works of American historical fiction, *Black Thunder: Gabriel's Revolt: Virginia, 1800*. Bontemps had fled the South in large part because of the oppressive racist atmosphere, which helped him understand why his parents had moved west back in 1906. Thurman spent a little time in Utah and tried to break into Hollywood, unsuccessfully, before returning to New York, where he wrote a final, cynical novel on the New Negro Renaissance crowd and succumbed to tuberculosis. Hughes would become, effectively, a citizen of no particular place but a citizen of every African American community. Bontemps would later join Aaron Douglas at the historically black Fisk University in Nashville, where he continued to write and to keep alive the memory of the New Negro Renaissance.

THE NAACP CONVENTION OF 1928

The black West unofficially came of age when, in 1928, the NAACP held its annual convention on the West Coast—in Los Angeles—the first time the convention had been held anywhere west of the Mississippi River. It was about time. The national headquarters focused too much on the East in exclusion of the West, but the Northern and Southern California branches were emerging as large and prosperous branches, and everyone at the 1927 convention seemed to think it time to arrange a West Coast meeting. What sealed the deal for Los Angeles, however, was a specific promise made by the local race man, Dr. John Somerville, a founding member of the local NAACP, and a friend of Du Bois. Somerville promised the national headquarters that if they came to L.A. for the national meeting, he would build a fine, new hotel to house the delegates (see the sidebar below).

THE HOTEL SOMERVILLE, 1928

The Hotel Somerville was beautiful, especially on the inside. From Central Avenue, one merely saw a new and handsome brick building. But the main entrance led to an open-air courtyard, highlighted by Spanish tile, with a lovely fountain in the middle and leafy palms arching from each corner. The Mediterranean theme continued throughout the interior. The spacious dining room and ballroom, which occupied most of the ground floor, sported classy décor and chandeliers. Staircases to the second floor, where the guest rooms began, had elegant metal railing, again in the Spanish style.

W. E. B. Du Bois called the Hotel Somerville "a jewel done with loving hands," and added that "it was all full of sunshine and low voices and the sound of human laughter and running water." He had been prepared, he confessed, for "something that didn't leak and was hastily clean and was too new for vermin." Instead, he and the delegates "entered a beautiful inn with soul" (Flamming, *Bound for Freedom*, 287).

By choosing to build his hotel at 41st and Central Avenue, John Somerville ruffled some feathers in the black community. At the time, the community was centered around 12th and Central, a good distance north of the hotel site. Critics said it was too far removed from the rest of black L.A. But Somerville stood firm on the location, and well he did. The price of land was much cheaper there, because the area was still largely undeveloped. What's more, the hotel soon acted as a magnet for the community. Before long the community's entrepreneurs and professionals had built their own new offices and businesses near the Hotel Somerville. It became the new heart of black L.A. Although Somerville lost the hotel in the Great Depression, it was soon under black ownership again and renamed the Dunbar Hotel. It served as the center of the community—especially the jazz and entertainment scene—from roughly 1930 to 1950 (Flamming, *Bound for Freedom*).

Somerville came through and Los Angeles delivered a grand convention. The delegates were stunned and delighted by the beauty of the Hotel Somerville. The convention itself went very well: serious issues were discussed in daily meetings, and the evenings were filled with entertainment, including, most strikingly, the jazz-dance revue of Carolyn Snowden, known as the Josephine Baker of the West. Los Angeles got the glory, but the event was, in a larger sense, a defining moment for the black West. In the realm of African American life, it marked an important bridging of East and West. Many delegates had not traveled to the West Coast before, and what they found there was a city running full tilt and a local branch of the NAACP that had the size, the organization, and the clout to pull off a grand event. The black community of Los Angeles no longer seemed a distant and marginal group. The NAACP had at last become truly national.

THE GREAT DEPRESSION AND THE NEW DEAL

In late 1929, the American economy took a dive, first in the stock market and then in all sectors of the economy—retail, manufacturing, agriculture, transportation, banking, construction, service. The whole ball of wax melted down. That this was no ordinary economic slump became clear in 1930 and 1931, when the doldrums persisted and even worsened. By 1932, the nation that had seemed so confident and prosperous in the Roaring Twenties suddenly seemed broke, stunned, and hungry. Among wage earners nationwide, unemployment reached 30 percent. For African Americans, the last hired and the first fired in most wage-earning circumstances, unemployment was higher. In many black communities, especially in the larger cities, unemployment stretched toward 50 percent.

The Great Depression blew the lid off American politics and gave rise to a new and powerful liberal wing of the Democratic Party, which had always been dominated by southern conservatives. In the 1932 elections, there was a massive mobilization of new voters—mostly members of the white American working class. Previously alienated from the political arena, these newly active voters swept liberal Democrats into office at all levels of government. They also gave a landslide victory to the new president, Franklin D. Roosevelt (FDR), the governor of New York, who promised America a "New Deal." In the first three months of FDR's administration—the famous "First Hundred Days"—the federal government took unprecedented action to help its citizens survive the economic crisis and rebuild the economy. New Deal liberalism included direct emergency relief payments to people in dire straights, and it gave hope to ordinary Americans everywhere.

Everyday Americans loved FDR—and his wife, Eleanor, who became the first politically active first lady in American history. She was one of the few first ladies ever to have connected so comfortably and sincerely with the working class and the poor and destitute. She also interacted easily and with no apparent condescension with African Americans, and struck up a lasting and friendly professional relationship with Mary McCloud Bethune, the famed African American educator in the South. Many white southerners were outraged by her social interaction with blacks, but she simply carried on as usual while they fumed. She even went on personal visits to the slums of Washington, D.C., with an eye toward improving living conditions there (she also tried unsuccessfully to get other politicians' wives in the capital to go there with her). Eleanor was probably one of the very few white *racial* liberals in the nation.

There was a big difference between the New Deal *economic* liberalism and the kind of civil rights or *racial* liberalism espoused by African Americans. The white leaders who created and promoted New Deal liberalism were focused on economic well-being. In the past, the classical liberals in the United States were economic conservatives who stood for free trade and unfettered production; they promoted a laissez-faire approach to the nation's political economy, meaning that the government, especially the federal government, should leave the capitalist system free of regulation to ensure the liberty of the individual. New Deal liberalism, by contrast, insisted that the government, especially the federal government, had to regulate and stimulate the capitalist system to preserve the liberty of the individual. As the New Dealers saw it, the laissez-faire approach had created an undemocratic system of corporate capitalism, in which the wealth and power of the few was wrung from the labor and impoverishment of the many, and which, left unchecked, had led the nation into the Great Depression.

Early New Deal leaders did not see race discrimination in and of itself as a problem. Instead, they saw race prejudice as a product of economic

PERSONAL AND CONFIDENTIAL.

THE WHITE HOUSE
WASHINGTON

March 19, 1936

Rec'd.W.W. 3-21-36

My dear Mr. White: Ref. to _____

        Before I received your letter today I
had been in to the President, talking to him about
your letter enclosing that of the Attorney General.
I told him that it seemed rather terrible that one
could get nothing done and that I did not blame you
in the least for feeling there was no interest in
this very serious question. I asked him if there
were any possibility of getting even one step taken,
and he said the difficulty is that it is unconstitutional apparently for the Federal Government to
step in in the lynching situation. The Government
has only been allowed to do anything about kidnap-
ping because of its interstate aspect, and even that
has not as yet been appealed so they are not sure
that it will be declared constitutional.

        The President feels that lynching is
a question of education in the states, rallying
good citizens, and creating public opinion so that
the localities themselves will wipe it out. However, if it were done by a Northerner, it will
have an antagonistic effect. I will talk to him
again about the Van Nuys resolution and will try
to talk also to Senator Byrnes and get his point
of view. I am deeply troubled about the whole
situation as it seems to be a terrible thing to
stand by and let it continue and feel that one cannot speak out as to his feeling. I think your next
step would be to talk to the more prominent members
of the Senate.

                    Very sincerely yours,

                    Eleanor Roosevelt

*Eleanor Roosevelt was a strong advocate of racial liberalism in the White House. In this
letter to NAACP leader Walter White, she talks strategy in favor of antilynching legislation.
(Library of Congress)*

conditions. They believed African Americans were looked down upon and discriminated against because they were poor. The general economic programs of the New Deal would surely give them a lift out of poverty and into the nation's blue-collar mainstream—at which point, their race would cease to matter to white Americans. Or so they thought. Looking back, their views appear almost shockingly naive about the depth of race in the white American mind, especially the southern white American mind. FDR's early "brain trust" was largely a collection of northern white intellectuals who had little firsthand experience with the southern way of things. Almost immediately, they encountered the full force of Jim Crow emotion in the U.S. Senate, where southern Democrats controlled the key committees. And in many states of the nation, they saw their economic programs segregated along racial lines that had nothing to do with economics.

It took time for some New Deal leaders to accept the fact that their logic was backward. Blacks were not subject to racism because they were poor. Instead, most blacks were poor because of racism. Race prejudice, New Dealers gradually learned, was an independent variable in American life. Blacks faced the double discrimination of class *and* caste. This was what black leaders had been saying all along, but white New Deal liberals had been slow to see it. African Americans in the North and West made sure that they did see it, and, in time, Democratic Party liberalism would include civil rights.

But in order for blacks to put civil rights on the agenda of the Democratic Party, they first had to leave the Republican Party—the party of Lincoln and emancipation—and move into the house of their political enemies, the Democrats. For many African Americans this shift in party loyalty was difficult, but overwhelmingly blacks in the North and West did move into the Democratic Party in the late 1930s. That fateful shift in political loyalties permanently changed the black civil rights movement and the nature of American politics.

Black voters had several reasons for joining the party of Roosevelt. For one thing, the Republican Party had been taking the black vote for granted. At election time, Republican candidates would show themselves in African American communities in the urban North and West, raising the banners of Lincoln and Emancipation. After the election, those politicians were more difficult to find and did not seem so interested in black civil rights or the legacy of Lincoln. Most white Republican leaders figured they had the black vote in the bag. Where, after all, were African American voters going to go? To the Democratic Party—the party of the Confederacy, the party of white supremacy?

As far as black civil rights were concerned, the Republican Party had gotten lazy. For decades, black leaders had been protesting against such apathy, occasionally threatening to cross party lines. Sometimes large numbers of African American voters had voted for the Democrats, but these shifts were temporary. Generally, black voters stayed true to the party of Lincoln. In the 1930s, however, the situation had changed. The triumph of the *liberal* Democrats suddenly gave black voters new motivation to vote Democrat—and a way to punish the Republican Party for its apathy toward civil rights.

New Deal aid did indeed reach African Americans, saving their homes, giving them jobs, and putting food on the table. Quickly after he took office in January 1933, Roosevelt sent a flood of emergency legislation to Congress, and it all sailed through. The Federal Emergency Relief Act provided emergency cash payments for people who had run out of work and out of money. The Civil Works Administration created public works projects to put the unemployed to work. The Civilian Conservation Corps put young men to work on huge outdoor projects, such as road building, and provided them with training (e.g., engine repair) for future employment. There were programs to help people hold on to their homes. Day care centers were established for children. Not all of these New Deal programs treated African Americans fairly, but blacks were included in the aid, and in the immediate crisis it saved livelihoods and won black support for the Democratic Party.

A third reason for the realignment had to do with the Roosevelts themselves: Franklin and Eleanor Roosevelt made a special effort to welcome African Americans into the Democratic Party and, in a larger sense, into the life of the nation. In large part because of Eleanor's prompting, Franklin became more attuned to the cause. Although his belief in black civil rights never matched that of Eleanor, the president did meet with black leaders and established the "Black Cabinet"—an unofficial committee of African American leaders who advised him on issues concerning race in the New Deal. When his reelection campaign rolled around in

1936, Roosevelt openly courted the black vote, even though he was so popular that he had no real need for it. His reelection was in the bag, black voters or not.

Still, for African Americans who had been long-time Republicans, a shift to the Democratic Party was not easy. A story from Seattle conveys some of the emotions. A young man, Revels Cayton, came home on election day to find his father—Horace Cayton Sr., a leader in the black community—sitting rather dejectedly on the front porch. Revels said, "Hey, Dad, what's wrong?" His father answered, "I just voted for a Democrat." Revels countered: "Well, what's so bad about that. Roosevelt's gonna feed ya." Yes, replied the father, "but the Republican Party *freed* me" (Taylor, *Forging*, 104). Younger blacks such as Revels Cayton did not have the partisan roots of their parents and grandparents; they moved into the Democratic camp without much hesitation. For older Republicans, switching sides was difficult. One way to get through it was to claim that the liberal Democrats were now carrying the torch the Republican Party had lighted long before. In the 1930s, black voters claimed to be upholding the spirit of Lincoln by voting the party of Roosevelt.

Los Angeles was one of the few cities in the West in which the black population was large enough to have real political clout—and there the shift from Republican to Democrat was dramatic. The most heated contest for black voters occurred in the 62nd Assembly District, which was the Central Avenue district, broadly defined. Since 1918, the district (formerly the 74th) had elected an African American to the state legislature. That man was Frederick Madison Roberts, a progressive Republican who had made some modest but nonetheless significant improvements in the state's civil rights code—including a stronger law against racial discrimination in public places. By the late 1920s, though, it was hard for Roberts to make much headway in Sacramento, and perhaps he had grown a bit too comfortable with his dependable Republican vote. He won reelection in 1932, but large numbers of white, blue-collar workers in his district had mobilized for that election—and in the general election that November, they nearly put a black Democrat in office over Roberts.

When Roberts sought reelection in 1934, he wound up facing a young black Democrat in the November election. That newcomer was

Augustus "Gus" Hawkins, a native of Shreveport and a recent graduate of UCLA with a degree in economics. His economics and politics were strongly New Deal and strongly in favor of organized labor. He put together a new kind of biracial coalition in the Central Avenue district, a political alliance between white working-class voters and blacks who were eager for a change. In so doing, he unseated Fred Roberts (see the sidebar below). An African American Democrat now replaced an African American

THE ELECTION OF GUS HAWKINS, 1934

In 1934, with the New Deal in full swing, a young black Democrat in Los Angeles successfully challenged the Republican political icon, Fred Roberts (see the sidebar in Chapter 4), for the state assembly. Gus Hawkins had graduated from the University of California, Los Angeles (UCLA) and soon became frustrated with the lack of opportunities caused by the Great Depression. Angry at the state of things, he and his friends took aim at the Republican Party, and they began in their own neighborhood, promoting Hawkins for the 62nd Assembly District (formerly the 74th).

Hawkins won the Democratic primary by the slimmest of margins. Three other black leaders were serious contenders, including John Somerville (see the previous sidebar), but only Hawkins courted the district's white votes—the blue-collar Democrats whose political activism had surged since the rise of Roosevelt in 1932. Hawkins narrowly won the primary by winning this working-class vote on a pro-labor platform.

In the November general election, Hawkins faced Fred Roberts, who, everyone knew, would win most of the district's black vote. Blacks were still largely voting for the party of Lincoln, not the party of Roosevelt. Hawkins was going to win the white vote. The question was: Could Hawkins win enough of the black vote to unseat Roberts? The answer was yes, because just enough blacks voted Democrat. Hawkins's election foreshadowed the nationwide shift of black voters to the Democratic Party, which began in earnest in 1936. Hawkins had created a new biracial alliance, one that featured African Americans and working-class whites: the essential coalition of New Deal liberalism.

Republican in the state assembly. This was part of a national trend of great importance. All over the West and all across the North, blacks were becoming Democrats.

In the 1936 presidential election, Roosevelt won a large percentage of the black vote, and that trend grew stronger in the years and decades ahead. Throughout the West and the North, some black leaders remained committed to the Republican Party—Fred Roberts being one of them until his death in 1952. But after a while, there just were not many African Americans left in the GOP. Looking ahead in the story, Gus Hawkins never lost an election and remained in the California statehouse until 1962, when he was elected to the U.S. Congress—just in time to vote for the critical civil rights legislation of the mid-1960s. Conservative Democrats from the South fought black civil rights to the end, but in their effort to reshape racial law in America, the Liberal Democrats won out.

Like many other black Democrats in the West and North, Gus Hawkins would help to make racial liberalism a part of Democratic Party liberalism—and ultimately a part of mainstream America. But it would prove to be a long, hard road from the early New Deal to the victories of the civil rights movement, and beyond that to mainstream acceptance of equal opportunity in daily life. A critically important part of that journey began elsewhere, when Adolf Hitler's Nazi Germany invaded Poland in 1939. This invasion sparked World War II, which would, in unexpected ways, significantly alter African American history—especially black history in the American West.

BIBLIOGRAPHIC ESSAY

The opening vignette is from Douglas Flamming, *Bound for Freedom: Black Los Angeles in Jim Crow America* (Berkeley: University of California Press, 2005), 259–261.

On the Tulsa race riot, see Scott Ellsworth, *Death in a Promised Land: The Tulsa Race Riot of 1921* (Baton Rouge: Louisiana State University Press, 1982), and James S. Hirsch, *Riot and Remembrance: The Tulsa Race War and Its Legacy* (Boston: Houghton Mifflin, 2002).

On the second Ku Klux Klan in the West, see Richard White, *"It's Your Misfortune and None of my Own": A New History of the American West* (Norman: University of Oklahoma Press, 1992); for Los Angeles and California, see Flamming, *Bound for Freedom*.

Quintard Taylor's *In Search of the Racial Frontier: African Americans in the American West, 1528–1990* (New York: W.W. Norton, 1998) provides an overview of Garveyism in the West, including a list of places where UNIA chapters were established. Emory Tolbert, *The U.N.I.A. in Black Los Angeles: Ideology and Community in the American Garvey Movement* (Los Angeles: Center for African American Studies, 1980), remains useful. Flamming, *Bound for Freedom*, focuses on middle-class dissatisfaction with Garvey in the wake of the 1921 convention and seeks to place the episode in the larger context of economic self-determination in the 1920s.

On the Harlem Renaissance generally, see David Levering Lewis, *When Harlem Was in Vogue* (New York: Penguin, 1997). See also Arnold Rampersad's *The Life of Langston Hughes*, vol. 1, 1902–1941 (New York: Oxford University Press, 1986). On African American literature (and the arts generally) in the West, the essential starting point is Blake Allmendinger, *Imagining the African American West* (Lincoln: University of Nebraska Press, 2005). For the NAACP's 1928 convention, see Flamming, *Bound for Freedom*. On Arna Bontemps and the Renaissance, see Flamming, "A Westerner in Search of 'Negro-ness': Region and Race in the Writing of Arna Bontemps" in Valerie J. Matsumoto and Blake Allmendinger, eds., *Over the Edge: Remapping the American West* (Berkeley: University of California Press), 85–104.

On the Great Depression and the New Deal in the black West, see Walter Nugent's *Into the West: The Story of Its People* (New York: Alfred Knopf, 1999); Taylor, *In Search*; Josh Sides, *L.A. City Limits: African American Los Angeles from the Great Depression to the Present* (Berkeley: University of California Press, 2003); and Flamming, *Bound for Freedom*.

Chapter Six

WORLD WAR II
AND THE GREAT
TRANSFORMATION

When the Japanese attacked Pearl Harbor, on December 7, 1941, Fanny Christina Hill was living in Tyler, Texas, a classic East Texas town in which southern customs prevailed. Jim Crow was strong in Tyler, and opportunities for young women like Fanny Hill were severely limited. Basically she could work as a domestic—a maid—for a white family, and that was about it. Pay was very low, and it would stay low as far as one might imagine, but change was in the air, and everybody in every city, town, and hamlet of the South knew it. By late 1940, well before Pearl Harbor, defense industries throughout the country started humming, and the lingering cloud of the Great Depression began to clear away. Before long, word got around. Defense plants on the West Coast were hiring African Americans—even African American women.

In 1942, Fanny Hill left Tyler and Texas behind and made her way to Los Angeles. In doing so, she also left her husband, but her chance to become a Rosie the Riveter was apparently too good to pass up. Within days after her arrival in L.A., she got work at the North American Aviation plant, where one day of wages earned her more than most southern domestics earned in a week. She quickly learned that racial equality did not extend throughout the plant, however. Jobs were basically segregated, and white women got better, cleaner jobs than black women. Nonetheless, she was there, earning good wages, first as a riveter and later in the glass-installation department. And she found that her labor union, the UAW-CIO (United Automobile Workers-Congress of Industrial Organizations), would push for her rights on the job. Before long, she bought a home for $4,000 in the Central Avenue district and settled in. After the war, she stayed on at

North American (most Rosies went home after the war), and what's more, her husband then joined her in L.A. and also got a job with the company. Looking back at her experience, she used the same phrase used by black women up and down the West Coast: "Hitler was the one who got us out of the white folks' kitchens" (Chamberlain, *Victory*, 124–125).

The story of Fanny Christina Hill exemplifies many of the trends that shaped the black western experience during World War II. Leaving the dead-end Jim Crow South for high-wage defense work on the West Coast—even as a woman alone—Hill experienced both the opportunities and challenges encountered by hundreds of thousands of black southerners in the wartime West. For the American West generally, and for African Americans in the West especially, World War II and its aftermath marked a great transformation—demographically, economically, and politically. This chapter explores that transformation, focusing on the West Coast.

Every West Coast state exploded with growth during the war. Massive shipbuilding and aircraft plants popped up seemingly overnight. Millions of Americans back East flocked to the coast for defense jobs; huge numbers of these migrants were southerners, black and white. Labor unions swelled in power. Cities scrambled to provide housing for the unprecedented population boom. Army bases expanded, and new naval yards went into operation up and down the coast. In this decisive moment, the West Coast ceased to be on the periphery of American life and shifted to the center of the nation's political and economic development.

In the history of African Americans in the West, World War II forms the great watershed. The black population skyrocketed, restructuring virtually every aspect of urban life for the small black communities in the West. This Second Great Migration turned the loosely clustered, mixed-race neighborhoods of the black West into overcrowded, mostly black ghettos. Newcomers poured in because hundreds of thousands of high-wage industrial jobs had finally been opened to African Americans—not without some pushing by black activists and the federal government. The crush of black migrants during the war sparked a white backlash and brought black–white racial tensions to the forefront of the multiracial West. On the positive side, it created lucrative opportunities for black-owned businesses, placed racial discrimination in the center ring of western politics, and dramatically enhanced African American voting power.

For African Americans, these trends were not merely the by-products of another war. Black Americans saw World War II as another chance, indeed a better chance, of winning equal rights for themselves. That hope was not new. When the United States entered World War I in 1917 to make the world safe for democracy, African Americans saw in the global conflict the possibility of democracy within America itself. That faith had been bitterly dashed by the racial violence of 1919. But hope is not easily killed altogether, especially in America. The New Negro Renaissance of the 1920s and black inclusion in the New Deal coalition in the 1930s kept hope alive. Roosevelt's "Four Freedoms," enunciated in 1940 did not specifically include freedom from racial discrimination, but "Freedom from Fear" and "Freedom from Want" was rhetoric that could be seized upon by civil rights activists. Then, before the United States even entered the war, FDR issued Executive Order 8802, prohibiting racial discrimination in federally funded defense plants.

Once the United States entered the war, hopes flamed even higher. U.S. propaganda excoriated Nazi Germany for its evil doctrines of racial superiority. The point was not lost on African Americans. Surely, many thought, these official American ideals of racial equality and racial justice would be applied to America itself. Black leaders nationwide saw that the time was ripe, and, unlike Du Bois during World War I (who had urged blacks to "close ranks" with white Americans in the war effort), civil rights leaders in the early 1940s, including those in the national office of the National Association for the Advancement of Colored People (NAACP), called on black Americans to speak out, protest, and press hard for their rights. Across the nation, blacks heard the motto: Victory overseas against the fascists; victory at home for black civil rights and full democracy. This "Double-V" campaign became a vital part of African American life during the war.

This chapter examines African Americans in the urban West during World War II. The emphasis throughout is on the West Coast cities, which were most intensely affected by the wartime transformation. The chapter begins with the defense boom, which began before the United States entered the war itself. It then examines migration, jobs, organized labor, and housing—the key issues of the era—as well as the enduring conundrum of black military life and patriotism.

THE DEFENSE ECONOMY

The United States entered World War II when the Japanese suddenly attacked Pearl Harbor on December 7, 1941, but America's wartime mobilization had begun nearly two years before that, as President Roosevelt and Congress had quietly and tentatively eased the nation toward full-scale war preparations. By mid-1940, the Nazis had taken virtually all of continental Europe and Scandinavia, and they had Great Britain on the ropes. In Asia, Japan's invasion of China continued its bloody course, and Japanese imperialists sought full control of the South Pacific and southern Asia. The American public, still smarting from the outcome of World War I and still isolated from the fighting itself, wanted to keep American boys out of these wars. In 1940, FDR ran for an unprecedented third term in office, making American peace part of his platform.

Roosevelt understood that Great Britain needed massive emergency aid to survive, however, and he rightly believed America's entry into the war was inevitable. Defense production in the United States, therefore, could serve multiple purposes: it could save America's most important ally, boost the sluggish U.S. economy, and place America on a firm foundation of military preparedness—for when the time came. Congress worked with FDR on the famous Lend-Lease Act, which set in motion an unprecedented ship-building and airplane-building program to help England. Simultaneously, the United States instituted its own military draft with the Selective Service Act of 1940, the nation's first peacetime draft. The building up of the U.S. Army naturally drew working-age men away from the factories, even as the outfitting of the American military created even higher demand for industrial production.

By mid-1940, the U.S. government was issuing huge contracts to a wide array of manufacturers in all parts of the country. These contracts, it bears noting, were cost-plus contracts, meaning companies were guaranteed their full contractual profit in advance, just so long as they came through with their deliverables. The costs of production—labor, machines, buildings, raw materials—were effectively paid for by the federal government. In return for guaranteed profits, defense contractors had to accept organized labor in their plants without resistance—and why wouldn't they, since the federal government was picking up the tab for labor costs. For its part, organized labor agreed to a no-strike pledge for the duration of the war. Workers would sometimes go on strike anyway, usually over difficult or dangerous shop-floor conditions or to protest the sometimes impossible pace of wartime production. And in plants throughout the country, blacks sometimes walked out to protest racial discrimination, and white workers sometimes walked out (or rioted) because blacks were *not* discriminated against. All told, however, the system worked, overcoming unbelievable pressures to get the job done. American industry boomed as never before. The nation's workers, engineers, and industrial managers performed heroic feats of production during the early 1940s—and therefore made it possible for the American military forces to defeat the fascists in Europe and Asia.

The American West came in for the lion's share of defense contracts, especially along the West Coast. Seattle, Portland, the Bay Area, Los Angeles, San Diego—all of these cities and the larger metropolitan areas surrounding them witnessed stunning industrial development. From C-rations to B-12 bombers, the West Coast made it. The truly huge firms were the shipbuilding and aircraft-production plants. Almost overnight, small airplane plants in Southern California and Seattle were transformed into massive, assembly-line airframe plants. Humble strips of Pacific coastline suddenly became the foundation for sprawling shipyards, which built everything from merchant ships to destroyers. Steel manufacturer Henry Kaiser, to give only one example, landed a mammoth federal contract to build more than 30 merchant ships for Great Britain in 1940. He chose little Richmond, California, for this project and proceeded to build four massive shipyards in the East Bay's stubby peninsula, where the rough-around-the edges industrial town had been plodding along for nearly two generations. Richmond exploded with building, people, and chaos. And so it went. A full year before Pearl Harbor, unemployment had all but vanished in the West, and Americans everywhere were repositioning their lives around defense production.

Then Pearl Harbor sent the already rapidly running industries into an almost impossibly high gear—total mobilization and industrial production, around the clock, with no clear end in sight. The American and Allied armies (which now included the Soviet Union) needed everything: boots, barracks, bullets, bombs, uniforms, parachutes, tents, office supplies, food, gasoline, radios, rifles, and all the big stuff—tanks, trucks, destroyers, bombers—which required more steel and specialty production than could be imagined. Depression-era surplus labor had filled the plants in 1940 and 1941, but by 1942 the reservoir was empty. The military draft became less a vehicle for securing soldiers than for balancing manpower between the army and industry. Selective Service worked with the War Manpower Commission to keep enough skilled men and foremen in the war plants. Still, by mid-1942, military demands absorbed most of the male labor pool. Enter Rosie the Riveter. In the beginning, many defense contractors in heavy industry would not hire women; but as the labor crisis deepened in early 1942, they ran out of other options and began to hire white women. Finally, even the most racist companies began to hire African Americans, men and women alike.

A few companies on the West Coast, Kaiser notable among them, hired African Americans from the beginning. Kaiser had huge shipyards and steel mills up and down the Pacific Coast: three shipyards in and around Portland; four shipyards in Richmond, California; and a steel mill in Fontana, California, a rural area east of L.A. Its labor needs were huge. At peak production, the Richmond yards alone employed nearly 100,000 workers. Early on, the company aggressively recruited workers back East, sending company representatives throughout the North and South, promoting patriotism and high wages and handing out free tickets for the company's special "Liberty Trains" that ran to the West Coast plants through 1943.

Other companies hired blacks begrudgingly, only when labor demands forced their hands. And, as Kaiser discovered, elaborate recruitment efforts for African Americans were not necessary. Most black migrants learned about Kaiser and other defense jobs through friends and family and the grapevine, not through company recruiting. Some, as it happened, left the South and came to the West through the efforts of the War Manpower Commission. Regardless, once the West Coast plants began to hire African Americans, black migration to the West ceased to be a Modest Migration. It became a Great Migration.

African American women working as welders in the Kaiser shipbuilding yards of Richmond, California, in 1943. (National Archives)

THE SECOND GREAT MIGRATION

The Great Migration of World War I bypassed the West. In the North it continued full-tilt through the 1920s and then slackened a bit during the Depression decade. Historians use the term "Second Great Migration" to distinguish the southern exodus of the 1940s and 1950s from that of the 1910s and 1920s. For industrial centers of the North, the contrast between the First and Second Migrations was not too noticeable, save for the greater numbers involved in the second surge. Nationally, the biggest change in the 1940s migration was its pronounced movement to the West. This was true not just for African Americans but also for white Americans, and it sparked a national surge westward that would continue through the 20th century. For the West, though, the Second Great Migration was really the region's first, so the label is misleading and confusing. Still, this chapter will use the traditionally accepted term "Second Great

Migration," with the caveat that this really was a first-time event in the West.

Hundreds of thousands of black job seekers came West in the early 1940s. They came by train, gradually moving forward out of the Jim Crow cars as the train moved west. And they came by car, camping along road-sides when no hotels would take colored people. Most of them made the journey in 1942 and 1943, when the labor shortage required all hands on deck, regardless of what color those hands were. In the most eye-popping example, 12,000 African Americans arrived in Los Angeles in a single month—June 1943. Twelve thousand in one month!

In the northern California Bay Area, the numbers were equally stun-ning. In 1940, the black population of San Francisco and three main East Bay cities—Richmond, Berkeley, and Oakland—*combined* was only about 17,000. Ten years later, the black population of these four cities stood at roughly 117,000. And that was not the half of it. In the midst of the wartime crunch, a University of California study reported that, in the six Bay Area counties, the number of African Americans had increased by a total of 324,000 between 1940 and 1943.

Between the late 19th century and World War II, the black popula-tion of San Francisco had grown very little; the 1940s changed that. At the beginning of the decade, the city's black population was just shy of 5,000. By 1945, a special study by the U.S. Census Bureau counted 32,000 blacks in San Francisco. By 1950, the number had reached 43,500. Represent-ing less than 1 percent of the city's population at the outset of the war, African Americans represented 6 percent of the city's population 10 years later. There was no major shipyard in San Francisco itself; black migrants were moving into San Francisco but working at the shipyards built in other cities, including the Marin Shipyards in Sausalito, just north of the city, over the Golden Gate Bridge, and, of course, plants in the East Bay cities. Kaiser's yards in Richmond were perhaps the main employer of San Francisco's black migrants.

The black community in Oakland, the largest in northern California before the war, experienced similar growth. With an African American population of about 8,500 in 1940, Oakland saw about 37,000 more settle there by 1945. West Oakland's black community, which had been a mixed-race area not unlike the Central Avenue community in Los Angeles

THE RICHMOND BOOM

Before World War II, Richmond, California, was a small industrial city, an East Bay peninsula at the northeast end of San Francisco Bay. In 1940, its population was roughly 24,000, with only 270 African Americans. Then came the war and the Kaiser shipyards, which swelled Richmond's population to 100,000, including some 15,000 black newcomers, most of them from the South.

African Americans from the South (and California itself) poured into Richmond for shipyard jobs. Kaiser initially hired blacks equally with whites. The shipyards were giant assembly lines, where workers required little to no training to get started, and wages were high. Problems emerged, however, when the American Federation of Labor's (AFL) Boilermakers' Union gained control of the hiring and promotion process for most of the workers in the yards. In fact, all workers had to join unions to work in the yards, and the Boilermakers segregated black members, standing proudly for exclusionism and effectively quashing any possibility of skilled jobs and upward mobility for blacks in the yards.

Tensions on the job were mirrored in the city. Blacks were crowded into inferior housing. Most white newcomers were southerners who opposed black advances. The Richmond NAACP was established in 1944 to fight union segregation and housing discrimination. Even so, black workers earned good wages during the war, and compared with the South, racial conditions were an improvement.

After the war, racial tensions between blacks and white intensified. As happened in many cities, working-class whites began to leave Richmond for suburban developments that were off limits to blacks, and the African American population continued to grow steadily through the 1950s (Moore, *To Place Our Deeds*).

in its ethnic composition, now became overwhelmingly black, pushing northward into south Berkeley in the process.

And then there was little Richmond, which did not remain little. Richmond had been an industrial town since its origins in the early 20th century, with manufacturing plants geared toward railroad services, not maritime production. Despite its industrial roots, the town's neighborhoods had maintained an almost rural feel. Its scattered blue-collar homes, some of them self-built, had some breathing space; many had gardens or even a couple of cows and chickens. The handful of African American families who lived there before the war liked it that way. Middle-class blacks in San Francisco and Oakland tended to look down on Richmond folks—too small town, too rural-minded, too poor—but Richmond's residents had their own ideas about the good life. Everything about Richmond changed in 1940, when Henry Kaiser decided to build his new shipyards on Richmond's undeveloped bay side.

The building of Kaiser's four shipyards in and of itself was such a huge and hasty construction project that the economy and demography of Richmond were instantly changed. The shipyards necessitated other industrial developments: two dozen shipways, an equal number of outfitting births, and a factory for making prefabricated parts for the ships. All told, the Kaiser facilities covered 900 acres along the East Bay. During the war some 100,000 newcomers crammed into the Richmond city limits. All of these people were desperate for housing—shacks, tents, trailers, apartments, home, anything. Plus, they needed basic services, such as grocery stores, restaurants, and building contractors—and plenty of bars and thinly disguised brothels, much to the displeasure of the established Richmond residents.

By 1943, Richmond's black population had reached 5,700. This in a city that counted only 270 black residents three years earlier. Kaiser did not specifically recruit African American workers, but it hired them from the beginning, and from there the grapevine took over. Richmond's traditional neighborhoods were overrun and changed quickly. Mixed-race areas that had casually included blacks, Italians, Mexicans, and more were suddenly washed over by newcomers. Newly arrived blacks crammed into a section of town called North Richmond, which became somewhat of an all-black slum area. Still, the wages were excellent. Blacks working at Kaiser earned lower wages than white workers, but the average black wage was nonetheless nearly a dollar an hour—an unthinkably high wage in Dixie. No wonder blacks who lived in Oakland and other parts of the Bay Area also commuted to Kaiser, which at its peak employed some 8,000 African Americans, roughly 10 percent of the Kaiser workforce.

Far to the north on the West Coast, Seattle witnessed similar trends. Puget Sound became a major center for shipbuilding and aircraft production. War contracts sent nearly 90 shipyards into production in the Seattle area! Boeing Airplane Company employed 50,000 workers by 1944. Meanwhile, Seattle's Pacific Car and Foundry Company hired 4,000 hands to build Sherman tanks. All told, the Seattle area won $5.6 billion worth of military contracts during the war.

But would African Americans get their share of jobs in the Seattle boom? The answer was yes, but not always immediately and seldom without confronting blatant discrimination. Pacific Car and Foundry hired blacks at the outset, but black employees had to protest to get management to abolish its segregated restroom policy. A similar protest was held at Doran Brass Company, which responded by firing the black workers.

Hiring policies at the huge Boeing plant did not help. Initially, Boeing refused to hire African Americans at all. (The company also initially refused to hire any women.) Only after protests by the local black community, insistence by the local machinists union, and pressure brought to bear by the federal government did Boeing agree to hire African Americans. Boeing did not relent until spring 1942, when it opened doors just a crack by hiring two black women. Even at peak production, Boeing employed only about 1,600 African Americans.

Even so, black Seattle grew rapidly. At the outset of the war, the city counted fewer than 4,000 residents. A decade later, the number stood at 16,000. As in Los Angeles, previous housing patterns in Seattle largely determined the location of housing for black migrants. The newcomers crowded into the Central District, where most blacks in Seattle had lived for decades, but, like the Central Avenue corridor in L.A., Seattle's Central District had been a singularly mixed-race section of town, in which black residents were not the majority. Now the Central District became increasingly black, and, in keeping with the usual wartime pattern on the West Coast, it became increasingly crowded and run down. Older patterns of community life were overwhelmed, even though the traditional patterns in housing restrictions were in large part what facilitated the creation of West Coast ghettos.

Who were the wartime migrants who flooded into the established black communities of the West Coast? From Seattle to L.A., the answer was the same: In the main, they came from the western tier of southern states—Texas, Louisiana, Arkansas, and Oklahoma. In this respect, they resembled the black middle class of the Modest Migration era, who were predominately from that part of the South, and they were also like the flood of southern whites who moved west for the defense jobs. That black and white southerners from basically the same states were vying for the same jobs in the same places presaged racial conflict, to say the least.

The extent to which the black newcomers were rural types is harder to determine. The terms "rural," "backward," and "uneducated" were interchangeable insults flung at the black newcomers. Whites fearful of the suddenly large black sections of their cities used "rural" as a blanket accusation; they said these "backward" people were not ready for city life, did not know how "civilized" people behaved, and were a blight on the city not to be tolerated. Blacks who were old-timers used the terms as well, in part to distance themselves from the newcomers and in part as an indignant response to what they perceived as the uncouth public behavior of the newcomers. Government officials also used the "rural" label as a way to explain rising racial tension in the West Coast cities and defense plants. Terms such as "rural" were therefore loaded, whoever happened to be using them at the time.

Narrative sources (such as oral histories) and statistical sources (such as U.S. census analyses) complicate the collective portrait of the newcomers and show them to be less rural than contemporary critics suggested. Without question, many of the migrants had been living in cities before they moved west; they were from large urban areas such as Houston, New Orleans, or Dallas or from smaller cities, such as Little Rock, Shreveport, or Tulsa. Some were from the countryside or small-town South but had received government training in skilled industrial work as a prelude to their migration. A postwar survey done by Berkeley students who studied Richmond (not a particularly thorough survey) found that only 50 percent of the southern blacks who arrived during the war were from rural backgrounds. In his far more rigorous and recent study of U.S. Census data on Los Angeles, the historian Josh Sides concluded that "the vast majority of black migrants to Los Angeles . . . came from metropolitan areas rather than rural and farm areas" (Sides, *L.A. City Limits*, 39). Indeed, he states that figures for 1950 reveal that nearly 9 of 10 recent black migrants to Los Angeles had moved from cities, not farms.

One aspect of the newcomers was indisputable: young women were heavily represented. A study of Bay Area migrants described the average black newcomer as married and 23 years old; and there is little doubt that young couples—with and without children—were indeed numerous. But another Bay Area study found that female migrants outnumbered males by a margin of 6 percent, and this figure too carries an important grain of truth. The Second Great Migration was driven by newly created jobs in heavy industry, just as the First Great Migration was, but this time around, the migrants were not overwhelmingly male. Young black women were moving out of the South and into the West—on their own, of their own volition—in strikingly large numbers. Nothing quite like it had ever happened in America. This aspect of the migration might well be thought of as a kind of triple liberation movement—liberation from Dixie, liberation from low-wage work, and liberation from male control over their lives.

THE ROLE OF THE FEDERAL GOVERNMENT

As in the First Great Migration, black migrants of the Second Great Migration relied heavily on word-of-mouth information. Letters from family and friends, along with the national grapevine, spread vital information about jobs, wages, housing, and racial conditions. And also like the First Great Migration, manufacturers were driven to southern black labor not by ideology or ethics but by labor-supply emergencies. But quite unlike the First Great Migration, the World War II movement saw the pointed engagement of the federal government in the migration process.

The federal role began in early 1941, when A. Philip Randolph, the well-seasoned and tough-minded leader of the Pullman porters' union, insisted that the White House take a stand for black workers. With lucrative contracts in hand, the defense industries were booming by 1941, and the costs of production and the workers' paychecks were being paid for, of course, by the federal government. Black taxes helped pay for that, but in most cases, black people were pointedly excluded from employment in the defense plants. To protest racial exclusion, Randolph called for blacks to join him in a march on Washington, where an orderly, highly visible march for jobs was to take place in early summer. The event caught on, and some observers estimated that more than 100,000 black protesters would converge on the nation's capital.

Franklin Roosevelt did not want such a protest and cut a deal with Randolph. If Randolph would call off his marchers, FDR would issue an executive order outlawing racial discrimination in hiring in those companies operating under federal defense contracts. Randolph agreed, and the president delivered. In late June 1941, FDR issued his now famous Executive Order 8802 (see the sidebar on page 173). Ostensibly, a defense company could be stripped of its contract if it refused employment on account of race. But 8802 was more a statement of principle than it was a statement with enforcement potential. The possibility of punishment was virtually nil, and everyone knew it. Companies that did not want black workers, or who were certain that their white workers would not accept black workers, made no effort to change their policy until serious labor shortages in 1942 forced their hands.

To increase pressure on employers, in the spring of 1943 FDR followed up on Executive Order 8802 by issuing Executive Order 9346, which created a Fair Employment Practices Committee (FEPC), a kind of watchdog group that monitored racial discrimination in the defense plants. The FEPC could not actually do much to thwart discrimination in hiring, but it could bring a moral imperative into the discussion and could bring into the clear light of day the racism African Americans faced on the hiring line. The federal government had never taken such action on behalf of its black citizens; quite likely, no nation on earth had ever done so. However tepid the FEPC might seem in hindsight, and however much it disappointed black Americans at the time, it was nonetheless true, and black Americans could sense it, that New Deal liberalism was finally moving toward the question of *racial* liberalism.

As it happened, the West Coast FEPC was especially active and especially vocal in its support for African American rights. The director of the West Coast FEPC was a white racial liberal, Harry Lees Kingman, who had taken an interest in black civil rights and collaborated with the Bay Area's black leadership before the war. Kingman had few resources at his disposal, but he was indefatigable in his FEPC work and collaborated closely with both the NAACP, the Urban League, and San Francisco's interracial civil rights organization, the Bay Area Council against Discrimination. West Coast blacks had been fighting for civil rights for a very long time, mostly without influential white allies.

EXECUTIVE ORDER 8802

In the summer of 1941, nearly half a year before the bombing of Pearl Harbor, President Franklin Roosevelt issued Executive Order 8802, an executive proclamation prohibiting racial discrimination in the nation's defense plants. Roosevelt issued the order as a way to prevent a threatened march on Washington to protest defense-plant discrimination. The opening statement of Executive Order 8802 is printed here.

June 25, 1941

WHEREAS it is the policy of the United States to encourage full participation in the national defense program by all citizens of the United States, regardless of race, creed, color, or national origin, in the firm belief that the democratic way of life within the Nation can be defended successfully only with the help and support of all groups within its borders; and

WHEREAS there is evidence that available and needed workers have been barred from employment in industries engaged in defense production solely because of considerations of race, creed, color, or national origin, to the detriment of workers' morale and of national unity:

NOW, THEREFORE, by virtue of the authority vested in me by the Constitution and the statutes, and as a prerequisite to the successful conduct of our national defense production effort, I do hereby reaffirm the policy of the United States that there shall be no discrimination in the employment of workers in defense industries or government because of race, creed, color, or national origin, and I do hereby declare that it is the duty of employers and of labor organizations, in furtherance of said policy and of this order, to provide for the full and equitable participation of all workers in defense industries, without discrimination because of race, creed, color, or national origin; . . .

Source: EEOC official Web site (http://www.eeoc.gov/abouteeoc/35th/thelaw/eo–8802.html).

One positive aspect of the FEPC, then, quite apart from its role in security employment opportunities, was that it brought people like Kingman into prominent and highly visible positions, suggesting to African Americans that a new day in interracial liberalism was indeed dawning.

The other federal agency that played a role in fostering the Second Great Migration was the War Manpower Commission (WMC). The commission's goal was to match the nation's labor supply with the needs of the defense industry. In doing so it relied on state employment offices, which, during the New Deal, had directed unemployed workers to public works projects and other gainful employment. Now employment officials faced a different challenge: finding workers for defense contractors who were strapped for labor. The "federal" image of what became the United States Employment Services (USES) was misleading, for local officials basically controlled operations, and as for racial discrimination, they tended to favor it, especially in the South but also in the West.

But Roosevelt's executive orders, especially the creation of the FEPC, did bring new federal pressures to bear on state and local branches of the USES. For one thing, activists who were seeking to broaden the vision of the USES officials now had FDR as an official ally in the cause. For another, the USES reported to the WMC, which had practical reasons for getting every American to work, regardless of race, and which, in any case, was bound to support FEPC directives. There was one extra bit of pressure the FEPC could bring to bear on racist corporations: they could tell the USES offices to no longer fill the labor needs of a company in violation of 8802. Plus, as it turned out, the WMC had on its staff a good number of white racial liberals who would work hard to give special training and good work to African Americans.

Federal directives and local control clashed most violently in the South, where the WMC and the planter elite held incompatible ideas about what should be done about surplus black labor in the region. The planters wanted inexpensive black labor to remain in the South, so it could be available at harvest time. The WMC saw a huge supply of underemployed workers who were desperately needed out West—and who were eager to get out of Dixie. To the outrage of southern planters, the WMC pulled ahead in this contest, as national needs eventually trumped local privilege. Under pressure from the NAACP and other black activist organizations, as well as the WMC, southern offices of the USES even began to train blacks for skilled industrial work, and when southern defense plants refused to hire these newly trained black workers for skilled work, the WMC arranged for those workers to get skilled jobs out West and gave them train tickets to the West Coast. As it happened, defense contractors eventually welcomed the newly arrived black workers more hospitably than did white workers, if only because their interest was production, not the protection of their own jobs.

RACE AND ORGANIZED LABOR

Labor unions in the United States grew strong during the war, and they had a significant influence—for worse and for better—on the experiences of black workers in the defense plants. The two major labor organizations held different positions on racial equality. The older, more decentralized American Federation of Labor (AFL) had survived the lean years in part by fiercely excluding colored workers and focusing on bread-and-butter issues (e.g., wages) instead of taking on a larger social or political agenda. Each AFL union had the autonomy to set its own policies, including policies that excluded colored people from membership in the union. The recently formed Congress of Industrial Organizations (CIO) took a different path. The CIO sought to organize all industrial workers—black, white, or otherwise; male or female; skilled or unskilled. The CIO was highly centralized and aggressively political (it was pro-New Deal), and, in theory at least, it was devoted to racial equality—on the job and in society.

Black defense workers obviously favored the CIO over the AFL, but they were not in a position to choose their unions. Most of the defense industries had already been organized by either the AFL or CIO before the United States entered the war. One or the other controlled each company. Black workers thus had no impact on which labor organization controlled their particular defense plant. They simply had to make the best of the labor situation that was awaiting them. That situation was seldom favorable to their interests, especially when the AFL had control.

Consider the Kaiser shipyards in Richmond, where the Boilermakers' Union, Local 513, controlled the labor setup. An AFL union, the Boilermakers had negotiated a closed shop, meaning that all workers who got jobs in the Richmond shipyards automatically became union members, and they had to pay union dues or lose their jobs. From the get-go, Kaiser hired black workers in the yards; all to the good, but the Boilermakers had a strict whites-only membership policy. That meant, among other things, that black employees had no choice but to pay union dues to a union they could not actually join. Under criticism of this bla-tant injustice, the Boilermakers finally agreed to create an auxiliary union for Negroes only—Local A-36—which would have no real say over any union policy set by Local 513. The auxiliary system was a tried-and-true AFL strategy for dealing with colored workers, but Richmond's African American workers were in no mood for such games.

The black community in Richmond organized to fight the system. Workers themselves established a group calling itself Shipyard Work-ers Against Discrimination. They were joined by an activist organiza-tion called the United Negro Labor Council. Together they demanded that Local 513 be fully integrated; they used strikes and picketing, among other tactics, to force the Boilermakers' hand. The Boilermak-ers did not budge. In 1943, the federal government held hearings on racial conflicts in the West Coast defense plants. In those hearings, Richmond came off as having especially volatile relationships between blacks and whites. The open racism of the Boilermakers was one rea-son why.

Indeed, if there was one labor organization that stood front and cen-ter for white supremacy during World War II, it was the Boilermakers, whose metal-working skills placed them atop the labor hierarchy in heavy industry. Even in Los Angeles, where the black community had political clout and a tradition of civil rights activism, the Boilermakers proved vir-tually unbeatable. Of the numerous wartime shipyards built in the L.A. harbor, on a strip of land known as Terminal Island, some of the smaller yards hired African Americans without incident. In those yards black wage earners joined the CIO union—the Union of Marine and Shipbuilding Workers of America, which openly sought equal opportunity for black and Mexican employees. But the Boilermakers controlled the city's "Big 3": the California Shipbuilding Corporation (or Calship), the Western Pipe and Steel company, and Consolidated Steel. Significantly, the AFL Boilermakers had not bested the CIO in a standard union election.

CLAYTON RUSSELL AND THE NEGRO VICTORY COMMITTEE

Throughout World War II, African Americans embraced the Double-V campaign—victory over fascism overseas and victory for racial democracy at home. At the local level, home-front activism operated through organizations created by community leaders. In Los Angeles, this occurred primarily through the efforts of the Rev. Clayton Russell, who in 1942 organized the Negro Victory Committee (NVC).

Russell was the dynamic pastor of the People's Independent Church, which had been organized in Los Angeles 30 years earlier. It was an influential church, an offshoot of the First African Methodist Episcopal Church, and one whose members were generally more affluent and whose ministers were expected to be community leaders. Russell had taken the reigns of the church during the Great Depression and had prioritized social welfare programs. He embraced the left-leaning CIO labor union as a partner in advancing black economic and civil rights.

In July 1942, the USES responded to charges of discrimination against black women by issuing a statement that black women were not interested in defense-plant jobs. Russell then called a mass meeting in conjunction with the CIO and the NAACP, where the NVC was organized. One week later, Russell led a direct-action protest at the USES office, in which hundreds of African American women arrived at once to apply for defense-plant jobs. The USES gave in, and Washington, D.C., sent officials to ensure fair hiring. The LA Victory Committee also worked with blacks in the Bay Area, including those in Richmond (see the sidebar on page 167), to oppose racial segregation within the Boilermakers' Union. (Chamberlain, *Victory at Home*; Sides, *L.A. City Limits*).

Instead, the Big 3 colluded to keep the more aggressive and liberal CIO out of their yards. With their federal contracts in hand, they bypassed the normal labor election process and met behind closed doors with AFL leaders. In what became known as the "Master Agreement," the Big 3 signed identical contracts with the Boilermakers, giving them a closed shop for the remainder of the war. The CIO cried foul to no avail.

This meant of course that virtually all of L.A.'s black shipyard workers—10,000 worked for the Big 3—faced an unfair and hostile situation as soon as they walked into the shipyards. To keep their jobs in the closed shop, blacks had to pay union dues to the Boilermakers, but, again, the Boilermakers had a whites-only membership policy, which they were not about to change merely for a war to save democracy. As a compromise, the Boilers created a black auxiliary, which, like the one in Richmond, had no power whatsoever. To add insult to injury, and perhaps to divide and conquer, the Boilermakers in L.A. expanded their whites-only policy to include virtually every racial and ethnic group except Negroes. Mexicans, Filipinos, and even the rare Chinese worker could all join the union.

Protests against the system rose and fell and made little headway. One major protest was led by the black activist Walter Williams, who had worked as a CIO organizer earlier in the war. After a he took a job at Calship, he organized the Shipyard Workers Committee for Equal Participation, which, at its peak in late 1943, counted some 4,000 members—nearly half of all black workers employed by the Big 3. Meanwhile, the FEPC came to Los Angeles to investigate charges of racial discrimination. (This was during the same West Coast swing in which the FEPC found trouble between blacks and the Boilermakers in Richmond.) In Los Angeles, the FEPC called on the Boilermakers to appear at the hearings, but the Boilermakers simply refused to attend. Management for the Big 3 could claim, accurately enough, that they had given contractual control over such matters to the AFL, so their hands were tied. The only threat the FEPC could make was to demand that the local USES office block all requests from the Big 3. The USES had no incentive to do so and continued to give the Big 3 all the labor they could get. Blacks who refused to pay union dues at Consolidated were fired. Walter Williams filed for a court injunction to stop such firings but only won a short-lived victory.

African Americans who fought the Boilermakers eventually won a string of legal victories. In each cluster of West Coast shipyards, black leaders emerged to lead the fight. Walter Williams in Los Angeles was just one example. In the Bay Area, the president of the San Francisco NAACP, Joseph James, took a job at the Marin Shipyard in Sausalito;

Walter Williams of Los Angeles fought for equal rights within labor unions during World War II. (Library of Congress)

there he rallied black workers against Boilermaker policies. In mid-1943, the whites-only union struck back, winning a private agreement with West Coast shipyard companies to dismiss black workers who protested union policies and refused to pay dues. In Portland, the Bay Area, and L.A., hundreds of African Americans were fired. Walter Williams and Joseph James were both fired. But James was not president of San Francisco's NAACP for nothing, and regional director of the FEPC, Harry Higgins, was a friend and fellow activist. The FEPC charged the shipyards and the Boilermakers with violating the provisions of Executive Order 8802 and mandated that conditions be righted. The shipyard companies, concerned about meeting their hiring schedules for their contracts at a critical junction of the war, were inclined to go along with the FEPC ruling. The Boilermakers flatly refused, insisting that the FEPC had no authority in the matter. Williams and James, among others, then filed law suits against the shipyards and the Boilermakers.

The black plaintiffs ultimately fared well in these cases. *James v. Marinship* went to the California Supreme Court, which ruled in favor of Joseph James: a closed shop could not arbitrarily exclude a group of workers from joining the union. A federal district court in Portland, in a separate but similar case, essentially concurred. In Los Angeles, the Big 3 responded to the *James* decision by effectively capitulating; collectively, they announced that they would no longer fire black workers who refused to pay dues to the Boilermakers. A few months later, in June 1945, black workers received further legal sanction for their rights on the job. In *Shipyard Workers v. Boilermakers International and Local 92*, a case brought by Walter Williams, a superior court judge in Los Angeles ruled, essentially, that the union could not maintain both its closed shop and its unequal union policies; if the Boilermakers wanted to force blacks into an auxiliary local, then that auxiliary had to have the very same rights and privileges as the white local. Put another way, separate really had to be equal.

For many wartime workers, these victories came too late to be helpful. By mid-1945, black employment in the L.A. shipyards was down to 5,000—a 50 percent decline from peak production—not because of discrimination but simply because war production was winding down. When Japan surrendered in August, the Big 3 shut down their shipyards altogether and moved into other industrial sectors in the postwar era. The Kaiser yards in Richmond stayed in business and found new life in postwar prosperity and Cold War military contracts. Boilermaker racism, however, also stayed in business, and for a time, the union insulted African Americans by trying the separate but equal approach.

In the long run, however, these wartime victories against union auxiliaries were important. They were yet another reason black Americans had rising expectations for civil rights in the postwar era. They also set a legal precedent that eventually forced the nation's whites-only AFL locals to concede equal union rights to African Americans. One battle in the war for democracy at home had been won.

THE PORT CHICAGO DISASTER

The worst tragedy of the Western home front involved navy men stationed at the Port Chicago Naval Magazine, which was located some 25 miles east of Richmond, where the northern waters of the Bay Area snake inland to form a low-lying, swampy area. (This is currently the Concord Weapons Naval Detachment, and a National Memorial for the Port Chicago disaster was erected there in 1994.) The navy facility was located in a sparsely populated area, and for good reason: it was loaded with bullets and bombs. Most of the navy men stationed there were blacks, and they served their nation as stevedores, loading ordnance into cargo ships bound for the Pacific Theater. As the crunch of war intensified, the troops loading the ships began to voice concerns about safety. Tensions were already high between the all-white navy authorities and the mostly black stevedores when the worst happened—although the exact details cannot be known, for there were no survivors. On July 17, 1944, during the night shift, two cargo ships were docked, filled with nearly 10 tons of bombs and depth charges and taking on more. Then a loud cracking noise, a little explosion, and another, followed by a massive explosion, strong enough to shake the ground in San Francisco and to be felt in Nevada, strong enough to lift a massive cargo ship into the air and hurl it nearly 200 yards into the ship channel. The explosion fully disintegrated an entire cargo ship and utterly leveled the Port Chicago facility, instantly killing everyone within 300 yards and more.

The blast killed 320 men—202 of them black and 118 white; most were navy personnel, but some were civilians—making it the deadliest home front disaster in American history. But the story was not over.

This photo of Port Chicago, California, taken after the tragic explosion of 1944, shows that the bustling U.S. Navy yard was instantly reduced to rubble. (Bettmann/CORBIS)

A few weeks after Port Chicago was destroyed, the navy brought fresh ordinance to the navy shipyard on Mare Island, located at the town of Vallejo, some 15 miles west of Port Chicago. The stevedores who were not on shift that fateful night were understandably reluctant to load the cargo ship until the safety issues hanging over the Port Chicago tragedy had been adequately addressed. After considerable cajoling and jabs about patriotism from navy officials, most of the men proceeded to load the explosives. Fifty black men refused. They did not see themselves as unpatriotic or unmindful of the men on the front lines; rather, they saw themselves as rational people who wanted to prevent another disaster. The navy had other views. The 50 men were arrested, court-martialed, and found guilty of mutiny. All were given dishonorable discharges. All were sentenced to 15 years of military detention. About a year later, in early 1946, the detentions were ended without public notice, in exchange for the men's continued service in the navy. And so, quietly, the story of the Port Chicago mutiny (or Mare Island mutiny, as it is sometimes called) faded from public memory.

Other soldiers in the West had more positive experiences—or at least less-disastrous ones. Many men and women—about 14,000 in all—were stationed at Fort Huachuca in Arizona, and, by and large, their experiences there were positive. Unlike in World War I, African Americans stationed at Huachuca during World War II were as likely to serve under black officers as white. In addition, two units of the Women's Army Auxiliary Corps (known as WAACs) were also stationed at the fort, thus providing an outlet for patriotic service among black women, particularly well-educated, middle-class women who possessed the clerical and educational skills needed to keep the base running smoothly.

Phoenix and the surrounding area attracted its share of military installations, including Luke Air Field, where some Tuskegee Airmen were stationed after their graduation from the now famous all-black flight training center in Alabama. One of those Tuskegee men was Lincoln J. Ragsdale, who later recalled that "Phoenix was unquestionably the Mississippi of the West" (Whitaker, *Race Work*, 77–78). In a secret experiment conducted by the U.S. military, Ragsdale and nearly a dozen more Tuskegee pilots were placed with white roommates—Ragsdale's white roommate actually was from Mississippi, and none too happy to have a black roommate. The tensions and conflicts involved at the air base and in Phoenix had the effect of hardening Ragsdale's resolve to actively promote racial equality and interracial understanding after the war. He would become one of Phoenix's foremost civil rights leaders in the postwar era.

Farther north, black troops were stationed at various bases around Seattle. Fort Lawton, a traditional base for black soldiers, saw an infusion of troops and energy. In the western creases of Puget Sound, black navy men were stationed at the Bremerton shipyard. Located in and adjacent to a booming defense center, black military personnel in the Seattle area could connect with the city's growing African American community. Being stationed near an urban area has its advantages—bright lights, churches, night clubs. There was a downside, however. Most of Seattle's restaurants and public establishments imposed Jim Crow exclusion on black soldiers, and the insult hurt. In one notable instance, black soldiers from Fort Lawton were enraged to find they were denied service in clubs and restaurants in which Italian prisoners of war were readily served. Insult and anger collided and combusted, the result being a riot by Fort Lawton's soldiers, one in which an Italian prisoner of war was murdered by black soldiers.

African American soldiers stationed at Huachuca—the 93nd Infantry of the U.S. Army—served overseas in the European theater. After training at Huachuca, the black division got its military assignment: the troops would ship out and take part in the African campaign, as General Patton drove the Germans eastward across the desert. Then it was on to Italy, where the 93rd engaged in the fighting in earnest. As they began to liberate villages from fascist control, the black troops were cheered on and welcomed as heroes by the Italians. At the time, they received enthusiastic commendation from white commanding officers. Later, back in America, as the realities of Jim Crow once again slapped them in the face, they found that their service in Italy had been slandered by lower-level white officers.

It is worth pausing here to reflect on the longer history of blacks in the military out West. The experiences of black soldiers in the 1940s had the feel of déjà vu. There was an uncomfortably familiar ring to Ragsdale's trials in Phoenix, the Port Chicago court-martial, the Fort Lawton riot, and the whitewashing of the service of the 93nd. Patriotic service by black Americans was, once again, under-rewarded, overlooked, or even resented. Military service for blacks in the West had often had an up side, without question, but all too often there was an underside that reflected the larger plague of race prejudice in America, including the West.

THE HOUSING CRISIS

In many respects, the black housing crisis during the war foreshadowed challenges that would confront African Americans in the West for the rest of the 20th century. The housing issue is rightly considered the last topic in this chapter because the crisis did not abate after 1945, and because it rapidly and permanently altered the black communities of the region. By 1950, the black communities in the urban West looked markedly different than they had in 1940. By 1950, they looked dishearteningly like northern ghettos.

Racially restrictive real estate covenants were at the root of the problem. As discussed in previous chapters, blacks in the urban West had fought against restrictive covenants as fervently as whites had tried to use them. This was especially true in Los Angeles, where real estate was more important to the black economy, where home ownership was such a vital component of black middle-class culture, and where the black population was large. But in cities throughout the West, conflicts over race and housing had popped up on an erratic basis. The Second Great Migration moved all of those tensions front and center and transformed them into what became, in effect, a seemingly permanent racial crisis.

The attack on Pearl Harbor brought on an immediate racial crisis for the Japanese, who were heavily concentrated in San Francisco, Portland, Seattle, and, especially, Los Angeles. Japanese adults who had immigrated to the United States were not citizens, and indeed by federal law they could not become naturalized citizens even if they hoped to do so. Their children born in the United States were American citizens by virtue of their birthplace, as specified in the citizenship policy in the 14th Amendment to the U.S. Constitution, but citizenship status did not help. In early 1942, all people of Japanese ancestry on the West Coast were hastily rounded up and relocated to large internment camps in the interior West. In all, about 110,000 Japanese were moved out of their homes. Those homes would not remain empty for long.

In virtually every West Coast city, African Americans quickly occupied the neighborhoods previously occupied by the Japanese. In Los Angeles, black migrants moved into the suddenly vacant spaces of Little Tokyo, a none-too-prosperous section of downtown, just north of the Central Avenue district. To place their own demographic stamp on it, blacks in Little Tokyo unofficially renamed it "Bronzeville." In San Francisco and Seattle, the Japanese population had been more widely dispersed, but here too blacks moved in—sometimes at the invitation of their Japanese neighbors, who passed along the property before their eviction.

In L.A.'s Bronzeville, migrants quickly outnumbered available dwellings. Before long, Little Tokyo was an overstuffed slum. Perhaps 30,000 Japanese had lived there. By 1944, according to one estimate, 80,000 African Americans lived there. The small apartments of the district were basically operating on shifts, just like the round-the-clock factories. Activists, community-welfare organizations, and public officials all voiced concern about the slum conditions and the inordinate number of bars, brothels, and liquor stores that popped up amid the brick blocks. Bronzeville was the wildest place in town, where sex, drugs, and jazz flowed freely all night long—and most of the day, too! Residents of the traditional Central Avenue community were none too happy about the Bronzeville scene, but the club owners, pushers, and pimps of Bronzeville showed no inclination to follow the lead of the middle-class Central Avenue crowd. The wild side of Bronzeville, it seemed, was proud to be wild.

But Bronzeville's overcrowded tenements and poverty were a serious problem that had to be addressed, and L.A.'s government leaders took action. The city established a community center—Pilgrim House—to provide child care, healthy entertainment, and other services in an effort to alleviate some of the obvious problems facing Bronzeville residents, but the problems were overwhelming. What would happen, asked L.A.'s worried mayor, Fletcher Bowron, when the Japanese returned? He sought some kind of plan to prevent racial violence between the two racial groups. As it turned out, some serious tensions did arise between the African American newcomers and the Japanese who returned in late 1944 and early 1945. In the end, however, most Japanese did not return to Bronzeville, which had become almost unrecognizable from what it had been before the war.

Little Tokyo became overcrowded because the Central Avenue district became overcrowded, and Central Avenue became overcrowded because restrictive covenants and resistance in white neighborhoods prevented black migrants from living elsewhere. To be sure, the housing crisis was nationwide. Wherever new plants were built, chaotic tent-and-trailer migrant settlements followed. In every defense center, in every big city, government officials at all levels—local, state, and national—scrambled to house wartime workers. The U.S. Army pitched in with engineers and labor. In both Los Angeles and the Bay Area, large public housing units were constructed, and not on the cheap: they were thoughtfully planned and nicely built. So the housing crisis slowly abated—for white workers. Race, as a legal reality, would not go away.

Whites could escape declining neighborhoods; blacks could not. The racial inequalities built into the New Deal housing programs of the 1930s naturally prevailed through the war and beyond. Privately developed industrial suburbs openly promoted their new units as being reserved for whites only. For the most part, public housing officials insisted on segregating the projects along white and black lines, even when those projects were located in traditionally mixed-race neighborhoods. Black activists and white liberals fought these policies and witnessed some limited successes. Perhaps the key word was "limited."

Before the war, virtually all black westerners had lived in mixed-race neighborhoods. Even in the so-called Negro districts, blacks made up less than half of the population and usually far less than that. Blacks, Asians, a broad array of less affluent white folks from all across the United States and Europe, and, in Southern California, ethnic Mexicans—these people bumped elbows on a daily basis and did so, all things considered, rather tolerantly. In a few short years, however, these diverse neighborhoods had vanished. The Japanese were moved out, and then the Second Great Migration overwhelmed the homes and apartments. Whites moved out, and Mexicans moved out or got pushed to more marginal areas. By war's end, the "Negro districts" of the West had became exactly that—residential sections that were virtually all black. Hemmed in by housing restriction, the Negro districts of the West came to resemble northern ghettos, in which African Americans were essentially trapped in increasingly overcrowded neighborhoods. As migrants outnumbered available housing units, and as human needs exceeded public services, these newly created all-black neighborhoods began to deteriorate.

The same pattern held in every major West Coast city, not just Los Angeles. In Seattle's Central District, African Americans numbered fewer than 4,000 when the war began and were a rather dispersed minority population within the district; the wartime influx made blacks the dominant and fastest-growing group in the Central District, which was well on its way to being a fully Negro ghetto. In San Francisco, small clusters of blacks had been scattered through the city before the war. At war's end, African American newcomers were packed into the Fillmore District. San Diego's Logan Heights followed a similar trend, and North Richmond was another packed ghetto. West Oakland and South Berkeley had grown together to form a larger black ghetto, just as Watts and Central Avenue had grown together in Los Angeles.

LIBERTY SHIPS

For all of the problems that confronted blacks in the wartime West, it was also clear that the Double-V campaign had been successful in many respects—especially when contrasted with the racial outcomes of World War I. At no time in history had more high-wage industrial jobs been available to African Americans, and blacks seized the opportunities of the moment. Outside the South, the wall keeping black workers out of the factories was basically brought down for good, and the major West Coast industries that now employed African Americans—aircraft, auto, and shipbuilding—were all well positioned for postwar growth. What's more, the war had strengthened the NAACP and the Urban League and had fostered the rise of a new generation of white racial liberals. FDR's Executive Order 8802 and the subsequent creation of the FEPC made equal opportunity for black Americans an official federal principle. At all levels of government, black grievances were heard and, increasingly, acted upon in positive ways.

Liberty ships, appropriately enough, became an important symbol of the growing visibility and influence African Americans won during the war. In a miracle of industrial engineering, and with the hands of determined workers, West Coast shipyards could produce a Liberty ship in less than one week. The launch of each ship was a justifiable celebration. Late in the war, the federal government and the navy began to recognize the historical contributions and achievements of its African American citizens by naming Liberty ships after historic black leaders and choosing present-day black leaders for their christening. In Richmond in 1943, for example, the 90th ship produced in Yard #1 was named after the black scientist and inventor George Washington Carver, and it was launched by black entertainment star Lena Horne. At Terminal Island in Los Angeles, the local black activist Charlotta Bass broke the champagne bottle over the bow of the S.S. *Booker T. Washington*.

What about these Liberty ship honors? On the plus side, tens of thousands of blacks on the West Coast were earning high wages in the yards, and the white establishment was actually acknowledging this contribution to American history and to the war effort. All of this was new and important. On the other hand, the African Americans who helped build those ships usually held the dirtiest, hardest jobs, regardless of their skill level. To keep their jobs they had to pay dues to an all-white Boilermakers' Union that explicitly, even proudly, blocked blacks from joining. Was recognition in the Liberty ship celebrations just a sop to distract African Americans from the discrimination they confronted daily? Or was it a sign that America was changing, that the Double-V home front battle was slowly being won? As Americans everywhere celebrated V-J Day in August 1945, African Americans found it difficult to determine exactly what had been won and what had been lost during the great transformation. What was clear to all, however, and perhaps especially to blacks living on the West Coast, was that the postwar years would be a critical period for civil rights in America.

BIBLIOGRAPHIC ESSAY

This chapter's opening vignette—the story of Fanny Christian Hill—is taken from Charles D. Chamberlain, *Victory at Home: Manpower and Race in the American South during World War II* (Athens: University of Georgia Press, 2003), 124–125.

On wartime migration to the West, see Walter Nugent, *Into the West: The Story of Its People* (New York: Alfred Knopf, 1999). Quintard Taylor's *In Search of the Racial Frontier: African Americans in the American West, 1528–1990* (New York: W.W. Norton, 1998), chapter 9, surveys the period.

Information on specific West Coast cities is found in the following: Shirley Ann Wilson Moore, *To Place Our Deeds: The African American Community in Richmond, California, 1910–1963* (Berkeley: University of California Press, 2001); Kevin Leonard, *The Battle for Los Angeles: Racial Ideology and World War II* (Albuquerque: University of New Mexico Press, 2006); Josh Sides, *L.A. City Limits: African American Los Angeles from the Great Depression to the Present* (Berkeley: University of California Press, 2003); Quintard Taylor, *The Forging of a Black Community: Seattle's Central District from 1780 through the Civil Rights Movement* (Seattle: University of Washington Press, 1994); Marilynn S. Johnson, *The Second Gold Rush: Oakland and the East Bay in World War II* (Berkeley: University of California Press, 1994); Gretchen Lemke-Santangelo, *Abiding Courage: African American Migrant Women and the East Bay Community* (Chapel Hill: University of North Carolina Press, 1996); and Albert S. Broussard, *Black San Francisco: The Struggle for Racial Equality in the West, 1900–1954* (Lawrence: University of Kansas Press, 1993). See also the salient essays in Quintard Taylor and Shirley Ann Wilson Moore, *African American Women Confront the West, 1600–2000* (Norman: University of Oklahoma Press, 2003); and Lawrence B. de Graaf, et al., *Seeking El Dorado: African Americans in California* (Seattle: University of Washington Press, 2001).

On the Port Chicago disaster, the essential book, originally published in 1993 but recently reissued in paperback, is Robert L. Allen, *The Port Chicago Mutiny* (Berkeley: Heyday Books, 2006).

Chapter Seven

THE ERA OF RACIAL LIBERALISM, 1945–1965

In 1948, Sylvester Gibbs left Mississippi for good. He and his fiancée loaded up his Chevy, drove west, and scarcely stopped until they reached Los Angeles. World War II had changed Sylvester Gibbs, but it had not altered the racial code of his hometown of Lauderdale, Mississippi. Gibbs had served in the U.S. Navy during the war, and when he returned he was 21 years old—free, black, and 21, as it were. His demeanor was different now. When he was in the presence of white men, he simply acted and talked like a man, not a Negro man in a Jim Crow town. And Gibbs expected to be treated like a man in return. His changes in attitude and behavior were not lost on white Lauderdale, and that meant trouble for Gibbs. As he later recalled, "The bad part about this was that the white folks, when they can't be the chief and you the little Indian, they'll do something to you" (Sides, *L.A. City Limits*, 199). Gibbs did not wait around to find out what they would do.

In L.A., Gibbs landed a job in heavy industry, which was positively booming in the postwar era. Perhaps because of his naval experience, he first sought work in the harbor area. On the docks, the white longshoremen of Los Angeles were adamantly opposed to opening their local union to black workers, but the steel mills nearby had opened their doors to both black and Mexican hands. Fortunately, Gibbs landed a job in the scrap steel industry, which offered blacks better opportunities for advancement than did basic steel manufacturing. His union—the International Longshoreman's and Warehousers' Union (ILWU), Local 26—actively supported racial equality in wages and promotion. Gibbs became a crane operator, a skilled, relatively clean, high-wage position. He hired on with the nation's leading scrap-steel recycling company, so the paychecks kept coming.

By 1952, Gibbs and his new wife were secure enough financially to afford a newly built home in Compton, a suburb of Los Angeles that was emerging as a residential jewel for Southern California's middle-class blacks. Only a decade earlier, Compton had been an all-white town fiercely determined to remain off-limits to blacks, but after World War II, this began to change. In the mostly undeveloped western part of Compton, real estate developers began building large, new bungalows that were *not* restricted to white buyers—a rarity at the time. The Gibbs family settled in. It was a far cry from Lauderdale, Mississippi.

Of course, the larger story was not so simple. Gibbs himself would be the first to say that L.A. had its share of racists and racism and that blacks in the postwar West often had a difficult time of it. Not everyone found good jobs or helpful unions. Housing proved a major crisis for lower-income African Americans. The transition of Compton from an all-white to a majority-black suburb was itself fraught with racial tension. Blacks moving into white neighborhoods often met angry crowds of hostile whites and occasionally experienced extreme violence: During the 1950s, six homes of black Angelenos were blown up and four others were burned down. And if Compton was a new and relatively pleasant place for more affluent Afro-Angelenos, it was also true that residents of the Central Avenue district, and the Watts district especially, were trapped in neighborhoods that were increasingly overcrowded and run down. The city's African American residents still had to fight far too hard just to get access to restaurants, hotels, and basic public spaces.

In the two decades following World War II, blacks in the West faced this dual reality: ongoing racism and new opportunities. Basic jobs in industrial plants and basic clerical jobs in offices were opened to African Americans for the first time, giving black westerners a new measure of economic stability and a new sense of dignity. For the black middle class, better neighborhoods opened up, and yet these very gains for blacks in the West too often came at the price of white hostility. Indeed, many whites in the West seemed to view black advancements as an outrage, as a government betrayal of the principle of white privilege. White resistance to black neighbors reached a kind of frenzy region wide, with the result that blacks were increasingly hemmed in to older neighborhoods; and as black migration to the West surged, the loosely clustered multiethnic neighborhoods of the prewar West turned into overcrowded, mostly black slums. What was singularly "western" about black communities in the urban West began to disappear, replaced by communities that functioned like northern ghettos.

Black westerners showed a strong resolve to gain basic civil rights. Riding the wave of wartime transformation, African Americans carried the home front side of the Double-V Campaign into the postwar era. They fought for basic housing rights. They fought for basic employment rights. They fought for equal treatment in factories and in labor unions. By joining together in civil rights organizations old and new, they pushed to gain the basic rights that most American citizens enjoyed. Although most Americans think of the civil rights movement as a movement of southern blacks in the 1960s, we do well to look outside the South and to an earlier period. In many respects, the civil rights movement identified with Martin Luther King Jr., the civil rights movement that climaxed in the mid-1960s, was already running in 1945, and it was very apparent in the urban West.

Racial liberalism now came to the fore. The liberalism of Franklin Roosevelt's New Deal was, in the beginning, *economic* liberalism. The goal was to put people to work, to save homes, to repair the economic system, and to provide an economic safety net for ordinary people. The New Deal intellectuals who devised these policies for FDR were northern men with little understanding of the history of American racism or Jim Crow; they did not see race prejudice as a problem in its own right. These New Dealers learned better once the New Deal was in full swing, and every piece of their economic policy was subjected to examination by southern Democrats, whose primary objective was to maintain their system of white supremacy.

By the end of the 1930s, however, it was clear to all that the southern Democrats were losing control of the Democratic Party, and it was increasingly clear to white liberals in the North and West that civil rights for blacks needed to be on the Democrat agenda. Black voters had shifted decisively to the party of Roosevelt and had become an important part of the Democratic Party outside the South. Black activists vigorously insisted that racial equality be part of the liberal agenda. They promoted *racial* liberalism. Increasingly, white liberals got the point, and in 1948, the Democratic Party added black civil rights to the official party platform—causing a firestorm of protest among southern Democrats determined to preserve the "southern way of life." The delegations from some Deep South states left the Democratic national convention and formed their own third party in 1948: the State's Rights Democratic Party whose followers were often called "Dixiecrats." From that point until the civil rights victories of the 1960s, the ideal of racial equality moved slowly toward political reality.

After 1948, when the Democratic Party added civil rights to its party platform, the party was split between the racial liberals of the North and West and the racial segregationists of the South. In this political cartoon from 1952, the Democratic donkey tries to cover up the conflict, but divisions remained until the passage of the Civil Rights Act of 1964 finally defeated the southern wing. (Library of Congress)

AN EVEN GREATER MIGRATION

The pace of black migration to the West, so rapid during the war, continued in the late 1940s and then skyrocketed in the 1950s. Black veterans had something to do with this. Men like Sylvester Gibbs, who had left the South during their military service, and were disinclined to accept it once they returned, accounted for some measure of continued migration. Single women, too, continued to leave Dixie for the West, joining relatives and girlfriends who had been Rosie the Riveters during the war. The West offered better wages and freer lives than Jim Crow could offer.

Then there was the mechanical cotton picker. Southern planters had long sought a machine that could pick cotton, but cotton picking was a human skill not readily mechanized and, besides, black labor in the fields came cheap. By the time World War II arrived, however, various types of mechanical pickers had in fact been invented. They were neither cost-effective nor efficient, but their appearance in the cotton fields of the South coincided with the defense-industry boom, which made labor—even black labor—increasingly scarce. By war's end, the planters' enthusiasm for mechanized picking was strong. Research and development quickened. By the 1950s, the future of cotton picking was clear. Planters still needed enough black field hands to plant and hoe and prepare the fields for harvest, but the mass of surplus African American labor that was traditionally needed at picking time was simply no longer needed. In thousands of instances, black sharecroppers and farm laborers were cut loose, effectively evicted. They moved to southern cities. They moved to the North. They moved to the West.

Through most of the late 1940s and 1950s, black newcomers found plenty of jobs. The western economy roared into the postwar era and kept running full tilt. Pent-up savings fueled mass consumerism in America, international trade flourished, suburban homes required everything new and an extra car to boot, the baby boom created its own economy, tourism emerged as a huge industry throughout the West, and commercial air travel became increasingly common. All of these peacetime trends kept the factories humming. What's more, the Cold War required a new round of defense contracts in high-wage industry. Before the war, virtually none of these jobs had been open to blacks. During the war they opened up, and after that, for the most part, they remained open. African Americans usually got the worst jobs in the manufacturing plants, but for newcomers from the South such jobs looked good. And so the push and pull went. Even as the mechanical cotton picker pushed blacks out of the South, the ongoing industrial boom of the West attracted African Americans from all walks of southern life—city, town, and country.

Some general statistics can help one appreciate the magnitude of black migration into the West during the two decades after the war. The cities of the coast witnessed the largest influx. By 1945, the black population of Los Angeles had topped 100,000; 20 years later it was closer to 500,000—and that is not counting the black community in nearby Compton, which had itself topped 50,000. Down the coast a bit, San Diego counted more than 50,000 by the end of the 1960s. Up in northern California, the Bay Area cities combined to form a huge African American community. Twenty years after the war, Oakland's black residents numbered roughly 120,000. Richmond counted nearly 30,000. Over the mountains to the east, the state capital of Sacramento had a black community nearly 30,000 strong. California, obviously, was the place to be. The black population of the state rose as follows: from about 124,000 in 1940 to 462,000 in 1950; 880,000 in 1960; and 1,400,000 by 1970. By 1970, fully 75 percent of all black westerners were living in California.

There was noticeable growth in the interior West as well—again, mostly in the larger cities. By the mid-1960s, Denver's community was pushing 50,000. Another 15,000 African Americans were scattered throughout the state; Colorado Springs had developed a sizable community. By 1970, Phoenix counted nearly 30,000 African Americans among its residents, and another 20,000 were residents of Tucson. The black communities in Salt Lake and Albuquerque were clearly growing. And then there was Las Vegas, which grew rapidly as a gaming/entertainment mecca during the late 1940s and just kept on growing. The rise of the casinos created a massive service economy in which thousands of blacks found employment. By the end of the 1960s, more than 25,000 blacks were living in Nevada, mostly in and around Las Vegas.

In the Great Plains states, the cities of east Kansas remained the center of the black population. West of the Missouri, no state other than California had more African American residents than Kansas—which counted more

In the years after World War II, Los Angeles continued to be an attractive city for African American families, as this casual neighborhood snapshot attests. (Library of Congress)

than 100,000 blacks in the 1970 census. Topeka was still tops, but Wichita had witnessed major growth in the postwar decades; its black population reached 25,000 by the end of the 1960s. The black community in Kansas City, Kansas, also continued to grow.

All across the West, the African American population grew rapidly during the postwar decades. The Second Great Migration of World War II had altered the course of black western history, and that migration only got greater after 1945. The results were profound, and they began with the basic question of race and living space.

THE HOUSING CRISES

Take a second look at the title of this section. The key word is *crises*, with an "e." In the postwar era, blacks in the West did not face merely one housing crisis; rather, they faced several. Those housing crises occurred at roughly the same time and involved both private and public housing. There was, first of all, the problem of overcrowding. Virtually every major western city had experienced unprecedented overcrowding during the war, true enough. Even so, by the 1950s, every major urban area had adjusted to its new residents—at least its nonblack residents. For most people in the urban West, overcrowded neighborhoods became a thing of the past. This was especially true for the white middle class and working class, who soon had access to homes in new suburban subdivisions, but the new suburban housing was almost all off-limits to African Americans because of the way in which the federal government helped to finance the construction of these suburbs and the way it underwrote the mortgages people needed to purchase them. After the war, the U.S. government was willing to direct funds and financial backing into the housing industry—construction, financing, and real estate development—and into the hands of ordinary Americans who wanted to buy new homes.

A good portion of these funds were channeled through the famous G.I. Bill, which offered economic advantages to returning veterans. The G.I. Bill, for example, paid veterans one year of unemployment income after they returned home; it also paid for their college education and provided long-term, low-interest, low down-payment home loans for purchasing approved housing. The key to that last point on housing was the word "approved" housing. In keeping with the federal policies for home construction in the 1930s, the postwar government worked closely, and generally secretly, with private banks and financial institutions to determine what property would gain official approval. The Federal Housing Administration (FHA) would underwrite only those housing developments or personal mortgages that banks approved. The federal government and the banks were determined to make safe investments. Nationwide, banks used a uniform system of grading—designating loan applications as safe or not safe. This system, as it turned out, was determined by race. If blacks—even one—lived in an area of the city, bankers classified that area as unsafe for investment—and thus ineligible for FHA backing. What that meant for the inner city was that older areas that needed redevelopment were simply excluded from all of this federal largesse. Central Avenue in L.A., the Central District in Seattle, and the Fillmore District in San Francisco—all needed new home construction and loans for remodeling. They were not going to get them.

For the same reason, new suburban developments explicitly restricted home ownership to whites only. In a very literal sense, this amounted to a massive government subsidy for white Americans. Contractors had the choice of excluding blacks and getting federal funding or admitting black buyers and being ineligible for funding. For that reason, even African American veterans eligible for the G.I. Bill could not actually use their mortgage benefits to buy a suburban home. Policies unknown to the general public made them ineligible for suburban housing. Almost without variation, suburbs were racially restricted; no blacks were allowed in. And in the inner city—the new western ghettos—plans for housing upgrades and new private housing developments were usually nipped in the bud by FHA regulations.

Meanwhile, the other people of color in the West's urban centers were also moving out of the ghetto. In a curious twist of fate, the Japanese returning from internment camps were treated with greater respect and acceptance than they had been before the war. Some conservative whites continued to denounce the Japanese, but public officials began to trumpet their virtues as hard-working and law-abiding residents. Oddly enough, many Japanese were now allowed into white neighborhoods and were accepted without incident. Laws prohibiting Japanese naturalization and Japanese ownership of land were dropped, and so was the antimiscegenation statute that prohibited marriage between Asians and whites. From the Central District in Seattle to the Central Avenue district in L.A., the Japanese became more closely associated with white society than with black society.

Residential trends among Latinos were more complicated, but the shift away from black neighborhoods was readily apparent. Whites tended to accept ethnic Mexicans of the lightest complexion, who now became rather "Spanish" or just blended with whites. White intolerance of Mexicans rose in direct proportion to a Mexican's skin color. The darker the skin, the lower the income, and the harsher the treatment. An inability to speak English or a heavily accented English mattered to whites as well. From the late 1930s to the late 1940s, there had been sporadic efforts to form black–brown coalitions in the urban West, as the leaders of both groups recognized their common needs and common oppression. During the 1950s, however, Latinos who shared neighborhoods with African Americans began to move elsewhere. Lower-income and darker-skinned residents were not welcome in the newly built subdivisions, but they tended now to congregate in ethnic enclaves, which in Southern California and the Southwest became sprawling urban areas in their own right. In Los Angeles, for example, ethnic Mexicans largely abandoned the Central Avenue district and moved eastward in huge numbers, into a relatively underdeveloped area of L.A. County that soon became known (and is still known) as "East L.A."— an appellation that became a synonym for Mexican Los Angeles. East L.A. was in many respects a Mexican ghetto, and parts of it clearly qualified as a slum, but for our purposes the important fact is simply that it emerged as an identifiably Mexican part of Metro L.A. and that, in the process, the Central Avenue lost its long-standing Mexican population.

Only a decade after the war ended, the West's old multiracial neighborhoods were gone. Residential blocks that once housed an eclectic population of Anglos, Asians, Jews, Mexicans, and African Americans had become, for the most part, black-only ghettos. In their low-rise, single-home appearance, these black western neighborhoods had a different kind of appearance than northern-style ghettos, with their cramped high-rise apartment buildings, but in many respects the western ghettos had begun to resemble the ghettos back East. They were noticeably more crowded and more black, and the infrastructure was generally going downhill as private contractors and county governments shifted their interests to the suburbs.

The public-housing crisis was, literally, a crisis within a crisis, and although it had well-intentioned beginnings, it eventually created a ghetto within a ghetto. Today, the very notion of "housing projects" conjures up negative images of crime, violence, and hopelessness, but when public housing was created, it did not carry such negative connotations. In the 1930s, the idea of public housing was an important part of urban liberalism. It was not considered "black" in any sense. Democratic liberals saw it as a way to provide temporary housing to families devastated by the Great Depression. White Americans who were down on their luck wanted the opportunity to live in public housing projects. Many of America's first housing projects were in the works when World War II broke out, and the national defense boom—with its population explosions in places like Richmond, California—created an unprecedented need for publicly built homes.

Almost immediately, the question of race and public housing flared into conflict. Whites flocking to West Coast defense plants, many of them white southerners, were not at all interested in having to share government housing with black people, yet blacks needed and demanded their fair share, and they certainly were not interested in being subject to Jim Crow laws in a war for democracy. In the Bay Area, political leaders tried to solve the problem with the principle of the "neighborhood pattern." The idea here was that the neighborhood racial traditions that had prevailed before the war would determine who got public housing during the war and whether it would be racially segregated. Given the wartime demographic shuffle, this idea was difficult to put into practice, but, so far as white Americans were concerned, they would not have to worry long about it.

The postwar suburban boom made public housing largely a "colored" problem. Fueled by federal housing and lending provisions, private suburban developments quickly opened for working-class whites. As a result, most whites moved out of public housing. But blacks could not participate in the postwar suburban boom because of those same federal housing and lending provisions. African Americans thus moved in increasing numbers into public housing, and areas with housing projects were thus defined as "colored" neighborhoods. Such neighborhoods were not eligible to receive federal help for new private housing developments. They were hemmed in and destined to decline. White Americans who might have favored public housing projects during the Great Depression or World War II now had no personal stake in public housing. Indeed, they basically viewed it as a waste of tax money—and for colored people, at that. By the time racially restrictive real estate covenants had been outlawed by the federal government (in the late 1940s and early 1950, as discussed later), the pattern had been set and "the projects" had acquired their negative connotation.

The Cold War further undermined the idea of public housing. It was vulnerable to charges of "communism," and real estate organizations (bitterly opposed to public housing) made the most of that vulnerability. In Los Angeles, for instance, the city government and housing authorities needed more public housing, and they planned for a massive and innovative public housing community in a mostly Latino area northeast of downtown—Chavez Ravine. A tightly united real estate bloc waged an unrelenting Red-baiting (and sometimes race-baiting) campaign to kill the project, and they succeeded.

Municipal authorities packed almost all of their public housing projects into neighborhoods that were mostly black or all black. By the late 1950s, Watts was almost entirely black and had become the poorest section of black Los Angeles. Developers who opposed public housing apparently had no interest in saving Watts from the Red menace. There was a need for public housing for African Americans, so city leaders put the housing projects in the ghetto. Indeed, the city constructed *five* housing projects in the Watts section alone. Unfortunately, once those projects were built, municipal funds for upkeep and improvement languished. Although many neighborhoods in Watts retained their bungalows and quaint charm, parts of the area became a slum. Poverty and its discontents took hold in Watts, especially around the "projects."

FIGHTING FOR CIVIL RIGHTS

African Americans in the West had always been firm in demanding equal rights, and the postwar era proved no different. Indeed, the pace of black activism quickened after 1945 as the fight for civil rights became increasingly visible nationwide. As before, the National Association for the Advancement of Colored People (NAACP) played a critically important role. The NAACP would focus its efforts on change through the legal system, and it would score landmark victories during the 1940s and 1950s. The Urban League continued its efforts to promote equal opportunities in the economic arena, and its influence grew as blacks in the West moved into the region's factories as never before. A newer organization—also biracial in membership—was the Congress of Racial Equality (CORE). It was mostly a younger crowd—with lots of college students in its ranks—and used a wide variety of tactics, including direct-action protests and civil disobedience. By the late 1940s, CORE had chapters throughout the urban West.

One of the most important fights was the struggle against restrictive real estate covenants. This fight took place in the courts and was supported by the NAACP. Opposition to restrictive covenants had deep roots in the black West, especially in California, as noted in earlier chapters. During the early 20th century, battles were won and lost, and by 1945, restrictive covenants were a hot issue in virtually every western city. In the battle against restrictive covenants, no person played a more important role than Loren Miller of Los Angeles, who steered the case against covenants to the U.S. Supreme Court. In *Shelley v. Kraemer* (1948), the Supreme Court ruled in favor of Miller's argument and rendered restrictive covenants unenforceable (see the sidebar on page 204). Five years later, the court closed remaining legal loopholes in a

James Farmer helped organize the Congress of Racial Equality (CORE), which was active throughout the West in the post-World War II era. (Library of Congress)

LOREN MILLER AND *SHELLEY V. KRAEMER*

For African Americans in the West, one of the main barriers to equal opportunity was the racially restrictive real estate covenant. Blacks constantly fought against these housing restrictions in the courts, but with only limited success. Finally, in 1948, Loren Miller of Los Angeles guided an NAACP court case to victory, with the 1948 U.S. Supreme Court ruling in *Shelley v. Kraemer.*

Miller, who had a brilliant mind, was a product of Los Angeles. Coming of age in the 1920s, he was part of the New Negro generation and in the early 1930s embraced the political Left. He also edited the city's newest race paper, the *Sentinel.* After World War II, Miller abandoned the left and moved into the liberal Democrat center; he took on the role of a classic race man and served as an attorney for the local NAACP. He took aim at restrictive covenants and pushed the *Shelley* case out of L.A. and, ultimately, in conjunction with other housing cases, into the U.S. Supreme Court. Miller won the case, arguing that restrictive covenants were not strictly private arrangements because they required state enforcement and were therefore a violation of the Fourteenth Amendment. The ruling in *Shelley v. Kraemer* was that restrictive covenants were unenforceable.

This ruling left a loophole that pro-covenant supporters in L.A. soon tested. When a neighbor sold to an African American, the pro-covenant families sued for breach of contract—the formerly signed covenant. Miller sought to close this loophole, again through the U.S. Supreme Court, and he was able to do so in the case *Barrows v. Jackson* (1953). Miller purchased the *California Eagle* from Charlotta Bass and was later appointed to a municipal judgeship, missing out on higher-level appointments because of his Leftist leanings in the 1930s (Sides, *L.A. City Limits*).

---

follow-up case, once again brought by Loren Miller, *Barrows v. Jackson* (1953).

Whites who favored racial exclusion would find ways to circumvent the laws, necessitating California's Fair Housing Act in 1963. And yet the victories in *Shelley* and *Jackson* were major achievements for African Americans, and they raised expectations that more victories would be forthcoming. The U.S. Supreme Court, which had so often dashed the hopes of black Americans, seemed suddenly on the side of black civil rights. The whites-only primary election had been struck down during World War II in a Texas case. Admission to graduate schools had also been decided in favor of black students, also in a Texas case. And now restrictive covenants were, on paper at least, banished from the American landscape.

Black leaders and their white allies in San Francisco and Phoenix also took aim at discrimination through courts in the early 1950s. In 1952, the NAACP of San Francisco tried to gain equal access to public housing. Since 1942, when wartime housing was being constructed, the city had held to the neighborhood pattern system, in which tenets for public housing were chosen according to the demographic tradition in each housing area. In other words, housing authorities would not give a black person a unit in a neighborhood that had been all white or mostly white. The policy had endured after the war. In *Banks v. San Francisco Housing Authority* the city had to defend the neighborhood pattern system against an NAACP challenge; in doing so, the commissioner of the Housing Authority as much as admitted that the policy was intended to keep black tenants out of white projects. Eventually, the San Francisco Superior Court judge, Melvyn Cronin, ruled that the neighborhood pattern was illegal and a violation of the Fourteenth Amendment of the U.S. Constitution. Moreover, the system was legally void, and Cronin ordered 20 percent of the units in a white-only project to be set aside for African Americans.

In Arizona, school segregation in Phoenix was a primary target. In 1951, state legislators passed a law that gave local school districts the authority to desegregate voluntarily, if they wished to do so. Most did—Tucson was the largest city to desegregate its schools. Phoenix, true to form, would not budge. Enter two of the most important white liberals in western history— Stewart and Daniel Udall. They brought two cases to the courts—one dealing with elementary schools in Phoenix and the other dealing with the city's high schools. Both cases were decided in their favor in 1952. In the case of Wilson Elementary School District, the county courts declared school segregation unconstitutional. The case regarding Phoenix Union High School was also decided in 1952, when a superior court judge ruled that Arizona's school segregation law was invalid.

THE RAGSDALES OF PHOENIX

In the postwar era, civil rights activism in Phoenix was strongly encouraged by Lincoln and Eleanor Ragsdale, who reflected the black middle-class leadership of the day. Dr. Lincoln J. Ragsdale Sr., was born in 1926 and in World War II was trained as one of the Tuskegee Airmen. He was later stationed at Luke Air Field in Arizona and subsequently made Phoenix his home. Eleanor Dickey, also born in 1926, graduated from Cheyney University in Pennsylvania—a historically black teacher's college—and moved to Phoenix in 1947, where she met and married Lincoln.

The couple devoted prodigious energies to civil rights activism and worked closely together. They were charter members of the local branch of the NAACP and the Phoenix Urban League and were key figures in a local liberal organization, the Greater Phoenix Council for Civic Unity. Like many civil rights leaders in the urban West, they focused their work on discrimination in housing, segregation in education, and opportunities within the mainstream economy. Largely through their activism, the schools of Phoenix desegregated in 1953, a year before the famous *Brown v. Board* decision.

During the 1970s, when they moved out of the limelight of activism, young radicals would label them (and virtually all middle-class activists) "sell-outs." During President Reagan's conservative revolution of the 1980s, they once again felt compelled to speak out forcefully against white supremacy and the economic consequences of racism for the black poor (Whitaker, *Race Work*).

Two years later, in 1954, a court case over school segregation in the West would reach the U.S. Supreme Court and become one of the best-known and far-reaching court cases in American history: *Brown v. Board of Education.* Topeka, Kansas's racial policies in its public schools were curious, to say the least. The local high school and junior high schools were already integrated—but in a strange way. At Topeka High, for instance, whites and blacks basically attended the same school building in segregated fashion. There were two football teams and two basketball teams—one black, one white. Similarly, there were black cheerleaders for the black teams and white cheerleaders for the white teams. There were two student governments. Students *did* attend mixed classes and walked the same halls, but interracial lunch tables were pointedly discouraged. The elementary schools were more straightforward: they were segregated by race, period. Topeka was a western town in which there was no stark black-only ghetto; some blacks lived in most every district in the city. Yet no matter how close to a white school black children happened to live, they had to make the trek to one of the city's four black-only elementary schools.

The NAACP chose its plaintiff carefully. The man who lent his name to the case, Oliver Brown, was a welder by trade and a part-time minister. He was well respected and had no reputation for civil rights activism—which was the way the NAACP wanted it. The parents challenged the elementary school system in the fall of 1950 by sending their children to enroll in the nearest school, which was designated as whites only. Naturally, they were denied admission, and the case was on. This was happening, it is worthwhile to note, before the Arizona cases had started. In the early 1950s, challenges to segregation were in the wind.

The *Brown* case was finally heard in federal court in June 1951. The federal judges held for the state, citing the infamous *Plessey* equation: separate but equal was valid. At the same time, however, the judges' hearts were clearly not with *Plessey*. Indeed, their decision included a harsh judgment against school segregation in general, stating that segregated schools, even with equal facilities, have "a detrimental effect upon the colored children" (quoted in Taylor, *In Search*, 283). This unusual addition to the judges' decision was an open invitation for the NAACP to push the issue to a higher court. And that, too, came to pass.

There were actually two *Brown* decisions, *Brown I* and *Brown II*. The first struck down the principle of the "separate but equal" doctrine, ruling that separate schools were inherently unequal. The second ruling, handed down by the court one year later, ruled that segregated school systems would have to desegregate with "all deliberate speed." The chief justice, who wrote both *Brown* decisions, was himself a westerner: Earl Warren, the former governor of California, who had been added to the Supreme Court by President Dwight D. Eisenhower, a Kansas man. When Earl Warren was governor of California, he actually showed little if any sympathy for black civil rights. Eisenhower was moderate to conservative on race as well, and he certainly did not anticipate Warren making such a radical decision as *Brown I,* much less pressing the issue in *Brown II.*

Brown was indeed a radical decision, however basic it may seem to Americans in the 21st century. Since the end of Reconstruction, the federal government had effectively sanctioned Jim Crow segregation, a legal fact that always weakened the power of any state and local civil rights ordinances that had been placed on the books. Building on the *Shelley* and *Barrows* decisions, the *Brown* decisions adamantly reversed federal policy. Throughout the nation, African Americans rejoiced. Throughout the nation, many whites panicked, and in the South, they organized the Massive Resistance movement to fight against this Second Reconstruction. *Brown* thus set the stage for the civil rights movement of the 1960s, which would move beyond the courts and into the streets.

DIRECT-ACTION PROTESTS

In 1955, only a year after the first *Brown* decision, a quiet act of defiance in a small southern city sparked a great change in the American civil rights movement. Rosa Parks of Montgomery, Alabama, was arrested for violating the city's bus segregation laws. She refused to give up her seat to a white man and accepted arrest over obedience to Jim Crow. Civil rights leaders in Montgomery moved quickly to protest Parks's arrest; the following morning, blacks refused to ride the city buses. It was a peaceful protest—a blanket boycott of city buses—and it would last for one year. It was accompanied by a rising spirit of civil rights fervor in the community, centered in the black churches and led by a dynamic young minister, Martin Luther King Jr., a native of Atlanta. The NAACP brought suit against the city's bus-segregation laws, and, as Montgomery's African Americans sustained their boycott, the case eventually wound its way into federal court. The NAACP won the case, and the black citizens of Montgomery had won a major victory against long odds.

The three television networks—ABC, CBS, and NBC (the only networks at that time)—all covered the boycott and had honed in on Martin Luther King, who rapidly emerged as a national figure. His melodic voice, good looks, and rhetoric of nonviolent social change gave black civil rights a new and positive image in America—outside of the white South, of course. The Montgomery Bus Boycott also brought into being a vitally important civil rights organization: the Southern Christian Leadership Conference (SCLC), composed primarily of black ministers, with King in the lead. One important fact about the Montgomery movement and the SCLC was that they were *southern*, not northern or western. Since the demise of Reconstruction and the black migration out of the South, civil rights efforts for blacks in the South had been waged primarily by activists outside the South. Within the South itself, civil rights agitation had been altogether too dangerous; northerners and westerners thus carried the banner for southern blacks, using national politics to attack Dixie's racial order. But by the mid-1950s, blacks in the South began to fight Jim Crow directly.

Numerous national and international trends contributed to the rise of the southern civil rights movement. The Double-V campaign of World War II and America's war against the Nazi ideology of racial supremacy brought questions of civil rights to the fore. The full disclosure of the horrors of the Holocaust further warned Americans of the evils of racism. Then there was the Cold War. Rapidly after 1945, the Soviet Union with its communist system and the United States with its capitalist system locked horns in a struggle to determine which system would prevail in the postwar world. In this struggle, ideology was front and center, and the United States tirelessly promoted itself as the leader and defender of the Free World against the totalitarianism of the Soviets. Stalin, the United States warned, was the new Hitler. For their part, the Soviets targeted America's weakest link in this chain of reasoning: the Jim Crow South. How, the Soviets asked, could America lead a Free World when its black citizens were not even free in America itself? Southern segregation therefore became more than just a regional problem. Jim Crow was now a full-blown problem for America's foreign policy makers. Something would have to be done about it.

Changes within the Democratic Party also sparked the southern civil rights movement. The Democratic Party was no longer controlled by southern conservatives, and it was no longer the party of white supremacy. It was a political party divided into two basic groups: the southern Democrats, who were willing to accept economic liberalism but were adamantly opposed to any form of racial liberalism, and the northern and western Democrats (the so-called "urban liberals"), who embraced economic and racial liberalism. These two wings of the Democratic Party had been in conflict over race relations ever since African Americans in the North and West had shifted to the party of Roosevelt in the late 1930s. This conflict continued during World War II, covered up only by the necessities of wartime unity. After the war it began to tear the Democratic Party apart.

Millions of new black voters in the West and North made a difference. In the South, African Americans were still virtually all disfranchised—thanks to the southern Democrats—but black political power within the Democratic Party grew as the Great Migration swelled the ranks of the urban liberals. African Americans outside the South successfully pressed black civil rights onto the Democratic agenda. The Democratic president Harry Truman, who had gained the Oval Office when FDR died in 1945, needed black votes to win election in his own right in 1948. Truman narrowly won, partly because of heavy black support in the Great Migration states. He rewarded black voters by desegregating the American military. The civil rights victories in the U.S. Supreme Court added to the feeling that the winds of national politics were finally blowing in favor of African Americans. Southern blacks were primed to take advantage of those possibilities. The Montgomery Bus Boycott of 1955–1956 was an early indication of the rising expectations and steely determination that now existed in Dixie. The Little Rock, Arkansas, school integration crisis of 1957, and President Eisenhower's willingness to send the U.S. Army to enforce *Brown* further reinforced the trend.

Then came the sit-ins. In 1960, a few young men attending a historically black college in Greensboro, North Carolina, decided to change Greensboro by sitting down at a lunch counter at the Woolworth Drug Store. In those days, all downtown drug stores and department stores had soda shop and hamburger luncheon areas. Blacks and whites alike could buy things in the stores, but the lunch counters were strictly for white customers. The Greensboro students were thus confronting a basic and visible manifestation of Jim Crow. Their simple act of civil disobedience struck a chord among black college students and their few white allies in the South. All across the South, thousands began to "sit in" where they had not been allowed: the lunch counter, the ground floor of movie theaters, and the white-only waiting room of bus stations. The protests were acts of nonviolent civil disobedience—based on the philosophy of Gandhi and preached by southern black ministers such as King and James Lawson of Nashville.

When attacked by angry whites, as the sit-in protesters often were, the protesters refused to fight back and would get up and return to the sit-in. When arrested in mass by local police, as they often were, the students would submit peacefully to arrest and walk single file to the paddy wagon, only to be replaced in the protest by a new group of sit-in students.

Before long, the students had their own organization—the Student Nonviolent Coordinating Committee (SNCC, usually pronounced "Snick"). It was a biracial organization rooted in the South, but chapters were soon organized in the North and West, where membership was mostly white liberal college students. SNCC would have a significant impact on the American West, especially California. In 1960, however, the focus was on the South, and SNCC joined with King's SCLC to engage in nonviolent protest in the South. An early target was Albany, Georgia, a notoriously racist town in south Georgia; the protest targeted Jim Crow generally and pushed for black voting rights.

The Albany campaign faltered for several reasons, but an important event occurred when Martin Luther King was arrested and jailed. The Democratic candidate for president that year was John F. Kennedy, and King's arrest presented a tricky situation for him. He vaguely supported black civil rights, both personally and politically, and he definitely needed black votes in the key northern states, but alienating the southern wing of the party could hurt his chances in November. Taking a political gamble, he made a personal phone call to King's wife, Coretta Scott King, at their home in Atlanta. Kennedy voiced his concern for Martin and his support for the cause. Kennedy would defeat the Republican candidate, Richard Nixon, but only by the slimmest of margins. Illinois, with help from a large Kennedy vote in black Chicago, put Kennedy over the top. The new president then pledged to send a civil rights bill to Congress during his first administration. Southern opposition and his razor-thin victory made him hesitate, but JFK's stance was yet another indication that push was coming to shove in the Jim Crow South.

Between the sit-ins of 1960 and JFK's assassination in November 1963, the southern civil rights movement dominated national news and national politics. The major organizations were constantly in the news. They launched legendary civil rights campaigns: the Freedom Rides, Mississippi Summer, Birmingham, the March on Washington, and Selma.

Images of those campaigns became icons of racial liberalism: buses set on fire, police dogs attacking protesters, fire hoses blasting young people, and King's "I Have a Dream" speech on the steps of the Lincoln Memorial. The drama, courage, rage, and tragedy of the moment captured the attention of the world.

After King's "I Have a Dream" speech in 1963, Kennedy met secretly with King and other black leaders of the March on Washington. He made only vague commitments to these leaders, but he was gradually converting to the cause. By late 1963, he had submitted his civil rights bill to Congress, but then he was gunned down in Dallas. Suddenly, Lyndon B. Johnson of Texas became president. Kennedy had once urged the nation: "Let us begin." Now LBJ consoled the nation with the admonition "Let us continue." But whether a Texas Democrat would continue toward a civil rights bill was uncertain.

DIRECT ACTION IN THE WEST

African Americans in the West had long taken direct action to gain and maintain their basic civil rights. As early as the 1920s, when Southern California's beaches remained segregated, a group from the Los Angeles NAACP occupied a beach (and the ocean water beyond the shore) in defiance of Jim Crow. They were quickly arrested but eventually won a victory over beach segregation. Later, during World War II, African American demands for equal opportunity in the defense plants and labor unions of the West were certainly met by direct action. After the war, and before Gandhi's philosophy became prominent, nonviolent acts of civil disobedience took place sporadically throughout the urban West. This was especially the case in university towns, where black and white students challenged the status quo at the local level. In Albuquerque, for example, students at the University of New Mexico successfully challenged restaurant segregation as early as 1947. The following year, about a dozen University of Kansas students—members of CORE—held a sit-in at the whites-only Brick Cafe. The campaign was brief and unsuccessful, and it had failed to win the support of the more established civil rights organizations in town, including the NAACP. But a decade later, in 1958, the NAACP did support a similar action staged by Wichita's NAACP Youth Council. This campaign to integrate the lunch counter at a local drugstore succeeded after one month of sit-ins, and by the end of the summer, most of the city's lunch counters had also abandoned their segregation policies.

Local activist groups sprang up to promote civil rights. These organizations were usually biracial in membership and flexible in their approach. One example was the Los Angeles County Commission on Human Relations, which bridged the 1950s and 1960s and sought the integration of public swimming pools and public housing units—all the while seeking to prevent racial conflict by organizing "community committees" to provide a constructive forum for resolving problems. In Phoenix, the Greater Phoenix Council for Civil Unity (GPCCU) was organized to eliminate discrimination through boycotts and direct-pressure campaigns. The NAACP and Urban League of Phoenix joined with GPCCU to bring suit against segregated schools.

One point to remember, then, is that blacks in the West were ahead of the curve in staging direct-action civil rights protests. But another point, equally important, is that the southern civil rights movement did in fact have a major impact on civil rights activism in the West. The movement in the South was so large and rapid—and so startling to most Americans—that it had no precedent in the nation's history. Civil rights activists in the West had long been accustomed to fighting for their own rights *and* for the rights of black southerners. Without question, the western push for racial liberalism after World War II played a significant role in the eventual victory of civil rights legislation in Washington, D.C. Even so, the South was now pushing national events forward. When the sit-in movement exploded in 1960, African Americans in the West suddenly found that the South was fighting for itself and was playing the main role in national civil rights. The southern movement of the early 1960s thus lit a fire under western activists, sparking new and larger campaigns in the urban West.

In Phoenix, where most public accommodations remained segregated, a wave of sit-ins and protest marches swept the city. The black middle class, with the Ragsdales and the Negro churches in the lead, pushed hard to shine a spotlight on Jim Crow in the West—and to eradicate it through persuasion and law. In an effort to win a state civil rights law with teeth in it, African Americans in Phoenix staged one of the more dramatic nonviolent protests in the West. Large numbers of African Americans gathered at the state capitol building. There they formed ranks and took their position at the door leading to the Senate chamber—a block of nonviolent disobedience that effectively prevented anyone from leaving or entering the state Senate.

Up and down the West Coast, college students—white and black—participated in the civil rights crusade. CORE, which had come West in the 1940s and had appealed largely to university students, was now joined by chapters of SNCC. In 1962 and 1963, the CORE chapter in L.A. set its sights on housing discrimination. The group staged nonviolent marches in Torrance, a suburb south of the city, where blacks had been virtually kept out and where real estate developers continued to promote white-only neighborhoods, U.S. Supreme Court decisions notwithstanding. In a more famous incident, students at the University of California at Berkeley organized a SNCC chapter and began to distribute information about SNCC and the civil rights movement in the South. As in most SNCC chapters outside the South, most of the students in the Berkeley chapter were white. When campus authorities barred them from promoting SNCC on campus, the students continued to do so. The administration therefore summoned local police to arrest the students, sparking a major protest on campus and, subsequently, the rise of Berkeley's Free Speech Movement, which is often seen as the springboard for student radicalism in the 1960s.

In Los Angeles, the major targets were school segregation and housing discrimination. Unlike Phoenix or Topeka, L.A. had not imposed a segregated school system on nonwhites, but a clear pattern of de facto segregation had emerged in the aftermath of World War II, and by the 1960s it was a thorn in the side of the black community. The multiracial schools that had characterized the city's Eastside before 1940 no longer existed. The Eastside was now overwhelmingly black, and the schools in the district reflected that demographic. That in itself was not the problem. The problem was that whites who lived in the same school district were almost always given official transfers to schools outside the district, schools where the students were virtually all white. That was true also in Compton and in the West Adams district, where blacks were only a slim majority in the district but attended schools that were overwhelmingly black. In other instances, black families who moved near a mostly white school would find, to their surprise, that the school district had designated them to attend a more distant school that was mostly African American. This de facto school segregation was a very public and government-sanctioned insult to African Americans. The message was that white students should not be forced to attend school with their inferiors and that close association with black students would some-how damage the lives and educations of the nonblack students. The school system pled innocent, of course, stating that neighborhood demographics, not race, shaped their designations and arguing that the burden of proof was on African American families, not L.A. Like unofficial housing discrimination, this kind of racism was difficult to fight.

But black Angelenos mobilized to fight the system, through an um-brella organization named the United Civil Rights Committee (UCRC). The UCRC was the brainchild of Marnesba Tackett, a community leader active in the school desegregation fight, and Christopher Taylor, president of the local NAACP. Inspired by Martin Luther King's visit to L.A. in spring 1963, they envisioned a large, direct-action coalition to target racial discrimination in their city. Under Taylor's guidance, the NAACP met with the local chapter of CORE, the local American Civil Liberties Union (ACLU), and individual leaders in the black community and the labor movement. They banded together to fight everything from police brutality to school segregation. In May, the UCRC aggressively asserted its intentions, which made the front page of the *Los Angeles Times*. Spokes-man Maurice Dawkins, a well-known minister and the former president of the local NAACP, pledged a nonviolent campaign, but made no bones about their aggressive goals: "We are not just asking for a small specific adjustment, but a total community integration" (quoted in Sides, *L.A. City Limits*, 163).

In June 1963, the UCRC staged the largest civil rights march the city had ever seen. The target was school segregation. A few black leaders thought it an unwise move, but the march had widespread support in the community. The marchers assembled—about 1,000 in all—at a well-known black church in the Central Avenue community; from there they marched north into downtown, eventually stopping at the building that housed the L.A. Board of Education. The marchers were well dressed and remained nonviolent; they carried signs and chanted slogans. Follow-up marches were held through the summer of 1963.

One surprising aspect of this campaign is that it was, until recently, all but lost to history. Its impact was limited; its imprint on historical memory slight. Had a march of similar magnitude occurred in Birmingham, or perhaps even Harlem or Chicago, it surely would have been an event in the national news—and a standard part of the national civil rights story. There were even white counterprotesters—the Committee Against Integration and Intermarriage, which was active in Southern California in the early 1960s. Yet it is hard to make history in Los Angeles, and perhaps the urban West as a whole. In cities relatively free of tradition, in which demographic and political changes occur so rapidly, and in which there is no real sense of a city core, events that should be remembered are often forgotten. Direct-action protest, it turned out, was most effective against blatant, officially sanctioned Jim Crow discrimination—and, indeed, most effective when white authorities in the South violently attacked nonviolent blacks, while the television cameras were rolling. Nonviolent protests in L.A. garnered little media attention and won no dramatic victories.

Sports and Entertainment

Not all gains for black civil rights in the West took place in courtrooms or protest marches. Athletic and cultural breakthroughs helped open white minds to black abilities, inspired the black community, and provided new opportunities for African American athletes and entertainers. The most visible breakthroughs came in professional sports, music, and Hollywood.

Most famously, Jackie Robinson of Pasadena broke the color line in Major League Baseball in 1947 (see the sidebar on page 217). Not only did he start at first base for the Brooklyn Dodgers, but he also brought a new brand of daring base running to the league (including stealing home) and won the Rookie of the Year award. The Dodgers went on to sign a string of legendary African American players. In 1957, the team moved to Los Angeles. Robinson retired that year, so he did not play professional ball on the West Coast. But the many talented black ballplayers who followed Robinson onto the Dodgers' roster did, including pitcher Joe Black and catcher Roy Campanella. Before long, San Francisco had lured its own National League team out West—the Giants from New York—which fielded Willie Mays and Bobby Bonds (father of Barry) in the outfield.

JACKIE ROBINSON

Jackie Robinson was born in Georgia but moved to Pasadena, California, at a young age. He starred at football, basketball, track, and baseball at Pasadena City College and then at UCLA. When he graduated from UCLA, World War II was on, so he enlisted in the army and entered an officer training program, where he encountered jarring experiences with racism at his training camp in Texas.

At war's end, he signed with the Kansas City Monarchs of the Negro Leagues, blacks having been officially banned from Major League Baseball for a long time. But Brooklyn Dodgers owner Branch Rickey wanted to change that, and he chose Robinson as the man to do it. Robinson had the right stuff: he was handsome and smart and had unparalleled athletic prowess. He had a quiet determination that indicated he could handle the intense racist pressure and would be unlikely to quit. After one year playing in the Dodgers' farm system in Canada, Robinson was promoted to the big leagues.

He was slated to start at first base on opening day in 1947. Baseball's opening day was then the most anticipated event in national sports, and this day the entire nation was focused on Robinson and Ebbets Field. Robinson's baseball performance that day was forgettable, but what he did by starting and finishing the game was of enormous importance. He went on to win Rookie of the Year in the National League and to have a Hall of Fame career (Robinson, *Jackie Robinson*; and Tygiel, *Baseball's Great Experiment*).

The postwar decade also marked a breakthrough in professional football. Since the Great Depression, blacks had been banned from the National Football League, but in 1946, the Los Angeles Rams ended this policy of exclusion by signing two UCLA stars, Kenny Washington and Woody Strode. Washington, like Robinson, had attended Pasadena City College for two years before moving to UCLA. In 1949, the Rams signed Paul "Tank" Younger, who was from an all-black college (Grambling) in the South—a signing with a decidedly South to West feel to it.

Change was also in the wind in basketball—amateur and professional alike. The London Olympic games in the summer of 1948 marked the first time African Americans were invited to play on the U.S. basketball team. UCLA's All-American, Don Barksdale, helped the United States win gold that year. The timing was important, because the Cold War was beginning and American policy makers needed the United States to field integrated teams to highlight the freedom of the Free World. In individual events, black athletes had long represented the United States in the Olympics—mostly famously Jesse Owens in Berlin in 1936—but it was another thing entirely to place black athletes on a *team* with white players, something that was still illegal in the American South.

The major turn in college basketball came in the 1950s. First, there was the rise of Bill Russell at the University of San Francisco (USF). Born in Louisiana, Russell's parents brought him to Oakland during World War II. He grew up in the Bay Area and received a scholarship to play basketball at USF. Nearly seven feet tall, Russell also possessed uncanny agility and almost overnight introduced a new kind of "big man" to the game. USF coach Phil Woolpert was a transplanted white southerner, but he showed no race prejudice in his coaching. In 1954, the USF team became the first major college basketball team to start three black players. Russell's famed teammate, K.C. Jones, was a Texan Woolpert recruited. Led by Russell and Jones, USF won national championships in 1955 and 1956. Russell was serious about civil rights and was reluctant to allow the U.S. Olympic team to use him as a public relations tool in the 1956 Olympics. In the end, President Eisenhower personally asked Russell to play on the U.S. Olympic team. He and Jones both played, and the team won gold; both became star players for the Boston Celtics.

A major event in college basketball occurred in El Paso in 1965, when Texas Western College (now the University of Texas, El Paso) fielded an all-black starting five. Western went to the national championship game, where they were to meet a traditional all-white powerhouse—the University of Kentucky. Few sportswriters gave Texas Western any chance of winning, and their stated assumptions carried racial overtones. Western then shocked the nation by defeating Kentucky and, in the process, initiated a slow change in traditional white assumptions about athletic superiority.

In professional basketball, the West witnessed a similar upsurge in black opportunities and team success. Most important, the Milwaukee Lakers moved to Los Angeles. Their main star, Elgin Baylor, had played for the University of Idaho and the University of Washington. Soon there-after, seven-footer Wilt Chamberlain, who had played for the University of Kansas, joined the Lakers. Throughout the 1960s, the Lakers consistently won the Western Division, only to lose to the Boston Celtics, led by Bill Russell and K.C. Jones. Eventually, after the Baylor-Chamberlain era had ended, the Lakers would sign Kareem Abdul-Jabbar and Magic Johnson, and "Showtime" basketball was born.

In the country-club sports—tennis and golf—changes came slowly, but pioneering black athletes did break barriers. In tennis, the key player was the legendary Arthur Ashe, who signed a scholarship at UCLA, led the team to the national championship, and then went on to a legendary career in professional tennis. In golf, the Professional Golfers' Association (PGA) was officially for whites only, but black golfer Charlie Sifford broke down that wall. He received special invitations to unofficial tournaments in Arizona and California and won a couple of them. In 1960, he was finally accepted into the PGA, which dropped its whites-only policy. Lee Elder, a Texas native raised in L.A., followed Sifford into the PGA. He became the first African American to be invited to play in America's most prestigious tournament, the Masters in Augusta, Georgia.

Beyond sports, in the larger world of entertainment, musical trends in the cities of the West Coast began to have a national influence. After 1945, nightclubs in San Francisco's Fillmore District and L.A.'s Central Avenue became the center of improvisational jazz. Known as bebop, this form of jazz rejected the popular big band style that had dominated previous decades and instead pressed the limits of tonal harmony and experimental instrumentation. Usually played by small groups of exceptionally talented players, bebop wasn't intended for the masses, for easy listening, or for dancing. It was about experimentation, about pushing traditional musical forms into a new universe of sound. It was—and remains—an avant-garde art form. The names of those who pushed the limits in the late 1940s and 1950s are still revered by diehard bebop fans: Cora Bryant, Buddy Collette, Sonny Criss, Eric Dolphy, Big Jay McNeely, Charlie Parker, Roy Porter, Lester Young, and many others.

On the more popular side of the ledger was Rhythm and Blues (R&B), which connected with postwar youth—white, black, and every other color—and led to the rise of rock and roll. Before the war, recordings by African Americans were generally known as "race records," but after the war producers and marketers abandoned that term—which perhaps seemed a bit too controversial for full public consumption—in favor of the term "R&B." A classic R&B story came out of L.A. There the successful and creative jazzman Johnny Otis went into production himself. Otis was by birth a white person, but growing up in Oakland he effectively decided to *become* a black person and to live his life that way. Music was the center of his world; moving to L.A. he became the leader of a big band and a tireless mover-and-shaker in Central Avenue music circles. In 1950, he discovered a powerful voice in "Big Mama" Thornton, an African American who was born in Alabama in 1926, traveled in the tough vaudeville circuit in her youth, and later became a fixture in the nightclubs of Houston. When Thornton moved to L.A. in the early 1950s, Otis lined her up for some R&B recordings. Two fledgling songwriters—white college students in L.A.—happened to hear Thornton's initial session. Floored by the power of Big Mama's voice, they dashed off a song made just for her. That song was "Hound Dog," and in 1953 it became a big hit on the R&B charts.

Three years later, a young white singer from Mississippi—Elvis Presley—cut "Hound Dog," and rock and roll took off. But the song itself was the product of California—the convergence of a white man who decided to be a black man and to promote black music, of an African American who left the South for a better life in the West, and of two young white men whose minds were blown by the power of a black woman's voice. Perhaps only in California could the stars have aligned to produce "Hound Dog."

Oakland contributed its share to new musical currents. A key player was Bob Geddins, an African American who came to the Bay Area during the war to work in the defense plants and then settled in Oakland after the war. Almost single handedly, he made Oakland into a blues town; he wrote, performed, recorded, and developed talent. He added his own touch to the Delta genre by adding a bit more playfulness to the lyrics and by placing more emphasis on the melody of the song than its rhythm. Both aspects of Geddins's style made his songs accessible to R&B performers. His song "Mercury Blues," on the glories of the automobile and the narrator's desire to have a Mercury in particular, has been covered by dozens of artists in many different genres—R&B, rock, folk, and country and western. Oakland gospel also placed greater emphasis on harmonies and melody than on the hard-driving rhythms that had characterized black gospel in the South. One influential gospel group from Oakland was the Andrews Sisters (not to be confused with the famous white group by the same name). The vocal expertise and lighthearted energy that the Andrews Sisters brought to recorded gospel in the 1950s were later echoed in the hit rock/pop records of the Jackson 5 and Sly and the Family Stone (itself a Bay Area group with gospel roots).

In American entertainment, of course, Hollywood was at the center of things, and finding a place in the studios remained an important area of black aspiration. Hollywood had been slow to integrate and reluctant to give up its demeaning portrayal of African Americans, but gradually conditions for African Americans began to improve. In the postwar decades, the image of blacks in movies improved over the *Gone with the Wind* stereotypes. In part, Hollywood was finally responding to NAACP protests. It was also a post-Holocaust world, and Hollywood began speaking to the dangers of racial hatred. A new generation of black stars arose in the 1950s, and Dorothy Dandridge, Sammy Davis Jr., Nat "King" Cole, and Lena Horne were prominent among them.

Sidney Poitier became a genuine black movie star—one who played complex and humane roles. In his films he was almost always the protagonist, not a bit player or a typical "Uncle Tom" character. Born in the Bahamas, Poitier came to live with family in the states in his early teens. From Miami to New York, he lived a rough-and-tumble life, dropping out of high school and showing no particular interest in the future. Then, somehow, he found acting. His life changed—and so did black characters in Hollywood films. In 1958, Poitier became the first black man nominated for an Oscar in the best actor category. In 1963, he won an Oscar for his role in *Raisin in the Sun*. In 1967, his success could scarcely be matched, as he starred in three major motion pictures. By that time, however, the Black Power movement was in full swing, and many young African Americans of the era turned against Poitier. They dismissed him as a tool of the white world.

That accusation was not fair to Poitier, but it did raise important questions. Could sports and entertainment really lead to black civil rights in America? Could they really be the great equalizer? Could the racial integration of athletic teams and the recognition of black talent really translate into greater respect and equal opportunity in other areas of American—and western—life? That was a question still unanswered as the civil rights movement crested in 1965.

THE POLITICAL ARENA

In the late 1950s and early 1960s, black activism within the Democratic Party produced huge dividends at both the state and national level. In the western states, the key civil rights issues involved fair employment, education, and housing. Because nearly three of every four African Americans in the West lived in California, the electoral influence of black voters was strongest there, with large blocs in Los Angeles and the Bay Area. Nationally, the focus of civil rights legislation was on the South, of course, and the issues were basic: segregation and the right to vote. In the end, however, the fate of black westerners and black southerners would both be strongly influenced by the federal laws passed in 1964 and 1965.

President Lyndon Johnson proved more than willing to continue with JFK's civil rights bill. He made it a priority and used his prodigious political skills to get it through Congress. Short of emancipation itself, the Civil Rights Act of 1964 was (and remains) the most important political act for civil rights in American history—for all people of color and, as it turned out, for all women as well. In the wake of King's "I Have a Dream" speech and JFK's assassination, the bill reached the floor of the House of Representatives, where it passed easily. Its primary aim was to end Jim Crow segregation. Gus Hawkins, the African American congressman representing South L.A., authored Section VII of the bill, which outlawed racial discrimination in employment.

Hoping to stall the bill, one southern congressman added a so-called "poison pill" amendment. The original version stated that employers could not discriminate in hiring on the basis of race, color, or creed. The poison pill was the addition of "sex" to this list. That is, employers could not discriminate on the basis of race, color, creed, *or* gender. Thus, all women, including white women, were now included in the provisions of Hawkins's Section VII. But the southern plan backfired. The bill passed the House anyway, and in the end, the provision for women's fair-employment rights actually gave it extra momentum for passage.

When the bill reached the Senate, southern senators dug in for a long filibuster to kill the bill. The quirky rules of the Senate are that senators given permission to speak about a bill may hold forth for as long as they want to, so long as they keep talking—reading a Dickens novel or a phone book or whatever. In a filibuster, a senator may drone on for 5 or 10 hours and will only yield the podium to an ally, who then drones on for another long stretch of nothing. The only way the other senators can stop this is by voting to end it—a process called "cloture." A successful vote for cloture is difficult, as it requires a large number of votes. LBJ leaned hard on key nonsouthern senators, urging them to get their fellow senators in line to vote cloture on the filibuster. In the end, he prevailed. The southern filibuster was defeated, and the bill passed the Senate in essentially the same form as it had the House. LBJ signed it into law in a famously biracial ceremony. The civil rights movement had won a great victory.

The southern struggle was not over, however, for the 1964 act was too weak on voting rights, which were still denied to many blacks in some parts of the South. This led to the dramatic voting rights campaign in Selma, Alabama. In the spring of 1965, local police and state troopers viciously attacked nonviolent protesters, many of them women and children. As law enforcement officers swung their clubs and fired tear gas into the crowd, network television cameras captured it on film. This event, known as "Bloody Sunday" in civil rights lore, was soon telecast to the nation and the world. LBJ called a joint session of Congress and delivered a live address in which he condemned the Alabama troopers and called for a comprehensive Voting Rights Act, borrowing the words of the movement itself: "We Shall Overcome." In early August 1965, Johnson signed the Voting Rights Act into law.

Meanwhile, out West, state legislatures had been moving forward on civil rights. In California, racial liberals in the statehouse had increased in number after the war. When the Japanese surrendered in 1945, Gus Hawkins of L.A. was still the only African American in the state legislature, and his main allies in Sacramento were those representatives who were part of the Congress of Industrial Organizations (CIO) labor bloc. These allies were few in number to begin with, and the postwar Red Scare weakened the power of the CIO and organized labor in general. In 1948, however, Hawkins gained a new African American ally: William Byron Rumford, a pharmacist from the Bay Area who represented a small portion of Berkeley and a large section of west Oakland. Through most of the 1950s, Hawkins and Rumford pushed civil rights legislation in vain, but they did gain some strong white allies, including L.A.'s Jesse Unruh, who would soon become the speaker of the House (and center of power) in Sacramento. There were also two important allies from San Francisco: the hard-driving liberal Philip Burton and the future governor, Edmund "Pat" Brown.

In the late 1950s, their time finally came. With the California Republicans suffering from internal divisions, California's liberal Democrats surged upward. The state Democratic Party became a tightly organized and highly effective machine, in part because of the creation of the California Democratic Council. Hawkins, Rumford, and other representatives interested in civil rights pushed Pat Brown for governor; when he won, he was ready to promote their civil rights plan. In the legislative session of 1959, several civil rights acts sailed through Sacramento. The Fair Employment Act established a California Fair Employment Practices Commission, something Hawkins and Rumford had been seeking for years. An updated and strengthened state civil rights statute, named the Unruh Act, passed as well; its key provisions increased the minimum fine for racial discrimination in public places. Finally, a fair housing act made it through, but Hawkins, for whom the act was named, thought it too weak. Still, in all of California's legislative history, there had never been anything like the racial legislation of 1959.

Democratic liberals pressed their advantage. Unruh became speaker of the House in 1961 and quickly consolidated liberal power. The election of 1962 saw the rise of two new African American legislators from L.A.— Mervyn M. Dymally and F. Douglas Ferrell. In this same election, Hawkins was urged by President Kennedy to run for Congress; Hawkins did so and won the seat, moving from Sacramento to Washington, D.C., where he arrived in time to vote for the civil rights legislation of 1964 and 1965.

The year 1963 proved especially fruitful for African American politics in California. San Francisco's Willie Brown, a native of Texas, was elected to the state assembly, beginning his long and distinguished career in state politics. The Rumford Fair Housing Act, a long-time goal of Gus Hawkins, was passed over fierce conservative opposition. In Los Angeles, three African Americans were elected to the city council, including the city's future mayor, Tom Bradley.

So, when LBJ signed the Voting Rights Act into law on August 6, 1965, it appeared that racial liberalism had won its major battles. The laws were aimed directly at Dixie's racial order and were largely prompted by the civil rights movement in the South, but black westerners and northerners had been essential in the long, hard process of pushing racial equality into the liberal agenda. What's more, the Civil Rights Act of 1964 directly addressed fair employment for blacks, promising a new day in job opportunities and, more broadly, in labor unions. Millions of black southerners would now join the liberal wing of the Democratic Party, which promised to strengthen legislative efforts to gain and sustain civil rights.

Liberals did not expect all problems to simply vanish. Of course there would be new obstacles to overcome, but great progress had been made: Federal law was now squarely on the side of equal rights and equal access—to an extent that would have seemed unlikely, if not downright impossible, only a decade earlier. By all appearances American race relations were looking up.

Appearances were deceiving, however. On August 11, 1965—only five days after LBJ signed the voting rights legislation—the black residents of Watts rose up in a violent rebellion against the white establishment. The Watts uprising shocked the United States. For several days, a bewildered and worried nation watched the burning and looting on television. When the smoke had cleared, it was apparent that African American life in the West had entered a new and turbulent phase.

BIBLIOGRAPHIC ESSAY

The opening vignette on Sylvester Gibbs is gathered from information in Josh Sides, *African American Los Angeles from the Great Depression to the Present* (Berkeley: University of California Press, 2003), 78, 126, 129, and 199–200.

Quintard Taylor's *In Search of the Racial Frontier: African Americans in the American West, 1528–1990* (New York: W.W. Norton, 1998), chapters 9 and 10 have key information; and Walter Nugent's *Into the West: The Story of Its People* (New York: Alfred Knopf, 1999), shows the population shifts of the postwar West. Lawrence B. de Graaf, et al., *Seeking El Dorado: African Americans in California* (Seattle: University of Washington Press, 2001), has excellent essays on the postwar decades, as does Quintard Taylor and Shirley Ann Wilson Moore, eds., *African American Women Confront the West, 1600–2000* (Norman: University of Oklahoma Press, 2003).

Excellent case studies abound for this period: Josh Sides, *L.A. City Limits*; Scott Kurashige, *The Shifting Grounds of Race: Black and Japanese Americans in the Making of Multiethnic Los Angeles* (Princeton, NJ: Princeton University Press, 2008); Albert S. Broussard, *Black San Francisco: The Struggle for Racial Equality in the West, 1900–1954* (Lawrence: Kansas University Press, 1993); Quintard Taylor, *The Forging of a Black Community: Seattle's Central District from 1870 to through the Civil Rights Movement* (Seattle: University of Washington Press, 1994); Matthew C. Whitaker, *Race Work: The Rise of Civil Rights in the Urban West* (Lincoln: University of Nebraska Press, 2005), which focuses on Phoenix; Shirley Ann Wilson Moore, *To Place Our Deeds: The African American Community in Richmond, California, 1910–1963* (Berkeley: University of California Press, 2001); Marilynn S. Johnson, *The Second Gold Rush: Oakland and the East Bay in World War II* (Berkeley: University of California Press, 1994); and Robert O. Self, *American Babylon: Race and the Struggle for Postwar Oakland* (Princeton, NJ: Princeton University Press, 2003).

On Jackie Robinson, see Jules Tygiel, *Baseball's Great Experiment: Jackie Robinson and His Legacy* (New York: Oxford University Press, 1983); and Rachel Robinson, *Jackie Robinson: An Intimate Portrait* (New York: Henry N. Abrams, 1996). For other sports, see Arthur Ashe Jr., *A Hard Road to Glory: A History of the African-American Athlete since 1946* (New York: Amistad Press, 1993); Charlie Sifford and James Gullo, *Just Let Me Play: The Story of Charlie Sifford, the First Black PGA Golfer* (New York: British American Publishing, 1992).

On trends in postwar music, see Cora Bryant, et al., *Central Avenue Sounds: Jazz in Los Angeles* (Berkeley: University of California Press, 1998); Bette Yarbrough Cox, *Central Avenue—Its Rise and Fall, 1890–c.1955* (Los Angeles: BEEM Publications, 1996); Jacqueline Cogdell DjeDje and Eddie S. Meadows, eds., *California Soul: Music of African Americans in the West*; Johnny Otis, *Upside Your Head! Rhythm and Blues on Central Avenue* (Hanover and London: University Press of New England, 1993); Roy Porter with David Keller, *There and Back* (Baton Rouge: Louisiana State University Press, 1991); and R.J. Smith, *The Great Black Way: L.A. in the 1940s and the Lost African-American Renaissance* (New York: Public Affairs, 2006). Larry Star and Christopher Waterman, *American Popular Music: From Minstrelsy to MP3* (New York: Oxford University Press, 2007), 181–182 provides the "Hound Dog" story. On blacks and Hollywood, see Donald Bogle's *Bright Boulevards, Bold Dreams: The Story of Black Hollywood* (New York: One World Books, 2006).

THE ERA
OF BLACK NATIONALISM,
1965–1980

In 1957, 13-year-old Marquette Frye moved with his family to Los
Angeles. He was just one among the tens of thousands of African Americans who migrated to L.A. in the 1950s, but his story was different from
most of the others. The vast majority of black migrants were from the
South, but Marquette Frye was from the West—the small coal-mining
community of Hanna, Wyoming, which, in the late 1950s, had fallen on
hard times. For Marquette's stepfather, Wallace, the Hanna mines and the
United Mine Workers had been his ticket out of the South. During World
War II, he had exchanged the cotton fields and segregation of Oklahoma
for the union wages and racial integration of Hanna, whose residents were
mostly Greek and who seemed not to mind at all that Frye was black. Wallace
had in fact been recruited by labor-union recruiters, who needed more miners when demand was high. But the economic recession of the late 1950s,
along with the increasing mechanization of the coal mining industry, made
Frye's mining skills obsolete. He had relatives living in L.A., and before long
he and his wife, Rena, had moved their family to Southern California.

Nothing could have prepared Marquette Frye for South Central Los
Angeles. The place was huge. There were more people in his junior high
school than there had been in all of Hanna—and they were all black. There
were no Greeks here, no white people at all, unless they were store owners or police officers. But what really hurt Marquette was his status as an
outsider in this community. This neighborhood was made up of newcomers from the South, and the students in the schools were the children of
those migrants. The school's culture was more southern than western, and
Frye was not a southerner. He did not understand the ways of southern

black culture—the jokes, the slang, or the little mannerisms everyone else seemed to take for granted. When he talked, he lacked a southern accent and used standard English. He was targeted and teased from day one. He later recalled one of the insults: "White boy, what happened to you? You fall in a puddle of ink and come up black?" (Conot, *Rivers of Blood*, 4).

Eventually, there was trouble. There were a few fights with those who ridiculed him and some misguided efforts on his part to fit in, including petty theft, which, during his high school years, pushed Marquette into the hands of the police and, eventually, into the penal system and prison—actually a forestry work camp. Frye worked his way out of the system and moved back to L.A. He and other family members lived in Watts, the poorest and most rundown section of black Los Angeles. Unemployment and underemployment were big, persistent problems that Marquette could not escape. He found only menial work and strung a few jobs together. Along with its poverty and its projects, though, Watts still had some pretty little streets with pretty little bungalows. It may have been an all-black ghetto, but it did not have the look of a big-city slum.

By the middle of the decade, despite some discouragement about jobs, Marquette seemed to be getting his feet on the ground. Then came August 11, 1965, which would change everything for Marquette Frye, for Los Angeles, for the black West, and for America. In early evening, a California Highway Patrol officer stopped Frye on suspicion of drunken driven. Frye was borderline drunk—and after a series of sobriety tests (there were no breath tests in those days)—the officer judged that Frye was intoxicated. Frye disagreed and noted that he was only two blocks from reaching his mother's home. While this was happening, a crowd of spectators gathered. Someone alerted Rena Frye, who went to the scene to see about her son. The highway patrolman needed a Los Angeles Police Department (LAPD) squad car to take Marquette in, so he called for that, plus a tow truck to haul away the car. But when the crowd on the sidewalk grew and began to heat up, he also called for backup. The backups were LAPD and they plunged into the scene with clubs flying. They began to use force on Marquette, Rena, and Marquette's cousin, who had just arrived in town for a visit and was simply a bystander. All three were hit and cuffed and then shoved into police cars. Within hours, thousands of people in the community were in the streets in full-scale revolt. The Watts riot of 1965 had begun.

The Watts upheaval of 1965 lasted nearly a week, and it shocked the nation. It drew all eyes westward. For six days, television news showed Americans in a virtual war zone in Los Angeles, as black residents of the Watts section fought against police, state troopers, fire fighters, and, eventually, U.S. soldiers. Scenes of violent confrontations, black people looting stores, and buildings burning—along with the outcry of young blacks, "Burn, Baby, Burn!"—filled the nation's newspapers and television screens. Americans were riveted, shocked, horrified, angry, and confused—all at once. Had not the civil rights movement secured unprecedented gains for Negroes? Had not President Johnson just signed the Voting Rights Act into law last week? Wasn't the race problem in the South? When did so many black people move to Los Angeles, and what were they so upset about? The answers to these questions were many and varied, but during the intense 15-year period that followed the Watts Uprising, the dominant answers came from a new generation of black nationalists.

Participants in the Watts (L.A.) uprising of August 1965 often exhibited a sense of jubilation, as shown in this photo taken during the riot. (AP/Wide World Photos)

THE BLACK WEST AS TRENDSETTER

Between the Watts riot and the early 1990s, the West became the primary trendsetter for African American politics and culture. For better and for worse, blacks who lived in the eastern half of the nation (especially those in the urban North) began to follow West Coast trends. Pause for a moment to consider what a major change this was in the black western experience. The black West had long been a kind of outpost of African American history and life—a place for exiles seeking better lives in a distant land. World War II rapidly changed the demographics of the region, as southern blacks flocked to defense plants throughout the region. This Second Great Migration and its continuation through the 1950s permanently altered the black West. The cities of the West developed black ghettos that, in their basic structure and entrapment, were northern in all but name. Western exceptionalism seemed at an end, as race relations in the urban West were channeled into the national stream.

After Watts, however, the black West began to regain its distinctiveness—not as an outpost, but as a leader in African American politics and cultural production. It seemed for a time as if everything that emerged in the black West spread eastward to the rest of the nation. This was especially true of the West Coast and, even more specifically, of L.A. and the Bay Area. Some of these trends were constructive, others destructive. Urban race riots, the Black Panthers, Kwanzaa, black studies programs, blaxploitation films, the expansion of the black middle class and professional class, and an increase in black political representation—all of these were products of the black West, and all had an influence back East. Many of the older leaders of the black West were rightly upset and dismayed by some of these developments and rightly proud of some others. Either way, the power to shape national race relations had clearly shifted to the West Coast.

REBELLION IN WATTS

Beginning with the arrest of Marquette and Rena Frye on Wednesday evening, August 11, and continuing into Sunday of that week, South Central L.A. was consumed in violence and destruction. It began with rocks and bottles being thrown at cars passing through the area. Young black men began to smash windshields and assault white drivers. By midnight it had evolved into sporadic gunfire and assaults on the police who were sent to stop the violence. There were African American police officers in the LAPD but proportionately not many. The LAPD officers, highway patrolmen, and sheriff's deputies who were trying to stop the riot were virtually all white men. The rioters began to turn cars upside down and set them ablaze; firefighters who came to put out the flames were then attacked with rocks and, subsequently, bullets. By dawn an uneasy cease-fire existed. That morning—Thursday—black leaders held a community meeting in the area in an attempt to quell the violence. Rena Frye herself made a plea for calm. But the meeting turned ugly as angry residents turned it into an indignation meeting. This venting session was not too unlike the old Sunday forums held in black L.A., but this one was very public, and white L.A. was watching it on television. When one young man briefly seized the microphone and yelled that they were going to march on the white neighborhoods, the tone for the day was set.

The violence escalated and spread. Retail stores were looted, put to the torch, or both. Molotov cocktails were flying. Dozens, then hundreds of buildings began to go up in flames. With thousands of rioters in the streets and police busy protecting the firefighters from bricks and gunfire, the looting of stores continued nonstop. Guns were everywhere it seemed, and neither the police nor the rioters showed any reluctance to use them. From the Watts area where the riot had begun, violence spread across south L.A. It did not spread like a wave, but like scattershot. It erupted at various intersections of major retail streets, spaced apart like beads on a chain. The old Central Avenue district, and the once-famous intersection at 42nd Street—where the Somerville Hotel had hosted the National Association for the Advancement of Colored People (NAACP) Convention in 1928, where the Golden State Life Insurance Company had built its impressive headquarters, and where the dentist and NAACP president H. Claude Hudson, who led a campaign against police brutality in 1925, had built his Spanish-style office—was almost utterly destroyed by arson. Eventually, the destruction found its way west of the Harbor Freeway, erupting in pockets along Vermont Avenue, a major retail artery.

The major destruction took place on Friday, before the National Guard was ordered into the riot zone. Army Guard officials had been put on alert early on, but on several occasions the LAPD believed it had the situation under control and thought the guard unnecessary; later, when the guard was necessary, top officials in the governor's office, the LAPD, and the army got their signals crossed and somehow bungled the logistics. Once the National Guard did arrive in force—about 4,000 soldiers strong, added to the 1,000 local law enforcement officers—the streets were cleared and the violence burned itself out by the end of the weekend.

The fire and chaos in L.A. were the focal point of television news for days, and Americans could hardly absorb the shock. Statistics were grim: 34 people died in the violence and 1,000 were injured. About 4,000 individuals were arrested, mostly for looting. Estimates of property damage varied widely—the initial estimate by the state of California was roughly 1,000 buildings damaged at a loss of $40 million.

What had happened in Watts? One answer was police brutality. Abuse of black Angelenos by police was nothing new, of course, but it did seem to increase as black neighborhoods got blacker and poorer. In addition, it had become less visible to the outside world, because the Latinos, Jews, Japanese, and Anglos who used to live there had now left the area. By the 1960s, African Americans who challenged the LAPD were viewed with skepticism, and Chief Parker, who seemed to have a special enmity for black residents, was an expert in deflecting criticism and lawsuits.

Economic decline increased the sense of anger and powerlessness that many black Angelenos felt. At the time of the riot, it was estimated that two-thirds of all people living in Watts were on welfare. The same percentage of adults in the district lacked high school diplomas, a surprisingly high percentage for black Los Angeles. African Americans with better jobs and more prosperous businesses lived elsewhere, and there did not seem to be much hope of economic improvement in Watts.

Even though it did not look like a northern ghetto slum, Watts had a poverty problem. President Johnson's War on Poverty was expected to help, but Watts got caught in a political conflict over how poverty funds would be used—or, more accurately, who would control the funds. The Johnson administration urged local community involvement, but L.A.'s increasingly reactionary mayor, Sam Yorty, was cool to that idea. He created a committee that included too few members of the Watts community and especially too few of the poor residents who were supposed to have some say in the matter. An activist coalition in Watts emerged to challenge Yorty's control: the Community Anti-Poverty Committee (CAPC). This group won the support of another powerful politician—Congressman Gus Hawkins. Yorty had no intention of letting a black Great Society Democrat distribute these funds, so he sat on the funds. When Hawkins returned from Washington, D.C., in early August, he noticed high tension in the air; the people of his district told him trouble was coming. Hawkins alerted city leaders, including Yorty, urging them to release funds for immediate distribution or risk an outbreak of violence. Yorty dismissed this warning as a political ploy—and the riot came.

THE AFTERMATH

The first major official report—*Violence in the City: An End or a Beginning?*—appeared in early December 1965, courtesy of the state of California. Governor Edmund "Pat" Brown, a liberal Democrat, had created a special commission to study the riot, a commission chaired by John A. McCone, a former Central Intelligence (CIA) director. The report became known to all as the "McCone Commission Report"—the appellation that is still used for it. Brown gave the commission 100 days to produce the report, which led to an intense campaign of interviews, sworn testimony, and data collection. Brown chose McCone in part because he needed a chairperson who would have the respect of California conservatives, who saw the riot, at the very least, as a means of taking back the state government from the liberal Democrats, who had been in control since the late 1950s. Personally, Brown was shocked by the violence and wanted to get to the heart of the problem. Politically, he was trying to save his party from utter disaster. Neither his personal nor political goal was served well by the report (see the sidebar on page 234).

The McCone report did not mention any disagreement within the commission, but a two-paragraph statement by one black commission member clearly showed it. Those two paragraphs were placed at the end of the report, as a kind of addendum. The unemotional and bureaucratic tone of the McCone report was singularly different in tone from the dissent, which "violently disagreed" with some of the language of the report and particularly with passages that seemed to condemn poor blacks as welfare freeloaders, basically blaming the victim.

THE MCCONE COMMISSION REPORT

The McCone Commission Report was the name given to the state of California's official report on the Watts Rebellion in 1965, published that December and titled *Violence in the City: An End or a Beginning?* Roughly 100 pages of text, with photos and a map, the report was immediately controversial. Although it claimed to seek balanced objectivity and to promote solutions to urban blight, it effectively absolved the L.A. police of the charge of brutality against blacks and urged blacks to solve their own problems. Although it outlined the daunting economic and educational barriers that kept poor blacks locked in the ghetto, it essentially blamed African Americans for their own problems—in the parlance of the time, it "blamed the victim." Although the report claimed that the people of Watts faced discrimination, it suggested that the riot was sparked and sustained by a small group of young troublemakers who were not engaged in meaningful protest.

The report's description of the riot itself reads as if its author were a military man fascinated with law-enforcement tactics: command posts, sweep tactics, chains of command, and the management of conflict. The report concluded that although blacks *perceived* that they were unfairly treated by the LAPD, there was no real problem. The tone and language of the report is a time capsule to the moderate-conservative mind-set of the mid-1960s. One of the commission's suggested solutions, for example, was that the LAPD should create a Youth Deputies Program, in which police officers would visit elementary schools to promote law enforcement and distribute badges to young volunteers. The final section, "Solutions and Leadership," claimed that the commission's proposals—basically better schools, less employment discrimination, and better public transportation—were "revolutionary" but necessary.

In a two-paragraph dissent, Rev. James E. Jones, an African American member of the commission, noted several problems with the report and stated "I do not believe it is the function of this Commission to put a lid on protest registered by those sweltering in ghettos. . . . Protest against forces which reduce individuals to second-class citizens, political, cultural, and psychological nonentities, are part of the celebrated American tradition" (Fogelson, *Mass Violence*, 95–96).

The McCone Commission Report reshaped the way many Americans thought about American race relations in their country. It changed the very meaning of the term "race riot." It inspired a heated and extended debate about ghettos; the police; urban poverty; and the proper role of local, state, and national governments in urban race relations. Most important, the report and the many critiques of it that followed gave rise to two poles of political thought. On the political right, most racial conservatives blamed the problems of the urban poor on the failings of the poor people themselves and emphasized the protection of white people's rights and liberties against unwarranted encroachments by black people and other racial minorities.

Racial liberals, by contrast, usually emphasized the long history of systematic racism against black Americans; they held that government action must be taken at all levels of government to redress this immoral past and to ensure that blacks (and other racial minorities) could at last enjoy their basic rights as Americans. Many conservatives insisted that police officers were heroes protecting good Americans (basically white) from bad Americans (basically not white). Liberals sometimes insisted that the police were a part of the problem, because they had brutalized Americans of color and served as the legal enforcers of white racism.

These two political positions sharpened in the late 1960s because Watts was the beginning of a national trend. Even as Los Angeles was burning, copycat revolts burst out in San Diego, Pasadena, and a few other small towns in Southern California. Two big-city riots exploded the following summer, in Chicago and Detroit. In the interior West, Phoenix and Omaha both experienced small but violent riots. For those who were counting—and it seemed that many were—some 150 race riots erupted in the three years after Watts.

"Black Power!"

The Watts Rebellion had the effect of breaking the final thread that had connected the older generation of black activists with the younger generation of black activists. Tensions between the two age groups had been growing noticeably in the climactic years of the southern civil rights movement. During the 1965 voting rights campaign in Selma, a split began to appear within the movement. On the one side were the ministers and established middle-class leaders of the Southern Christian Leadership Conference

(SCLC), led by Martin Luther King. On the other were the college students and young leadership of the Student Nonviolent Coordinating Committee (SNCC). In their economic and cultural backgrounds, the SNCC leaders were no less middle-class than the leaders of the SCLC, but like millions of other American college students in the mid-1960s—white, black, and otherwise—they increasingly rejected the leadership of their middle-class elders and embraced a more strident tone and a more radical political stance. Younger people in the Congress of Racial Equality (CORE) were following the same path as those in SNCC. Many Americans still viewed Martin Luther King as dangerously radical, but for young blacks who embraced Black Power, he seemed suddenly too moderate, too patient, too old.

The younger generation suddenly viewed "integration" as a sellout, and they promoted racial nationalism as the key to Black Power. Self-determination became the order of the day, and this could be achieved through "national liberation"—within the United States and the Third World. To them, capitalism had enslaved blacks in colonial economies; the answer, as the Black Power advocates insisted, was revolutionary nationalism, including anticapitalist revolution. One result of Black Power was that biracial civil

In the late 1960s, the antiwar movement and the Black Power movement often went hand in hand, as was evident at this 1966 antiwar rally at the University of California, Berkeley. (AP/Wide World Photos)

rights organizations—SNCC and CORE specifically—were torn apart. More accurately, the Black Power advocates within those organizations moved successfully to expel white activists from those organizations. Another result, of course, was a glaring generation gap between older civil rights activists and new Black Power recruits.

Nowhere was this generation gap more sharply exposed than in California—in L.A. and the Bay Area, both of which gave rise to militant black nationalist organizations. L.A. saw the creation of United Slaves, sometimes called the US Organization. Oakland witnessed the creation of the Black Panther Party for Self-Defense. Throughout the urban West, the basic pattern held: young militants embraced Black Power and racial separatism and moved away from older civil rights leaders. In Phoenix, for example, the local chapters of CORE and SNCC grew disdainful of the local NAACP and other middle-class organizations pushing for basic civil rights, such as Leadership and Education for the Advancement of Phoenix (LEAP) and the Phoenix Human Relations Commission. The youth councils of CORE, SNCC, and NAACP began to stage their own protests using militant Black Power rhetoric and some violence. College and high school students—and even some younger children—took part in these protests. As official organizations, neither the Black Panthers nor the US Organization made much headway in Phoenix, but their views and style of protest were taken up by the Black Power advocates of SNCC and CORE.

In the summer of 1967, Phoenix had its own miniature version of Watts. A race riot broke out on July 25 when a crowd of militant young people—some of them associated with SNCC and CORE—had a confrontation with police officers. Molotov cocktails and bullets flew. After a lapse, the violence erupted again on July 26, leading to, most notably, the burning of police cars. The police alleged that CORE had been involved, and that may have been the case. Either way, nearly 300 blacks were arrested during the riot. One positive consequence of the conflict was an expansion of social services in black Phoenix, including community medical centers. Local activist Jim Williams created a local branch of the Opportunities of Industrialization Center (OIC), which was intended to boost employment and income in the black community.

Another consequence, perhaps not surprisingly, was a severe white backlash against all things related to civil rights, to say nothing of things related to Black Power. What Phoenix needed, in the white conservative view, was not programs for poor black people but obedience to the law—and an enlarged police force. Throughout the West, white conservatives in the Republican Party used the Black Power movement as their rationale for "law and order" campaigns. They pointed to rioters, black nationalists, communists, and antiwar protestors to rally their own troops. The popularity of the law and order theme would bring two California Republicans to the White House: Richard Nixon in 1968 and Ronald Reagan in 1980. It is now clear that the law and order backlash against black civil rights and even more so against black nationalism gave rise to modern conservative politics in America. Racial liberalism was not easily rolled back, however, and the civil rights movement resulted in real and lasting gains for African Americans. Civil rights activists and black political leaders continued to push their agenda forward. After Watts and the rise of Black Power, however, their campaigns for equal rights were overshadowed by black nationalism.

KARENGA AND KWANZAA

One of the most unexpected results of the Watts riot of 1965 was the invention of Kwanzaa. Today, Kwanzaa is a routine addition to the holiday program in schools across the country, and few Americans would link its origins with a massively destructive urban rebellion. But history works in strange ways, and Kwanzaa did indeed spring from the uprising in Watts. More specifically, it sprang from the mind of Maulana Karenga, who wanted to create an Afrocentric alternative to Christmas (and a less consumer-oriented alternative as well). Karenga was born on the East Coast at the beginning of World War II and was given the name Ronald McKinley Everett. By his mid-twenties (the mid-1960s) he had repudiated his European name and taken a Swahili name: Maulana Karenga. While attending graduate school at the University of California at Los Angeles (UCLA), where he studied political science, Karenga also taught the Swahili language at Fremont High School in Watts.

Karenga's version of black nationalism came to be known as "cultural nationalism." It emphasized the African roots of black Americans—African languages, religions, foodways, gender roles, family, and warfare. Karenga believed it essential to liberate black minds from the narrow confines created by the white people's colonialization and enslavement of black

Maulana Karenga, a black nationalist leader in L.A. during the late 1960s. He organized the United Slaves organization, feuded with the Black Panthers, and invented the Kwanzaa holiday. (Bettmann/CORBIS)

people—a subjugation that was, in Karenga's view, still operating on the minds of African Americans. Black Power required a cultural separation, a cultural liberation. Blacks needed to create new and original traditions that were based on traditional African principles and culture. Hence, his emphasis on Swahili and his insistence that universities create black studies departments, which would, he argued, counter the limitations of a Eurocentric educational system. This, also, was where Kwanzaa fit in (see the sidebar).

Kwanzaa did not spread across the country by chance. Karenga and other members of United Slaves traveled eastward promoting the new

---

KWANZAA

Created in 1966, Kwanzaa appears on the surface to blend various holiday traditions that have long existed in the United States—Thanksgiving, Hanukkah, and Christmas—but its creator, Maulana Karenga, intended it to represent traditional African ceremonies and principles. Kwanzaa was not really "African" in a literal sense, because it originated in L.A., but it reflected the cultural nationalism flowing through California in the late 1960s. It provided a way in which African Americans could cherish and celebrate a lost heritage—a heritage Americans had never celebrated precisely because it was "black" and "African."

Kwanzaa is Swahili for "first fruits"—a reference to the celebration of the harvest in Africa's traditional agricultural societies. On each day of the holiday, which lasts for seven days, participants share dinner around a ceremonial centerpiece. The centerpiece consists of a seven-holed candleholder placed in the middle of the table on a Kwanzaa mat (often a straw mat) and surrounded by fruits, vegetables, and nuts, which symbolize the bounty of the harvest. The center candle is black, and the three on either side are red or green—the colors of the flag of Kenya, which was newly independent when Kwanzaa was created. Each candle and dinner is dedicated to one of seven key principles: unity, self-determination, collective work and responsibility, cooperative economics, purpose, creativity, and faith. Taken together, these principles form "Nguzo Saba," the necessary ingredients for black survival, identity, and prosperity. Dinners feature classic dishes from the black South, such as Hoppin' John, fried catfish, and, from the Louisiana side of the table, Creole dishes. Singing, dancing, and storytelling top off each evening.

---

holiday to African American communities, especially in the big cities. It was another instance of the black West emerging as a trendsetter for the rest of black America. Kwanzaa did not spread like wildfire, however. It took time for the message to spread—and for it to be accepted. Perhaps the most amazing thing is that it survived at all, but Karenga's holiday eventually caught on. Kwanzaa seemed to suddenly take off in the late

1980s. By the early years of the 1990s, New York City was hosting an annual Kwanzaa Expo, and Hallmark cards had introduced a Kwanzaa line—two sure indicators of mainstream acceptance (and commercial viability). By the end of the 1990s, more than 13 million Americans were celebrating Kwanzaa (some of them celebrated it in addition to Christmas). The holiday also spread beyond the United States and has been adopted by some 5 million people in other countries. Perhaps in the future Kwanzaa really will become a widely celebrated holiday in Africa itself. It started, however, in Los Angeles, a product of the youthful black nationalism that accompanied the Watts Rebellion of 1965.

To promote his black cultural nationalism, Karenga created United Slaves—the very name suggested both unity among African Americans and black opposition to white Americans. The name did not denote the victimization of blacks so much as it conveyed ideas about the potential power of black Americans—most of whom were descendants of slaves and, in Karenga's view, were still slaves of white culture. Instead of trying to straighten their hair to fit the mainstream, young blacks let their hair kink naturally and then forked it up to create an Afro look. Among women, large loop earrings added an extra statement to the 'Fro. Katangi cloth was "in" and other traditional styles of black Africa (real and imagined) quickly came into style, especially if they came in red, yellow, black, and green—colors that made up many of the flags in Africa's newly liberated countries.

Karenga organized the original Watts Summer Festival, which was held in the summer of 1966. The festival carried an explicit message about the uprising of 1965: It was not a haphazard "riot"; it was an issue-oriented revolt of the community. Blacks who died in the revolt were not merely victims; they were martyrs. Muhammad Ali, who was not yet the universally loved icon he has become, was the grand marshal of the festival parade. Ali was a highly controversial figure in America, because of his conversion to Islam and his refusal to submit to the U.S. draft for the Vietnam War. The festival drew an enthusiastic crowd estimated at 130,000, and it moved Karenga to the front and center of the community.

Nonviolence and tolerance were not part of Karenga's cultural package. He emphasized the male warrior tradition, and guns were the weapon of choice for his US Organization. The US Organization was no democracy; Karenga ruled with an iron fist. Group members did as Karenga said, without question or debate. Karenga himself became reclusive as the 1960s wore on. When he did appear in public, he always looked the same, and all the men in his organization adopted the very same look: shaved head, dark sunglasses, Kung fu–style mustache, African dashiki. Kwanzaa remains; the US Organization does not, largely because of the guns and violence. When the Black Panther Party opened a branch in L.A. an open and sometimes violent feud erupted between the US Organization and the Black Panthers, which both groups seemed to view as a struggle for the soul of their people. In 1969, that war for hearts and minds led to a deadly shootout—not on the mean streets of L.A.'s Southside, but on the lovely campus of UCLA in Westwood.

A black student union (BSU) had been established at UCLA, and both the US Organization and L.A.'s Black Panthers wanted to control its development and direction. Leaders from both groups attended the BSU meetings on campus, and tensions at those meetings began to escalate. Then at a meeting in Campbell Hall in January 1969, a fight broke out at the end of the meeting. Gunshots rang out. Exactly what happened may never be known, but the end result was that members of the US Organization shot and killed two of the Black Panthers—John Huggins and Bunchy Carter, who were the top officials of the L.A. Panthers.

THE BLACK PANTHERS

The Black Panthers were a revolutionary black nationalist organization that was founded in Oakland by Huey Newton and Bobby Seale, young black men who met late in 1966. The official name of their organization was the Black Panther Party for Self-Defense (BPP), and as the name suggests they were a paramilitary group committed to defending Oakland's ghetto residents from the Oakland police. They adopted a Marxist ideology and spoke in terms of liberating the black ghetto from white imperialist rule, like Africans throwing off the yoke of European imperialism. Before long, Oakland's BPP recruited Eldridge Cleaver, an ex-felon whose writings from prison would become a national best seller and favorite of college students: *Soul on Ice*, which was published in early 1967. At the time, the BPP was limited to the Bay Area and had about 30 members.

The Panthers' relative obscurity ended on May 2, 1967, when the Panthers arrived at the California statehouse in Sacramento, automatic

Young students give the Black Power salute at a Black Panther "liberation school" in San Francisco in 1969. (Bettmann/CORBIS)

rifles in hand. The governor, Ronald Reagan, was scheduled to make a speech, so the media was there, but the Panthers got the attention. Ostensibly, the BPP came to protest the passage of a new gun law that would make it illegal to carry a firearm on the street. On that day in Sacramento, the Panthers were all dressed in what would become known as the Panther uniform: all black clothing, including black berets, dark sunglasses, and black leather jackets.

The Panthers were arrested without a gunfight, but not before they had gathered in formation on the statehouse steps for one of the most famous photographs of the 1960s: the Panthers in full outfit, rifles in hand, directing hard, stoic gazes to the outside world. The photo was on the front page in newspapers across the country and the world (Angela Davis saw it in a newspaper in Frankfurt, Germany). As a result, the Black Panthers became known, and chapters soon popped up all over urban America. Even as the nation braced for ghetto riots in the summer of 1966, there was a new revolutionary force to be reckoned with.

After the Sacramento incident, the Panthers got out of jail and back to work, and trouble was not long in coming. In a shootout between the

BPP and the Oakland police, an Oakland police officer was shot and killed, and Newton was charged with the murder. The trial became highly charged, and both the law-and-order Right and the young-and-radical Left seized on it. The "Free Huey" campaign of early 1968 became a movement within the Black Power and New Left movements. Cleaver initiated the Free Huey campaign, but he and Seale now sought East Coast support and, in particular, an alliance with SNCC's Black Power leader, Stokely Carmichael. Carmichael and fellow SNCC leaders James Forman and H. Rap Brown decided to merge their organization with the rapidly growing Panthers. The merger did not last, largely because SNCC leaders found that the western radicals would not follow SNCC's lead. The Panthers were too independent, too headstrong for Carmichael to tolerate, so he and SNCC left the BPP. But during the brief merger the Newton trial had become a major national issue, and, like Watts three years earlier, it threw the national spotlight on West Coast race relations.

The trial continued through most of 1968, a year in which America nearly unraveled altogether. In late January and February, the Tet Offensive in Vietnam turned public opinion against the war. In March, a weary Lyndon Johnson announced on live television that he would not run for president again. In April, Martin Luther King was assassinated in Memphis, sparking riots across the country. In June, Bobby Kennedy, who was carrying the torch of civil rights after King was murdered, was assassinated in L.A. In August, the Democratic National Convention in Chicago exploded when the Chicago police attacked antiwar demonstrators in the streets. The liberal Democrats, split between hawks and doves over Vietnam, tore themselves apart. Nationally, conservative Republicans gained power. Richard Nixon, a California Republican, won the presidency that November on a law and order platform. "Law and order" was a political code word that meant, among other things, keeping blacks in their place. In the election of 1968, however, Nixon actually appeared to be a racial moderate compared with George Wallace of Alabama, who ran for president on a mostly antiblack platform for the American Party. The nation, exhausted, stumbled toward 1969 with racial liberalism in tatters.

Newton's leadership of the BPP was equally chaotic. Huey was convicted and incarcerated, and while he awaited his appeal, the Panthers grew nationwide. Then in 1970, Newton went free on a legal technicality. Some Panthers in Oakland probably wished he had not come back, for he

In 1966, Huey Newton of Oakland cofounded the Black Panther Party for Self Defense, a paramilitary nationalist organization that spread nationally and became highly controversial in the late 1960s and early 1970s. (Hulton Archive/Getty Images)

moved into a large penthouse apartment and became increasingly abusive and violent toward his fellow Panthers. His lover (and BPP leader) Elaine Brown believed he was falling into madness. She had privately decided to leave the Panthers, but when new legal troubles sent Newton into exile in Cuba, Brown decided to seize the top spot in the organization, and she took it—an astonishing feat for a woman in the hypermasculine BPP. One reason Brown found an opening at the top was that many of the leading men had been taken out through imprisonment, exile, or death.

With the male leadership increasingly gone, the women in the BPP began to take the helm. Known as "Sisters," women in the Panthers had occupied a tenuous and often unpleasant place within the party. The question of a woman's proper role in the BPP was a controversial issue almost from the beginning, and it was never fully resolved. The Panthers were macho men, and in the beginning the in-your-face assertion of their manhood topped the agenda. Women were allowed to join, but they could not expect to be treated with respect, much less as equals. If a time came for women to use their guns, then they should shoot, but, as the leading men saw it, cooking, cleaning, doing the party paperwork, and having sex were the main responsibilities of the Panther women.

The women's rights movement blossomed in the early to mid-1960s, pushing for equal opportunity. The civil rights movement, the antiwar movement, and the New Left Movement among college students—these overlapping movements eventually experienced an internal war between the sexes. Generally, activist women found that male activists fully expected their women to maintain the same old gender roles, to do the same old women's jobs. The men took it for granted that the women would do the cooking and cleaning, would remain quiet and take minutes at meetings, and would be willing to have sex for the cause. As the decade went on, women grew increasingly disturbed by this contradiction in values. During the late 1960s and early 1970s, many young women—especially middle-class white women—abandoned the racial struggle and the New Left to advance the cause of women. They developed their own brand of cultural and political nationalism, which came to be known as "radical feminism." The new feminists called for radical changes in gender roles and, in some versions, for a physical separation of women from men—not unlike the black nationalists who called for separation of blacks from whites. In the question of women's equality, then, the BPP was not unique, but the Sisters in the BPP had to make difficult decisions about race and womanhood.

Elaine Brown's decision to seize the Panthers' top leadership position was, as she knew, very risky, but she pulled it off. Before most Panthers knew Newton had fled the country, Brown sent out a call for local leaders around the country to come to Oakland for a vital meeting. At that meeting, Brown assumed the top spot in the Panthers' national organization. She took control with a dramatic and threatening speech, in which she insisted:

> I have control over all the guns and all the money of this party. There will be no external or internal opposition I will not resist and put down. I will deal resolutely with anyone or anything that stands in the way. So if you don't like it, if you don't like the fact that I am a woman, if you don't like what we're going to do, here is your chance to lead. You'd better leave because you won't be tolerated.

Brown also got in a dig at Karenga's United Slaves—"so-called black nationalists"—and then dismissed the conclave urging all to return home and "*make* the revolution" (Brown, *A Taste of Power*, 4–5).

Brown brought more women into the BPP's Central Committee, and as the 1970s progressed the Panthers gradually made public services a larger part of their agenda. Brown also moved into electoral politics, running for a seat on the Oakland city council. Eventually, however, Newton returned from Cuba, and the Sisters were soon marginalized again. One of Brown's loyal and hardworking Sisters in Oakland had told a group of Panther Brothers, in effect, to get to work. Insulted, they asked Newton's permission to punish her. He gave permission, and they beat her so severely that she had to be hospitalized. When Brown complained to Huey, he seemed unconcerned and said the issue of women in the party would soon be settled. Brown saw the writing on the wall and secretly fled Oakland and the Panthers, after which the trend toward community service in the BPP faded.

One last point about the Panthers bears on the evolution of black western history. The Panthers were a West Coast organization. They appeared in the West at a particular time and place, and the organization then spread across the nation. The Watts Rebellion can be viewed in the same light. So, too, can Karenga's United Slaves and Kwanzaa. These developments may be seen in many different ways, but they emerged at a critical and difficult moment in black western history. The black West had been a hopeful place outside of the racial mainstream; then, during and after World War II, it had begun to seem very similar to the northern ghettos; finally, in the 1960s, black southerners continued to pour into neighborhoods that were on their way down, not on their way up. The lingering optimism of life in the West collided with the increasingly brutal conditions of the western ghettos. The result was unprecedented racial conflict, black rebellion, and fiery black nationalism.

ANGELA DAVIS AND CHE-LUMUMBA

Of the many famous and infamous black revolutionaries of the post-Watts era, none achieved the kind of national notoriety that fell to Angela Davis, even though she did not want such notoriety. Davis was born and raised in Birmingham, Alabama, but she departed for New York before the civil rights movement really got started in Birmingham. She left for New York because she was an especially gifted teenager—precociously smart and ready to explore a larger world, even before she completed high school in Birmingham. As it happened, her desire to get out of Birmingham connected with an educational program sponsored by the Quakers, which gave scholarships to young and gifted African Americans in the South, whose schools could not offer the level of education a gifted child needed. It worked something like a student exchange program, only within the United States.

So, for her senior year in high school, Angela Davis left Birmingham and wound up living in a home and attending a private school in Greenwich Village, New York City—a place where communism was still a viable point of view among the parents and students of the district. It was her first exposure to the political Left, but there was no particular reason for her or anyone else to think that her life from that point forward would be lived largely on the Left and in support of communism.

From New York, Davis earned an academic scholarship to Brandeis University. The school was chock-full of white Ivy League-caliber students, and she was isolated from any city life. Although she was not happy in that environment, Brandeis introduced her to radical philosophy and to one of the leading radical philosophers of the era, Herbert Marcuse. Majoring in French and taking advantage of study abroad programs, Davis found her way to Europe, where she traveled widely and continued to explore

Angela Davis: radical black activist, communist, and philosopher. (Bettmann/CORBIS)

communism. Eventually, she decided to pursue a PhD in philosophy at the University of Frankfurt in West Germany. At the same time, however, the civil rights movement in the American South was exploding, and she longed to be part of it. Before she began her studies in Germany, she went home for a brief time, and that only sharpened her dilemma: She believed she should study philosophy in Frankfurt, but she also felt that she should be part of the black struggle in the United States.

In August 1965, Davis left the United States for Europe with a divided heart. Nearly a decade later, writing her memoir, she recalled, with a certain wistful pain, that "by the time I left [for Germany] in the summer of 1965, thousands of sisters and brothers were screaming in the streets of Los Angeles. . . . Watts was exploding, furiously burning. And out of the ashes of Watts, Phoenix-like, a new Black militancy was being born" (Davis, *Angela Davis*, 144). After two years in Frankfurt, she could no longer endure the separation, especially in light of the burgeoning Black Power movement, scattered news of which had reached her in Germany. She left Frankfurt to continue her studies in philosophy at the University of California at San Diego, where Herbert Marcuse had moved from Brandeis. She knew California was at the heart of the Black Power struggle, so there she could continue to study radical thought with Marcuse and also get political.

In the summer of 1967, Davis landed in Southern California, eager to hook up with a revolutionary group. Before long she found plenty of revolutionary groups in Los Angeles, and she began to take part in a Southern California ritual: the long commute. She divided her time between philosophy studies in San Diego and revolutionary politics in L.A. She continued that divided life until she passed her PhD qualifying exams (which allow a graduate student to proceed to the dissertation stage) and, before completing her dissertation, she received an academic appointment, teaching philosophy in UCLA's Philosophy Department. She would begin teaching at UCLA in the fall of 1969.

Between her arrival in San Diego and her appointment at UCLA, Angela Davis had been connected with every black nationalist organization in Los Angeles, and her experiences with them had not been particularly good. The men of the US Organization castigated her for transgressing her proper role as a woman, which was to support the black man. To them, she was out of line to speak out at meetings or take the lead in planning protests.

Having no patience with the men of the US Organization, Davis helped to build a Los Angeles chapter of SNCC. But because she and several of her fellow SNCC leaders were communists and had begun to build SNCC educational programs that taught the basics of communism, the national office in New York soon expelled them from the organization. Davis also thought James Forman and other national SNCC officials wanted the L.A. chapter to stop teaching in the ghetto and start holding fund-raising events; the national office needed funds, and getting that money was the proper role for L.A. group. The New York office essentially purged the communists from the L.A. chapter of SNCC, which also meant the L.A. branch quickly died out.

Davis was annoyed and troubled by the lack of planning and organization within the various Black Power organizations. When she attended a large Free Huey rally in L.A., she was thrilled to see so many Brothers committed to the cause and so many organizations coming together in unity. The speeches were brave and revolutionary, and she was all for that, but she was shocked when the meeting ended, because none of the speakers made any suggestions about how they might actually go about freeing Huey. No one proposed a plan, a rally, or an organized effort. For Davis— a highly analytical and highly organized person—this was unacceptable. Unorganized emotion accomplished nothing. A revolution had to have an organization, a standard set of tactics, immediate and long-term goals, and a plan—a big plan.

That was why she joined the Communist Party USA. Davis had long been drawn toward the Left, and, after spending some time at local communist meetings, she decided that this was the organization she had been looking for, the one that had a plan for revolution. She became a member of an all-black communist cell named the Che-Lumumba Club. This was a group of roughly a dozen card-carrying communists who organized independently within certain neighborhoods (in this case south L.A.), but with an eye toward the larger party organization and goals. The name was chosen to honor two revolutionary leaders: Che Guevara of Cuba, who was widely known, and Patrice Lumumba, who had led a revolution in the Congo, and who was mostly unknown. Davis devoted her political energies to this communist club, but it also brought her into a brief association with the L.A. branch of the Black Panther Party.

Initially, Davis joined the Panthers more or less at gunpoint. Before the Black Panther Party of Self-Defense opened a headquarters in L.A., Davis had become part of a group of radical intellectuals and professionals who called themselves the Black Panther Political Party, which was strictly a local group. One day at this group's headquarters, a drunken and profane Panther (from the Self-Defense group) barged in and stuck a gun in Davis's face. He demanded that they drop the name of their group and suggested they would all wind up dead if they refused. Reluctantly, the radical intellectuals changed their name (actually morphing into the L.A. chapter of SNCC discussed previously). Nevertheless, the death threat from the Black Panthers caused her to take a fateful step in her revolutionary life: She went out and bought guns to protect herself from the Panthers.

Che-Lumumba would later form a brief alliance with L.A.'s BPP—and Davis became good friends with some of the leaders, including John and Ericka Huggins, John being one of the Panthers killed at UCLA. Davis also desperately tried to organize the black community to save the L.A. Panthers when their headquarters was attacked full force by the LAPD and its new SWAT team in the spring of 1970. The Panthers underwent a wave of paranoia over Federal Bureau of Investigation (FBI) infiltration and experienced a purge that eventually included some of the communist members simply because they were communists. On principle, Davis cut ties with the BPP and stuck with Che-Lumumba.

Davis's communism, not her black nationalism, caught public attention after she was hired at UCLA. Governor Reagan and the University of California Board of Regents demanded to know her political affiliation. She decided the best defense was a good offense and soon issued a public statement that emphatically confirmed that, yes, she was a member of the Communist Party USA and that she intended to remain one. This statement created a massive backlash against Davis; death threats poured in, the UCLA police were on constant alert, and bomb scares were common. The regents ordered Davis to be fired. The Philosophy Department stood firm, stating that faculty could not be fired for their personal political views. Davis took the regents to court and won. She finished the first quarter of the school year, and the department granted her time off to complete her dissertation.

Politics would not leave Davis alone, however. In the spring of 1970 one chaotic event seemed to lead to another. The LAPD's assault on the headquarters of the L.A. Panthers was a large part of that. Davis flew into a frenzy of organizing protests in the street and later at the courthouse. The regents fired her a second time, this time for "unbecoming speeches" she had made off campus.

All the while, Davis had been trying to secure the release of the so-called "Soledad Three"—three black prisoners locked up in the Soledad penitentiary. They had been indicted for murder, but Davis thought it a fake arrest and police cover-up. She developed a particular affection for one of them, George Jackson, and began to organize rallies calling for the prisoners' release. In the meantime, she began to look after George's younger brother, Jonathan Jackson, whom she thought of as her own brother. A large protest in behalf of the Soledad Three was scheduled at the time of a critical court hearing in San Francisco in mid-August. Davis would be there, working for George's release.

Only days before that hearing, however, Jonathan Jackson walked into a courtroom in Marin County, a beautiful area north of San Francisco, carrying one of Angela Davis's guns in a sack. The case under review that day had nothing to do with the Soledad Three, but the prisoners on trial were African American and appeared to know Jonathan would be there. Jonathan pulled the gun and ordered the prisoners released. He gave them guns too, and they took some hostages, including the judge. In the parking lot outside the courtroom, Jackson had a van waiting as a getaway vehicle. He got in as the driver, and the other former prisoners got in with the hostages. Courthouse guards had followed the group outside and had their guns trained on the van. Jackson apparently hoped the presence of the judge in the van (with a shotgun taped to his neck and a string running from the trigger to one of the former inmates) would deter the guards from shooting. The guards did not wait, however. They fired into the van, killing all inside, hostages included.

Angela Davis was in Pasadena writing her dissertation at a friend's house when she saw the story on the news. She immediately went underground—it is still not clear exactly why, because she did not seem to have been involved in Jonathan Jackson's scheme and, given her desire to get his brother out of prison and her work toward the upcoming rally, she had no incentive to help Jonathan in this deadly game. Indeed, just the opposite: Jonathan Jackson's actions doomed any chance of his brother getting out of the penitentiary. Almost surely, however, Davis *would* have been arrested and interrogated—probably not politely—and she may have feared that the authorities would never release her, innocent or not. Perhaps she had simply had enough: one man she cared deeply about had just been shot to death, another was now doomed to remain in prison (indeed he was shot and killed by guards shortly thereafter), and she was bound to have serious trouble with the law no matter what.

With the help of a friend, Davis fled L.A. in disguise and reached Chicago, where she hid out with an old friend. The FBI opened a dramatic, highly public manhunt for Davis, who made its Top Ten Most Wanted list. The odyssey ended late in 1970 when undercover agents caught her in New York City. After a bruising time in a New York prison, she was rushed to the airport under military guard and flown back to California to stand trial for accessory to murder in the Jonathan Jackson case.

Two years later Davis was acquitted. Free again, she traveled to Cuba, where she received a hero's welcome. Later, she returned to the states and, in 1974, published her autobiography, *Angela Davis: An Autobiography.* She did get her PhD and was eventually rehired into the University of California system, at the notably progressive Santa Cruz campus. She has remained a communist and continues to protest against the prison system.

CIVIL RIGHTS IN THE WEST (CONTINUED . . .)

For all the black radicalism that exploded in California, the mainstream civil rights movement in the urban West did not simply vanish. Black Power seized the moment and the headlines, but the middle-class and working-class activists who had long been pushing for equal opportunities in the West kept right on pushing. Open housing, school integration, equal employment opportunities—all of these remained central goals of mainstream African American leaders. The tried and true strategies persisted. They worked through the court system, sought political power at the local and state levels, and held mass nonviolent protests against discrimination. But it would be wrong to say that nothing in these protests changed. Watts and the long hot summers as well as Black Power and violent black nationalism had jarred the entire political system. The context for civil rights had changed, and those who promoted equal rights had to adapt.

Yesterday's radicals became conservatives—seemingly overnight. The traditional civil rights leaders, such as Lincoln and Eleanor Ragsdale in Phoenix, had not moved politically, but their place on the political spectrum had. In the early 1960s, they were viewed as subversives; by the end of the decade, they were viewed as moderate, if not downright conservative. This change did not protect them from white anger, however. The Ragsdales experienced frequent harassment from whites who were determined to stop their civil rights activism. Still, they stuck to their work and maintained their allegiances with older organizations. In 1972, for example, the Phoenix Federation of Colored Women had its annual meeting, and, in what would have been seen by Black Panthers as a hopelessly anachronistic and middle-class gathering, Eleanor Ragsdale urged the city's club women to be more involved in the community and local politics. She placed a special emphasis on helping black women in Phoenix who were hard hit by poverty.

People like the Ragsdales found themselves attacked from both ends of the political spectrum. They were attacked by blacks on the left and whites on the right. In one way, the new black radicalism helped their cause, because equal opportunity suddenly seemed a relatively tame demand. On the other hand, middle-class blacks were criticized almost immediately for playing the "riot" card, that is, for making political demands and adding the proviso that "if not . . . riots will follow." On this point, civil rights leaders could not win. If they addressed the issue, some whites accused them of playing the riot card; if they did not, those same whites accused them of ignoring black crime. They had to push on as best they could in an explosive context. One way they pushed on was to seek more black representation in local and state politics.

THE ELECTORAL ARENA

In almost every western state, the number of blacks elected to office increased after 1965. This trend was partly due to the rising political consciousness that was part of the 1960s. The overcrowded inner-city neighborhoods that developed in the West after World War II had a mostly negative effect on the black western experience, but in terms of votes on election day, the numbers exerted a positive influence. Blacks in western cities still had to fight against gerrymandering—the drawing of city council districts, for example, in such a way that the black vote would be diluted. Still, in most cities, at least some African American office seekers were able to gain elective office.

Black representation at the state level had a lot to do with the less exciting but very influential process of political redistricting. Since the beginning of the American republic, state legislatures had always favored rural districts; the ways in which political districts were drawn, and the basic rules of the political game, were pointedly against the interests of the nation's cities. In any given state senate, representatives of underpopulated rural districts outnumbered representatives of heavily populated urban districts, leaving the interests of the cities badly underrepresented. Finally, in the early 1960s, the U.S. Supreme Court ruled in *Baker v. Carr* that state legislatures had to ensure that representation was fairly assigned throughout each state. The "one man, one vote" rule now had to prevail. This meant state legislatures quickly, and at long last, began to reflect the interests of urban America, including racial and ethnic minorities who were highly concentrated in urban areas. Now more seats in the state legislatures represented urban areas, and liberal Democrats sought to ensure that the new districts would lead to more African American office holders.

In Phoenix, several civil rights leaders won elections for local and state offices. Clovis Campbell Sr., owner of Arizona's foremost race paper, the *Arizona Informant*, and an outspoken advocate for black rights, was elected to the state senate in 1966 (the first black to earn a seat in the Arizona senate). Calvin Goode became a constant in Phoenix politics. A strong voice for equal rights in Phoenix, and a former chairman of the LEAP economic development program that met so much white resistance, Goode was elected to the city council and served 11 consecutive terms in office. In office, he placed special emphasis on at-risk youth, services in black neighborhoods, and equal employment. As early as 1974, he was made vice mayor of the city—a post he held again in 1984. One of Goode's fellow activists in Phoenix, Art Hamilton, was elected to the state legislature, where he promoted, among other things, the economic diversification of the inner city. He would remain in office into the 1980s

Tom Bradley, one of three African Americans who won seats on the L.A. City Council in 1963. In 1973, Bradley was elected mayor, a post he held for the next 20 years. (AP/Wide World Photos)

and eventually became the House minority (that is, Democrat) leader in the Arizona legislature.

The brightest political star in L.A., a much bigger stage, was Tom Bradley (see the sidebar below). Bradley was born into poverty in Texas and moved to L.A. as a child, early in the Great Depression. After two years at UCLA, he joined the LAPD and rose rapidly in the ranks. He read law on the side and eventually left the LAPD when he passed the bar. As a middle-class African American, he lived in the 10th District—the West Adams/Crenshaw area where the more affluent blacks moved in the 1950s. It was a diverse area—black, white, and Asian—and it was this constituency that elected Bradley to the L.A. City Council in 1963. Ten years later, he became mayor of the city, a post he would hold for 20 years.

TOM BRADLEY, MAYOR

After Tom Bradley was elected to the L.A. City Council, he became an outspoken critic of conservative mayor Sam Yorty and LAPD chief William Parker. In 1969, Bradley ran for mayor, losing narrowly in a campaign marked by Yorty's race baiting. That Bradley even came close was eye-opening, for the city's voters were overwhelmingly white. Bradley and his advisers saw the opportunity to fashion a winning coalition between South L.A. African Americans and West L.A. Jews—a biracial coalition of two groups that had long been marginalized in the city's centers of power and that was committed to racial liberalism. This Southside-Westside coalition triumphed when Bradley ran for re-election in 1973.

Bradley had downplayed race in his campaign, promising to be mayor for all of L.A. His administrations generally proved good on that promise. He tirelessly promoted L.A. as a global city and sought economic development by positioning the city as an essential center of the Pacific Rim economy. In the beginning, he actively sought federal funds to uplift the ailing economy of south L.A., where most African Americans lived, but over time he used less energy for this purpose. Critics within the black community complained, with some justification, that he ignored the needs of the black poor while promoting the city's pro-business environment.

In 1982, Bradley ran for governor of California and nearly won. In fact, major polls had predicted his victory. He lost by a narrow margin, prompting questions about the polls. Were the polls poorly conducted, or were white Californians not being honest about their willingness to elect a black governor? The polls, it turned out, were poorly run, but journalists nonetheless coined the term "Bradley effect" to mean that many white voters say they will vote for a black person when in reality they will not—a theory frequently raised on the eve of the 2008 presidential election.

The highlight of Bradley's 20 years as mayor was when he brought the 1984 Olympic Games to L.A. After that, a host of urban problems eroded his support across the political spectrum and among both blacks and whites. His ineffective leadership during the L.A. riots of 1992 sealed his political demise; he stepped down in 1993. (Sonenshein, *Politics in Black and White*).

Bradley's faithful coalition held until he retired in 1993, despite local disasters that Bradley proved unable to cope with. One of those was the deadly rise of gang violence on the Southside. A related problem was the seemingly intractable poverty and unemployment on the Southside, coupled with the trend of deindustrialization and the closing of large factories—especially auto and tire—on the edge of the black community. Still another was the rising tension between Korean immigrant store owners and the poor blacks they sold goods to. Conflict between the LAPD and the black (and brown) community endured and resulted, eventually, in the videotape of the Rodney King beating and, in 1992, the Rodney King riots, which made Watts seem small by comparison. Even after the riots of 1992, however, and even after all of the problems, opinion polls showed that, on the verge of his retirement in 1993, the people of the city continued to give Bradley a positive rating for leadership.

THE 1968 OLYMPIC GAMES

The 1968 Summer Olympic Games, held in Mexico City, unexpectedly brought national attention to West Coast race relations and sparked a national debate about race and sports that continues today. For African Americans on the U.S. Olympic Team, the games in 1968 represented a painful dilemma. The United States had long used the Olympics as a kind of global advertisement of American freedom. This had been something like an official policy since 1936, when Jessie Owens sprinted his way to Olympic glory and humiliated Hitler's "master race" athletes. And when the games resumed in the Cold War era, the face of a racially integrated and successful Olympic team became paramount. This placed black athletes in a moral bind. Overseas, for a few days, they were American heroes, but when they returned home everything reverted to the way it was before: they were no longer heroes but merely colored people, confronted with the same-old second-class citizenship. Plus, in those days, the Olympics were still amateur athletics; no one got paid to train or to compete.

Should African American track-and-field athletes use their talents to promote black civil rights in America? Should they threaten to boycott the games? What would happen if they withheld their athletic talent from the United States—until they could get a guarantee about improving black prospects for jobs and housing? In 1964, when the Olympics were held in Tokyo, these questions were not so hard for black athletes to handle. After all, in the fall of 1964 race relations in the United States seemed on the upswing. The Civil Rights Act had just become law, and Martin Luther King's "I Have a Dream Speech" was still reverberating across the nation and the world. Athletes concerned about being used by the American government could believe, not without cause, they were competing for a nation that actually did care about black rights. By 1968, however, black athletes faced a far more explosive situation. The Black Power movement and student radicalism forced black track-and-field stars to confront the issue directly. Black Power leaders demanded that black athletes boycott, that they not be tools of white imperialism.

Among the athletes themselves, the West Coast was the hotbed of the boycott movement. On the campus of San Diego State University—a track-and-field powerhouse at the time—a young, militant African American professor, the sociologist Harry Edwards, was promoting the idea and advising black athletes. Not all of them faced the same situation. In basketball, for example, UCLA's star player, the serious-minded and politically astute Lew Alcindor (later Kareem Abdul-Jabbar) could boycott the games, make an important political statement, and still be sure of a professional career in the NBA (National Basketball Association).

At the 1968 Olympic Games in Mexico City, American sprinters Tommie Smith (center) and John Carlos (right) shocked the world by giving the Black Power salute during the playing of the U.S. national anthem. (Bettman/CORBIS)

For track-and-field athletes, however, there were no professional leagues waiting, and no runner could really turn a personal boycott into political influence or economic gain. If they did not win, they would have no voice; if they did not compete, they obviously could not win.

The leading sprinters at San Diego State—Juan Carlos and Tommy Smith—decided to compete. With the blessing of Harry Edwards, himself an outspoken promoter of Black Power, they committed themselves to the team and to the games, but they also kept the idea of making some kind of political statement. To do that, they would have to medal in their races, so they could reach the winners' stand—which would be the prime spot for a protest. They ran, and ran well. In the finals of the 200-meter dash, Smith won, and Carlos placed third. They were headed to the medals stand, where they would receive their medals, where the national anthem of the United States would be played (in honor of the winner), and where an international television audience of many millions would be watching. Underneath the grandstands, waiting to be called onto the field, Smith handed Carlos a black glove.

On the winners' stand, when the national anthem was played, both men bowed their heads and raised a black-gloved hand in the Black Power salute. Whether Carlos and Smith fully appreciated the firestorm this would create, they were right about the basic strategy: Their winners' stand protest got more attention than a boycott would have. The uproar was immediate and fierce. Both runners were stripped of their medals and banned from any future Olympic competition. Few if any political protests in sports have been so controversial or, in their way, successful. The debate often sank to a low level of sweeping accusations and racial insults, but there was in fact a public debate over race and sports, and that was important. In a single, unforgettable moment (and a nonviolent one), Carlos and Smith had pushed the controversy to the center of the American table. It could never again be ignored.

BLACKS AND HOLLYWOOD

Black Power found its way into mainstream movie theaters in the early 1970s, as African American directors finally gained entry into the Hollywood studios and began to produce blaxploitation films. At first glance, the term "blaxploitation" seems to suggest that blacks were, once again, being exploited by Hollywood filmmakers—and many mainstream civil rights leaders condemned the image of black men and women that was presented in these films—but the blaxploitation movies were not invented by white filmmakers. They were made by African American producers and directors who were primarily targeting a black audience. Nor were these movies independent films produced outside Hollywood. They were the work of black filmmakers working *within* the Hollywood studio system.

Gordon Parks Sr., a native of Kansas, was the first African American to direct a film in Hollywood in 1969. By that time, he was arguably the best known African American photographer in the world. His first film was *The Learning Tree*, based on his novel of the same name. Virtually forgotten now, it is the (largely autobiographical) story of a hard-luck farm family trying to scratch a living from the High Plains. Parks hit pay dirt of a different kind in 1971, when he directed *Shaft*, regarded by many as the original blaxploitation movie, although Parks himself did not call it that. Whatever kind of film it was, *Shaft* struck a nerve in the moviegoing public and sold a lot of tickets nationwide. Then Gordon Parks Jr. followed his father's lead and produced a similar film, *Superfly* (1972). This one grossed more than $24 million.

The public response to blaxploitation films reflected America's changing racial culture in the 1970s. Middle-aged and middle-class blacks received them coldly; indeed, many were alarmed at the blatant ghetto violence shamelessly portrayed in these movies. After decades of seeking a more complex and realistic portrayal of black Americans in Hollywood films, civil rights leaders considered the creation of characters such as Shaft to be a leap in the wrong direction. In their view, the old *Gone with the Wind* stereotype had simply been replaced by a new and equally degrading stereotype. Young African Americans, on the other hand, usually received the blaxploitation films with unchecked enthusiasm. Whites also tended to split along generational lines. The older generations and parents watched with shock and alarm, but millions of white kids were enthralled with all things black and hurried to adopt the Afro hairstyles and super-cool attitudes that were on view in *Shaft* and *Superfly*.

After the Parks's one-two punch with *Shaft*, Hollywood poured forth the blaxploitation genre—well over 100 such films by decade's

Gordon Parks—famous for his photography—became the first African American to direct a feature film within the Hollywood system in the late 1960s and soon thereafter directed the box office smash, Shaft (1971). His son Gordon Parks Jr. followed with his own hit film, Superfly. (Christopher Felver/CORBIS)

end. They were copycat films and of varied quality. Black directors were not in control of all of them—not by a long shot—but in the larger sweep of western history, the more important point was that African American writers and directors had finally won the opportunity to secure a place in Hollywood, and they did secure a place. In the racially closed world of Hollywood production, securing that place was no small achievement.

In 1972, Motown Records moved from Detroit to Hollywood. This was no trivial relocation. Under the leadership of entrepreneur and producer Berry Gordy Jr., Motown had made Detroit the national center for popular black music in America. Motown, which took its name from Detroit's nickname, the Motor City, became one of the most successful black-owned businesses in history. Motown hits were in no way restricted to a black audience; the Motown sound crossed all racial boundaries (and national and economic boundaries for that matter). Indeed, Motown made the crossover hit commonplace in America. The statistics of success were staggering. Between 1961, when Smokey Robinson and the Miracles provided Motown's breakthrough hit, "Shop Around," until Gordy moved his company to L.A. in 1972, Motown notched more than 30 number-one hits and, to use a broader scale, more than 100 top-10 singles. Diana Ross and the Supremes, Stevie Wonder, the Jackson 5, and Marvin Gaye—all of these became household names in the United States, along with the name Motown itself.

Motown's move to L.A. in 1972, therefore, was a significant event in the history of black American culture and the black West. Gordy did not come to L.A. to make music. He came to produce films—and not blaxploitation films either. The company's first feature film was *Lady Sings the Blues* (1973), which garnered a best actress nomination for Diana Ross and was also a box-office smash. Here, at long last, was a black-made drama intended for the full spectrum of American moviegoers, in which the leading characters were African Americans whose roles involved no obvious or insulting racial stereotypes.

CONCLUSION

In 1965, the Watts Rebellion brought down the curtain on racial liberalism as the dominant theme in black political life. In its place, black nationalism took center stage, and a militant black nationalism at that.

The Black Panther Party that emerged in Oakland spread quickly and won converts all across the nation. This was an openly violent paramilitary nationalism: the Panthers saw more promise in bullets than ballots, and said so. They promised self-protection for the ghetto against what they saw as the racist law enforcement system. A different brand of black nationalism was represented by the United Slaves, founded in Los Angeles. The US Organization saw black salvation in cultural nationalism—the recovery and promotion of African culture among black Americans. This involved the creation of black studies departments in universities, the promotion of black history and culture in the public schools, and the spread of Kwanzaa and other cultural manifestations of black pride and heritage.

This Black Power movement took young America by storm, but many of the older political activists continued to do battle in more traditional arenas. The post-1965 civil rights movement in the West focused on integrating the public schools, creating equal access and equal opportunity in the job market, and establishing fair-housing laws. Others decided political representation was the ultimate key to racial equality, and politicians such as Tom Bradley and Willie Brown emerged to form biracial liberal coalitions. The political successes of these activists and politicians were never complete, but improvements came to pass for the black West. Those improvements tended to help the black middle class far more than they helped the black poor in the inner-city ghettos. That trend was not yet apparent in the late 1970s, when the militant phase of black nationalism waned. It would become apparent in the 1980s, when the inner cities fell into an economic and social crisis.

BIBLIOGRAPHIC ESSAY

The opening vignette for this chapter comes from Robert Conot, *Rivers of Blood, Years of Darkness* (New York: Bantam, 1967), chapter 1.

Quintard Taylor's *In Search of the Racial Frontier: African Americans in the American West, 1528–1990* (New York: W.W. Norton, 1998) and Walter Nugent's *Into the West: The Story of Its People* (New York: Alfred Knopf, 1999) shed light on the urban West in the decades after 1965.

On the Watts Rebellion, see Conot's *Rivers of Blood*, a contemporary journalistic account that still has power, and Gerald Horne's *Fire This Time: The Watts Uprising and the 1960s* (Cambridge, MA: Da Capo Press, 1997). The McCone

Commission Report is reprinted, with additional commentary, in Robert Fogelson, *Mass Violence in America: The Los Angeles Riot* (New York: Arno Press, 1969). Scott Kurashige, *The Shifting Grounds of Race: Black and Japanese Americans in the Making of Multicultural Los Angeles* (Princeton, NJ: Princeton University Press, 2008), and Josh Sides, *L.A. City Limits: African American Los Angeles from the Great Depression to the Present* (Berkeley: University of California Press, 2003) both offer important perspectives on the upheaval.

Community studies that deal with the post-Watts era outside of L.A. include Quintard Taylor, *The Forging of a Black Community: Seattle's Central District from 1870 through the Civil Rights Era* (Seattle: University of Washington Press, 1994), and Matthew C. Whitaker, *Race Work: The Rise of Civil Rights in the Urban West* (Lincoln: University of Nebraska Press, 2005), which focuses on Phoenix.

On black nationalism and radical politics in the West, see Robert O. Self, *American Babylon: Race and Struggle for Postwar Oakland* (Princeton, NJ: Princeton University Press, 2003), chapters 7 and 8; Elaine Brown, *A Taste of Power: A Black Woman's Story* (New York: Anchor Books, 1992), which gives an insider's look at the Black Panthers; Angela Davis, *Angela Davis: An Autobiography* (reprinted with a new introduction by the author, New York: International Publishers, 2006); Horne, *Fire This Time*; Gordon Wheeler, *Black California: The History of African-Americans in the Golden State* (New York: Hippocrene Books, 1993); and Jane Rhodes, "Black Radicalism in 1960s California: Women in the Black Panther Party," in Quintard Taylor and Shirley Ann Moore Wilson, eds., *African American Women Confront the West, 1600–2000* (Norman: University of Oklahoma Press, 2003), 346–362.

On Tom Bradley, see J. Gregory Payne and Scott C. Ratzan, *Tom Bradley, the Impossible Dream: A Biography* (Santa Monica, CA: Roundtable Publishing, 1986); Raphael J. Sonenshein's *Politics in Black and White: Race and Power in Los Angeles* (Princeton, NJ: Princeton University Press, 1993); Melvin G. Holli, *The American Mayor: The Best and the Worst Big-City Leaders* (University Park: The Pennsylvania State University Press, 1999).

On sports and entertainment, see Arthur Ashe Jr., *A Hard Road to Glory: A History of the African-American Athlete since 1946* (New York: Amistad Press, 1993), and Berry Gordy, *To Be Loved: The Music, the Magic, the Memories of Motown, an Autobiography* (New York: Warner Books, 1994); Jacqueline Cogdell DjeDje and Eddie S. Meadows, *California Soul: Music of African Americans in the West* (Berkeley: University of California Press, 1998).

THE AFRICAN
AMERICAN WEST SINCE 1980:
DECLINE AND SUCCESS

In the summer of 1996, "Shaq" came to Los Angeles, and his mere arrival ignited several months of frenzied enthusiasm in the city. At the time, no full name was necessary—Shaquille O'Neal was that famous. Like so many African Americans who had migrated to Los Angeles in the previous century, Shaq hailed from Louisiana. But his "migration" to the city was something altogether different. He had recently signed a $120 million contract to play basketball for the Los Angeles Lakers. Fully seven feet, one inches tall and weighing in at nearly 300 pounds, Shaq was a big deal. He had starred at Louisiana State University, and then in the professional ranks with the Orlando Magic. But there was more: Beyond basketball, he had released two rap albums, was frequently seen on television, and had starred in a made-for-Shaq Hollywood movie, in which he played a superhero named Shazaam. The L.A. media ate it up. Shaq himself seemed genuinely happy to be in Southern California. He bought a big home at Hermosa Beach. He handled the media overload with good humor, and he shouldered the city's super-charged expectations of him with a casual ease.

Shaq confidently promised championships for L.A., but the Lakers' front office made even bigger promises. As the Lakers' director of sales, Steve Chase, explained to the *L.A. Times*, Shaq would boost Southern California's sagging economy. The Los Angeles Forum (the home of the Lakers) would sell out for the season; Shaq jerseys would fly off the shelves; tourists would flock to see the "gentle giant"; and the people and entrepreneurs of L.A. would be energized by the Lakers' successes. As Chase said in an interview with an out-of-town reporter, "I really believe this is the best news this city has had in a decade. After Magic Johnson said

Basketball superstar Shaquille O'Neal signed with the Los Angeles Lakers in 1996, sending shockwaves of enthusiasm across L.A. (CORBIS)

he was HIV-positive, we had earthquakes, fires, mudslides and riots." The people of L.A. needed "a big superstar to hang our hats on." Shaq was the ticket. He was "going to create a trickle-down effect for the economy of the entire region" (Rachel Blount, "Shaq quake," [Minneapolis, MN] *Star Tribune*, September 29, 1996: 4C).

Less than a century earlier, the local chamber of commerce had promoted the city as an "Anglo-Saxon" dream come true, but now the city was pinning its hopes on the arrival of one larger-than-life African American. Whether or not Shaq could singlehandedly save the Southern California economy, his move to L.A. had boosted local spirits—which did indeed need boosting. The early 1990s had been disastrous for the city. The police beating of Rodney King, caught on videotape and broadcast repeatedly to the nation, scarred the city's reputation. The massive riots that followed the police officers' acquittal made the Watts Rebellion seem small by comparison. Large swaths of the city were burned to the ground. Then came the string of natural disasters alluded to by Steve Chase. The local economy sagged, and something happened to local real estate that had seldom happened since the boom of the 1880s: home values plummeted. In short, L.A. needed something good to happen. Shaq, in the summer of 1996, was that good thing.

Of course, Shaq was not a "migrant" in any meaningful sense of the term. Think back to the migration stories that have opened each chapter of this book: Hannah Smith and Biddy Mason were brought to Los Angeles as slaves, but they won their freedom. The Bontemps family left Louisiana to safeguard their hard-won prosperity and to improve their children's educational opportunities. Verna Deckard fell in love with Los Angeles and would not return to "bad old Texas." Fanny Hill came to get a job in the defense plants during World War II. Sylvester Gibbs left a small town in Mississippi because his wartime military service had broadened his view of what African Americans could be and had made him unwilling to accept the Jim Crow South. Marquette Frye came with his parents, who were leaving a declining mining town in the West for the city that seemed to have the best possibilities for employment. Shaq came from the South, yes, and he came for a new start, just as the others had, but obviously he was not a black southerner looking for a new start in the way they had been.

In fact, the Great Migration of the 20th century was over for blacks. Whether that migration began during World War I, as it had in the urban North, or during World War II, as it had in the urban West, the movement of African Americans out of the South had basically stopped by 1980. During the decade of the 1980s, more blacks actually moved into the South than moved out of it. Increasingly, the children and grandchildren of the Great Migrations were returning to their roots, and they were not, by and large, poor blacks who were desperate for jobs.

The civil rights movement had transformed the South, economically as well as racially. Once the shackles of Jim Crow had finally been broken, the South as a region experienced steady infusions of private capital, public investment, and educational improvement. Jobs were plentiful, and good jobs were common. Cities such as Charlotte and Atlanta attracted a new generation of black professionals and energetic entrepreneurs. These migrants to the South found that they could reconnect with their "home people" even as they could get ahead economically.

Had the West finally lost its magnetic pull on African Americans? In some ways, it had. The tarnishing of the western image in black America was linked to a series of painful trends and events that occurred in the West, especially in Los Angeles, during the 1980s and early 1990s. Not all the news was bad. Many African Americans in the urban West were prospering in the final decades of the century. The black middle class was expanding, an identifiable black professional class was emerging, and many thousands of black westerners were moving out of the city and into more prosperous suburbs. Still, it was not the case that these positive trends were "western" trends. They could be observed in the cities of the North and the South, too. Maybe black America no longer needed a "West," a region in which racial conditions were better, a last best place for the race.

"Maybe" is a key word in that last sentence, for historians are cautious about making claims about recent decades. They *should* be cautious, in any event. Historians need to have some chronological distance from events they consider. How much time must pass before "current events" become "history"? There is no specific rule, but most historians would probably agree that roughly 25 or 30 years must pass before a historian can safely make claims about events in their larger historical context.

This chapter, which covers the African American West since 1980, will therefore offer only a brief sketch of well-known events. It suggests how events and trends of these years might be understood, given the long view presented in this book—but it does so with the caveat that these interpretations are speculative, resting on thinner historical foundations than the interpretations presented in earlier chapters.

Without question, however, Shaq's arrival in L.A. in the late 1990s was greeted so enthusiastically in part because the city had witnessed a series of disastrous events in the years leading up to his arrival. Not all of those disasters were about race—wildfires, mudslides, and a severe real estate slump all brought their share of despair. But the worst blows to the city, both its people and its reputation, were related to race. They included the economic crisis of the inner city, a surge in gang violence, the Rodney King beating, the Rodney King riots, and the O.J. Simpson trial. Perhaps only someone as big as Shaq could have shouldered L.A.'s resurgence. It was no small thing, however, that L.A.'s newest savior was a black Superman.

THE URBAN CRISIS

The presidential election of 1980 marked the biggest shift in national politics since the New Deal of the 1930s. The winner in a landslide was the Republican candidate, Ronald Reagan, the most aggressively conservative president of the 20th century. Unlike the business-oriented conservatives of the 1920s, unlike the moderate Republican Dwight D. Eisenhower of the 1950s, and unlike the loudly but pragmatically conservative Richard Nixon, Reagan represented the new social conservatism that had gained control of the Republican Party in the mid-1960s. The conservative culture of Reaganism also pulled white working-class voters away from the liberal Democrats. In his inaugural address, President Reagan famously stated that "Government is not the solution. Government is the problem." This was political code that had ominous overtones for black civil rights and especially for the government programs aimed at inner-city uplift. Reagan had been elected governor of California in 1966, the year after the Watts Rebellion, in the midst of the state's white backlash, and he would continue to foster and benefit from the wave of white racial anger that swept California, the West, and the nation.

The president's "government is the problem" announcement indicated that his administration would seek major cuts in social-welfare programs, particularly those aimed at helping inner-city areas, which were heavily black. That is just what happened. Federal funds for social services were greatly diminished or simply eliminated altogether. These cuts included basic services—school breakfasts and lunches for poor children, psychological services for the poor and the homeless, welfare payments to the poor, and job-training programs. Inner-city neighborhoods that had been gaining a little economic momentum and a little hope were hard hit by these cuts. State, county, and city funds could not take up the slack, and the inner cities began to deteriorate.

As the 1980s progressed, and the cuts in social programs began to take their toll, it appeared that the inner-city poor (especially African Americans, but in the urban West, also Latinos and some newly arrived Asian immigrants) were stuck in poverty and had no real chance to get out. The term "underclass" found its way into the American vocabulary. It was intended to identify the urban American poor, those who had no jobs and no prospects and could not claim to be part of the working class. It was a label placed especially on single mothers living on welfare, high school dropouts, gang bangers, and people living in the "projects."

Both the term "underclass" and the condition itself (a class of permanently poor Americans) became matters of political and scholarly debate. Whose term was this, and what was the message? Were Reagan-era conservatives using the term to justify cuts in social programs—as if to say, "They're stuck and nothing can be done to change that, so why waste tax dollars trying to lift these people out of poverty." Or were political liberals saying, in effect, "This is the shame of America, and we must use our national resources to eliminate the conditions that have created an underclass"? And what about the residents of the inner city themselves, who often chafed at the terms "underclass" and "ghetto," even as they lambasted the Republican Party tax cuts that were undercutting the progressive programs in their communities.

Beyond the question of political language, another debate emerged about whether an urban underclass actually existed. Was the crisis of the inner city as bad as the liberal Left claimed? Were residents in underclass neighborhoods really trapped in a cycle of poverty? Or were some people within those communities actually moving up and out? Just how much distance was there between the underclass and the working class—or for that matter, the middle class? Was race really a factor in keeping inner-city residents down, or was this the same kind of situation other poor immigrant groups had endured and continued to endure? If race was indeed a factor, what about Asians in America, what about the Japanese and Chinese, who were both considered "model minorities"? Didn't they overcome racial discrimination to get their piece of the pie?

One newly arrived group of Asian immigrants—the Koreans—were right in the thick of the inner-city crisis. The Koreans owned and operated many of the little corner stores and markets that dotted the ghettos of the urban West. In doing so, they more or less took the place of the Jewish merchants who had owned and operated those markets before the 1960s. After the urban riots of the late 1960s—the Watts Rebellion key among them—Jewish businesses gradually left the black ghettos. That vacuum was partly filled by African American businesses, but by 1980 large numbers of Koreans had set up shop in South Central L.A., in black San Francisco, and in black Seattle. Strongly nationalistic, family centered, and tightly organized, the Koreans were in many respects well-suited to grab the shopkeeping niche that presented itself.

Other Asian newcomers—especially the Vietnamese, Cambodians, and Hmong, all refugees of the Vietnam War—were not able to match the shoestring economic progress of the Koreans, who thus became unintentionally embroiled in the underclass debate. The relationship between African Americans and the Korean immigrants was complex, as the black–Asian relationship had always been. The two groups were, at turns, cooperative and competitive. Relationships between blacks and Koreans could be cordial, and there were interesting cultural exchanges of the sort that often occur in the urban West; but there was also a wide cultural gap, lingering mistrust, and some open hostility. The black community was especially outraged by the killing of Latisha Harlins, an African American teenager shot dead by a Korean store owner, who claimed she had stolen a bottle of juice and, when confronted about it, had hit him. The store owner was convicted by the courts but was merely fined and slapped with a bit of community service. Interracial conflicts, both mild and severe, added another painful layer to conditions in the inner-city neighborhoods.

Within this new political environment, black youth gangs exploded with growth and became engaged in unprecedented violence. Before the 1980s, black street gangs had been relatively small and were basically involved in turf battles, theft, macho posturing, and the occasional explosion of tragic violence. In the 1980s, however, the character of black street gangs began to change into something more violent and coercive when they became connected with international drug-trafficking organizations. The gangs effectively took over the public housing projects. Crack cocaine, a highly addictive drug, hit the streets.

Big money was at stake now—although the wealth seems to have gone mostly to people at a higher level of operations than the gangs themselves. Two mega-gangs, the Bloods and the Crips, were eventually formed in L.A., and both spread to the other cities in the West and, ultimately, the nation. Conflicts between the police and the gangs escalated, and so did violence between rival gangs. Taken together, the cuts in social services, the decline of industry in the inner cities, and the rise of gang violence added up to an urban crisis.

THE RODNEY KING BEATING

As the cold realities of the urban crisis were sinking in, an event took place that immediately became infamous around the world and eventually blew the lid off of Los Angeles. On the night of March 2, 1991, Rodney King and a couple of friends spent a rather quiet evening drinking and watching television at his home in Altadena, a little community just north of Pasadena. An African American in his late twenties, King had experienced a tough childhood in Southern California, including some run-ins with the law, but in recent years he had found steady work in the construction industry and had settled down. Around midnight, though, he got the notion to take a nighttime drive for no particular reason. How much King and his friends had to drink and whether they had been taking hard drugs remains a matter of dispute. In any event, King and his two friends piled into his little car and hit a nearby freeway, heading north.

King was speeding and a California Highway Patrol car turned on its flashing lights. Instead of stopping, King sped up and tried to outrun the cops. Why? The answer may never be known for certain. Perhaps, being on parole, King feared the implications of a traffic stop; perhaps he was stoned. Whatever the reason, he initiated a high-speed chase that ended when he finally stopped, surrounded by several squad cars, most of them LAPD cars.

The arrest went badly. A Highway Patrol officer pulled a gun on King and was waved off by the LAPD. King was either very scared, giddy, or both and resisted arrest. An LAPD officer knocked him down with a club to the head. The supervising officer tried to subdue King by shooting him with a stun gun. Other officers beat him with clubs or kicked him. Dozens of other officers stood on the perimeter simply watching.

Someone else was watching, too. By chance, a resident who lived in an apartment near the arrest site, George Holliday, was awakened by the commotion and, having purchased a video camera that very day, decided to film the incident. Half awake, he shot video of the arrest and beating, and then went back to sleep. Later, when he reviewed the film, he was shocked by the brutality and decided he should give the tape to law enforcement authorities, the news media, or both.

When the tape hit the airwaves, it sparked outrage across the nation. One aspect of the videotape—one that proved to be deeply destructive to L.A.—went unknown until after the trial of the officers. The producer at KTLA-TV in L.A., the one who had the responsibility of airing the tape for the world to see, edited part of it out. The initial frames show Rodney King still standing, surrounded by officers. King appears to be in the process of charging in the direction of one officer. The officer is holding his club at the ready, much like one would hold a baseball bat when awaiting the pitch. On the original film, this brief image is followed by 10 seconds of blur—the camera being adjusted and moved—in which no action can clearly be seen. When the camera resettles, King is on the ground and the beating commences. One man in one studio made the arbitrary decision to cut everything before the end of the blur, because, he later explained, it made for a cleaner presentation of the story. More than a little defensively, he added that television news does this all the time—cuts to the heart of the matter—as if the tape of the King beating were just another bit of video of a local, short-lived story. All other stations got copies of the film from KTLA, which, apparently without any explanation, simply distributed the already edited version.

No one who saw the video on television, no one at all, actually saw the full film. Most Americans would probably say that the full film is no less incriminating. In terms of audience reaction, it is difficult to imagine that the full version would somehow have lessened the public's outrage against the LAPD, but the full version *was* viewed by the jury in the Simi Valley trial—and only by the jury and the attorneys: Not even the reporters covering the trial on a daily basis were shown the full tape; they did not even know there was more to see.

This all made a huge difference. It gave the officers and their defense lawyers all the evidence they needed to win exoneration from the all-white jury in a very conservative Simi Valley, California. Here, they said, was proof of two key points: (1) The officers were acting in self-defense against a raging, charging Rodney King; and (2) The liberal media had edited the tape to ensure that public reaction would be unfavorable to the LAPD. Had the full tape been shown, even at a later date, with an explanation of why it had been edited in the first place, the first argument would still have been suspect, and the second argument could not have been made. With their Simi Valley jury and their 10 seconds of extra video, the officers walked—all of them—on all counts, not guilty.

The judge, making a disastrous and inexplicable decision, allowed the verdicts to be announced live, just before a Friday afternoon rush hour. It was the end of April 1992, a little more than a year after the actual beating itself, but in many respects the beating had never really ended in the media and the courts, and certainly not in the hearts and minds of African Americans living in South Central Los Angeles. It is probably safe to say that, before the verdicts, most whites in Los Angeles and the nation expected some of the officers to be guilty on some of the counts, even in Simi Valley. And partly because most white people felt that way, most black people were hopeful for conviction.

THE L.A. RIOT

The L.A. Riot of 1992 began almost immediately after the "not guilty" verdicts were announced on April 29. The news spread quickly, and virtually everyone who heard the news knew a race riot would follow. Surely, L.A. authorities were prepared for this possibility. No, they were not. Far from it, Police Chief Gates immediately ordered all LAPD units *out* of the South Central area. Although this move may have saved the lives of some officers, most of them expressed bewilderment at the decision, and

A scene of destruction during the Los Angeles Riots of 1992. (Ted Soqui/CORBIS)

in any case Gates's decision cost the city and many of its residents dearly. For his part, Mayor Tom Bradley appeared to be completely blindsided by the verdicts and the riots that followed. South Central was already burning when an obviously shaken Bradley held a live press conference that showed, among other things, that he was not in control of his city.

For several days, seemingly without stop, the city witnessed violence, looting, and arson on an unprecedented scale. Not until Bradley lifted the nighttime curfew on May 4 was the riot over. The death toll was 54, and large numbers of people had been injured, beaten, or wounded during the melee. Property damage was estimated at almost $1 *trillion.* The Watts Rebellion had seemed big in 1965, but the explosion that rocked L.A. in 1992 dwarfed the Watts Riot and, indeed, all other urban riots in American history.

Whatever moral authority the rioters might have had was destroyed almost immediately at the intersection of Florence and Normandie in South Central L.A., when a group of black men beat a white man, Reginald Denny, nearly to death on live television—and did so with what appeared to be unrestrained glee, waving at the television camera and dancing in celebration over Denny's body. This beating was broadcast live from a helicopter. Not everyone in the city knew the verdicts had come in, and not everyone in their cars was listening to the radio, and as a result many people drove into the riot zone without even knowing what was happening. Denny was one of those unfortunate people, but a Latino man and some Asians around Florence and Normandie were also beaten nearly to death.

It is difficult to overestimate the impact of the Denny beating footage on L.A. and, more generally, on America. The video of the Rodney King beating shocked and galvanized America in one way; the video of the Reginald Denny beating shocked and galvanized America in another. The King incident and the 1992 riots were far more than just two videos, but both had a profound impact. Damian Williams and the others who attacked Denny were later arrested without much difficulty, as the television cameras were rolling, and they later stood trial, which followed the traditional L.A. patterns of media sensationalism. In the process, the so-called "L.A. Four"—the four attackers, not the four rescuers—gained brief notoriety.

For Denny and other innocent people being attacked by mobs in South Central, their only protection and rescue came from other African Americans who lived near the violence. The LAPD having abandoned the scene, and all other peoples of color subject to attack, good Samaritans from the black neighborhoods were their only hope. Four of those good Samaritans saved Denny: Terri Branett, Bobby Green, Titus Murphy, and Lei Yuille. They saw the event on television and raced to the scene. Denny was still alive, and they put him in his own truck. Bobby Green was a licensed big-rig driver and drove the truck to the hospital. Green in particular received public commendation for his actions and urged the people of L.A. to do right by one another.

It was tempting to view the 1992 riots as Watts revisited, but 1992 was not 1965, although it certainly began with black rage aimed at the police and at the larger establishment that kept African Americans down. The difference was not merely that the conflagration of 1992 was bigger and deadlier. There was a qualitative difference to the 1992 riots, which witnessed a diverse array of participants and raised new and different issues than Watts.

More important, the 1992 riot soon slipped out of control of the African American rioters and was transformed into something else. That "something else" is still difficult to pinpoint, but a tidal wave of looting swept over much of the city, and that looting was mainly by the poor Latinos who made up the majority of the population in South Central L.A. This group of Latinos was itself demographically diverse: Mexican immigrants, Mexican Americans, Salvadorians, Nicaraguans, and peoples from dozens of other Caribbean and Latin American countries. They did not appear to be motivated by outrage over the Rodney King verdicts. Instead, they appeared to be motivated by the desire to get a little something for themselves and their families in the midst of this chaos.

In many cases, the Latino looters exhibited a spirit of celebration. They had come to L.A. with dreams, and most of those dreams had not come true, but here was a chance to get a little of what was due. At the bottom of the working class and without the political control of their neighborhoods, which were usually represented by African Americans, people living in the poorer Latino neighborhoods represented a segment of the urban West that was rarely seen in the mainstream media and rarely supported by anyone in political debate. They were not really rioting for bread; they were out taking the kind of consumer goods they could not otherwise afford. They may have represented the city's actual underclass, but in any event their mass, unorganized participation changed the nature of the uprising and turned the riot into a multiracial, multi-issue uprising from below.

With Watts in mind, it is curious that the L.A. Riot of 1992 did not spark other riots in the inner cities of the West—or the North or South for that matter. To be sure, there were small conflicts and harsh words in most big cities, but there was no real duplication of the L.A. Riot. After Watts in 1965, as noted in an earlier chapter, there were copycat riots in cities throughout the region and the ghettos of the North. Not so after the 1992 riot. The Rodney King riots took place at the point of the not guilty verdicts, which was springtime; and that summer, the "long, hot summer" effect of the 1960s did not replicate itself.

Although neither journalists nor historians have explained why this was so, it is worth thinking about, and perhaps worth some speculations here. Swift government action helped, especially at the local and national level. Locally, Chief Gates was fired after the riot, and he was replaced by

an African American. This was no magic bullet, but it certainly demonstrated the city's willingness to put the Parker-Gates eras to rest and to
create an LAPD that actually had a genuine interest in addressing police
problems in the inner city.

For its part, the U.S. State Department acted quickly to charge
the recently acquitted officers with violating Rodney King's basic civil

---

THE RISE OF KAREN BASS

Out of the rubble of the 1992 Riots in L.A., there emerged
an upbeat community activist eager to rebuild her city—Karen
Bass. Bass was an Angeleno, born and raised, who had worked
her way through the public schools and had gone on to attend
Cal State Dominguez Hills, where she earned a bachelor's
degree in health sciences. From there she went to the School of
Medicine at the University of Southern California (USC), where
she was certified as a physician's assistant. While she worked at
USC Medical, she encountered a steady stream of low-income,
disadvantaged patients. She decided to try to improve the
overall health of inner city residents beyond the hospital walls.

After the 1992 riots, Bass organized the Community
Coalition, whose pragmatic goals included an effort to reduce
the number of liquor stores and low-rent hotels (used for
prostitution) in the area—and a simultaneous effort to bring in
more grocery stores and laundromats. These efforts to reform
and rebuild South Los Angeles led her, as it had led so many
others before her, into the arena of electoral politics.

In 1995, Bass was elected to the state legislature from the
47th Assembly District, a diverse section of South and West
L.A. that in many ways paralleled Tom Bradley's old base of
power in the 1970s and 1980s (see the sidebar in chapter 8).
It did not take Bass long to have an impact, and her rise within
the assembly was dramatic. She became the floor leader for the
Democrats in her second term, and in May 2008, she became
the first black woman in California (or anywhere else) elected
to be speaker of the State Assembly.

Source: Casey Nichols, "Karen Bass," online encyclopedia on Blacks in the
American West at Blackpast.org.

rights—and this in a State Department that served under George H. W. Bush's conservative Republican administration. Finally, 1992 was a presidential election year, and at the time of the riots the election was up for grabs. President Bush came to South Central to voice his support, but more important was the arrival of the Democratic candidate, Bill Clinton, who would go on to win the Democratic primary and then beat Bush in the general election. Other Democrat candidates came, too, of course, which meant people in power were constantly in and out of inner-city Los Angeles and were speaking to the larger issues of the nation's inner cities. Finally, other American cities got the message and moved toward reconciliation as a way to prevent riots of their own. Perhaps, then, the rapid and positive government responses to the L.A. Riot made other riots seem unnecessary.

The federal charges against the LAPD officers were a key component in dampening the festering discontent. Once again, the officers went on trial, and once again, LA gave itself to over-the-top media coverage. When the verdicts came in this time, the court wisely delayed the announcement of those verdicts until early on a Saturday morning, when most rowdy folks would be sacked out. The first of several verdicts was "guilty"—after that it was a mixed bag—but the city was spared further violence.

GANGSTA RAP

Out of the West Coast ghettos and conflicts with the police arose a cultural phenomenon that would shape American music: gangsta rap. At the time of this writing, rap music has been mainstream for some years now and has blended into a highly commercialized hip-hop culture, but in the beginning gangsta rap was radically antiestablishment. Those beginnings came in the late 1980s, when the pioneer rapper Ice T brought rap to Southern California. His first album, *Rhyme Pays*, appeared in 1987. Ice T has listed among his influences the bawdy African American comedians of the 1960s and 1970s, specifically the vulgar and sexually explicit stand-up routines of Redd Foxx and Richard Pryor. Whether Ice T knew it or not, Foxx himself had emerged out of L.A., sharpening his stand-up act on Central Avenue and cutting his first record in Watts—and, yes, it was an underground product, sold under the counter or out of automobile trunks. Although both Foxx and Pryor later made it in the mainstream with cleaned up acts, their roots in the business were as crude as crude could be. Ice T and other rappers followed suit with that, even though humor was not usually what they were after.

At this time, hip-hop culture was still largely an underground phenomenon, but it spread quickly in California. Its influence was felt and expanded in Compton, California. In the 1950s, the little town south of Los Angeles had been a prime neighborhood for black middle-class families who could afford to move out of the Central Avenue district. By the mid-1980s, it had become a symbol of black gang violence, poverty, and drug dealing. If the rival gangs were not shooting at one another, the gangs and the police were shooting at one another. Here was where a local rapper originally named Eric Wright (also, originally, a drug dealer), who took the name Easy E, founded his own record label, Ruthless Records—a name that reflected both everyday life in Compton and the violent current of early West Coast rap.

Along with three other young men—who had taken the names Dr. Dre, Ice Cube, and Yella—Easy E formed the hip-hop group "Niggaz With Attitude," or NWA, which soon attained notoriety and a growing following on the Ruthless Record label. The word "Niggaz" in the band's name set it apart—from both the black middle class, who were not from the "hood," and of course from anyone who was not black. That was part of the point. NWA was out to set themselves apart, to draw clear lines, battle lines even, between black residents of the inner-city neighborhoods and those who had not personally experienced what that meant. On a less philosophical level, the point was to be bad.

Rap songs told stories, and those stories reflected the cold realities of inner-city life. Violence, whether it was violence done to black people by the police, by the criminal justice system, or by government programs, kept black people, especially young black men, trapped in the nation's ghettos and jails. If not about that, rap songs were about sex, uncritically promoting the use and abuse of black women, who did not, in the male rappers' lyrics, actually qualify as women. They were merely "bitches"—problems to be dispensed with, sexual objects to be used and discarded. Early jazz lyrics had been filthy, too, before it became more respectable, but filthy or not, the jazzman's lyrics about women and sex usually came with a wink. In rap, by contrast, playfulness was not a part of the game. These days, as rap has itself moved in the direction of respectability, and as more women have themselves succeeded in rap, the misogyny of the early gangstas has faded (a little anyway) and become something of an embarrassment for the industry and its early icons. For many hard-core rap fans, however, outright and unapologetic expressions of disdain for black women remain essential to the genre.

Beyond its misogyny, the emotional roots of gangsta rap were not difficult to trace. Industrial plants near the inner city—the auto, steel, and tire manufacturing plants that had provided stable working-class jobs for a previous generation of African Americans, had begun to shut down in the 1970s. Corporate America had discovered outsourcing. Unemployment spiked, the Reagan and Bush administrations cut federal spending for inner-city social programs, and gangs became linked to the trade in crack cocaine. High school dropout rates for black males in the inner city soared upward, although exactly why that was so—apart from hopelessness—had not really been explained. The criminal justice system was stacked against the poor and the colored, so an unusually large percentage of young black men had spent at least some time in prison. There was little to stop young African Americans in South Central from becoming deeply alienated. Gangsta rap spoke directly to their condition and gave voice to that alienation. NWA became the personification of that alienation and rage.

Other West Coast stars soon emerged, along with a new rap label: Death Row Records, which soon became the center of the gangsta sound. Dr. Dre, formerly of NWA fame, helped to found the label in 1991; the chief executive officer was Suge Knight, who became a major talent developer. Dre's first solo album, *Chronic*, was an underground smash when it came out in 1992. The following year, a rising star out of Long Beach, Snoop Doggy Dog, released *Doggystyle*, also on the Death Row label. Another rising star, Tupac "2Pac" Shakur of Oakland, was literally bailed out of jail by Suge Knight in return for signing on with Death Row Records. On a trip to New York, however, Shakur was shot and robbed in the lobby of a rap recording studio. He survived, claimed the shooting was set up by East Coast rivals, and charged the well-known rap artists Notorious B.I.G. and Sean "Puff Daddy" Combs with having arranged the shooting. They denied it and exchanged bitter condemnations with the West Coast crowd by way of rap lyrics. The tension came to a head at the Soul Train Awards ceremony, held in L.A. in the spring of 1996, where the East Coast rappers and the West Coast rappers pulled guns in the parking lot. That fall, Tupac Shakur was shot and killed in Las Vegas, killer unknown. A few months later, Notorious B.I.G. was shot and killed in L.A., killer unknown.

These incidents and others forced rap stars and rap producers on both coasts to stop the rivalries and violence that were killing the industry. Those who survived the early days of gangsta rap have, in some cases, become mainstream stars in music, on film and television, and in the fashion industry. Ice Cube of NWA put in a stellar performance in John Singleton's breakthrough film, *Boys in the Hood*, and his star has been rising ever since. The music of Snoop Dog (he dropped the "Doggy") continued to do well, and he has diversified his entertainment ventures. Tupac Shakur became legendary in death and remains one of the best-selling rap artists, although in death, even as in life, legal disputes continue to entangle his portion (now his family's) of the profits.

Like rock and roll in the late 1950s and early 1960s, rap music took over the music industry very quickly. And, like rock, it has continued to expand and take on mainstream-friendly forms even as it has retained its rebel status. Unlike early rock, however, which was taken over by white

Los Angeles native Dr. Dre, a pioneering performer and producer of West Coast hip-hop and gangsta rap. (Neal Preston/CORBIS)

producers and white rock stars, in rap and hip-hop generally blacks themselves have maintained control of their creative sounds and the profits of production. There is now a deeply entrenched and highly successful black recording industry based in L.A., New York, and Atlanta—and more broadly a black-owned entertainment industry.

WILLIE BROWN: POLITICAL STAR

Willie Brown left Texas for San Francisco as a young man in 1951. He attended San Francisco State with an eye toward admission to Stanford, but he soon entered the arena of politics and never left. He caught the eye of Phillip Burton, one of the most powerful and savvy white liberal crusaders in California and, indeed, the nation. Burton would serve for years in the statehouse and then move on to Washington, D.C., where he took his "rage for justice" to a higher level. In the process, Burton taught Brown about the ways of white liberals and California politics, and he urged Brown to run for the California State Assembly in San Francisco's 18th Assembly District, which included the mostly black Fillmore District but also covered many neighborhoods that were mostly white. Brown did not need much prompting. He nearly won the seat in an upset bid in 1962, and then he won the seat easily in 1964. One key to his victory was his voter-registration drive in the Fillmore neighborhoods, which dramatically increased the district's African American vote. Another key to victory was his ability to appeal to the district's white voters. According to a recent biography of Brown, he won nearly all of the black vote but also 70 percent of the white vote in the 18th District (Richardson, *Willie Brown*, 100).

By the time Brown joined the California State Assembly, it was controlled by California's most powerful white liberal (yet another Texan), Jesse Unruh of Los Angeles. Unruh was speaker of the house and ran a tight ship; he could make or break Democrats in Sacramento, and it was partly his doing that had prevented Gus Hawkins from being named speaker of the house. (The other reasons included Hawkins's vote against socialized medicine, which alienated Unruh and other liberals, and President John Kennedy's urging Hawkins to run for the U.S. Congress in a newly created seat that included most of South Central Los Angeles. Hawkins ran for Congress in 1962 and won the election, serving in Washington, D.C., until his retirement several decades later.) Initially, Unruh

Willie Brown, legendary California politician and current mayor of San Francisco. (CNP/ Archive Photos)

scoffed at the young, bespectacled Willie Brown and tried to throw a wet towel on the young upstart. That conflict was short lived, however, for Brown impressed Unruh, who saw in the newcomer the same fiery ambition, the same commitment to liberalism, and the same kind of pragmatic political savvy that had propelled Unruh's own career. With the trust, support, and mentorship of Phillip Burton and Jesse Unruh, and being quick on the uptake himself, Willie Brown rose quickly in state politics.

In Sacramento, Brown produced controversy and positive results from the beginning. He and Burton openly opposed the Vietnam War, earning charges of treason from conservatives but winning widespread support among his San Francisco constituents and the California antiwar movement. He helped pass important new legislation that prohibited racial discrimination (and age discrimination) by insurance companies. He helped to create the Black American Political Association of California, which became a kind of civil rights coordination agency in the state. After the Republican Party gained a slight majority in the state legislature in 1969, Brown was instrumental in winning the assembly back for the Democratic Party. With Unruh, Brown helped to lead Bobby Kennedy's presidential campaign in California.

On the night Kennedy won the California primary, virtually making him the Democratic candidate, Unruh was with him at the victory celebration and was nearby when Kennedy was suddenly shot point blank several times by an Arab American assassin who claimed he did it for Palestine. In many respects, Unruh never really recovered from Kennedy's assassination; he lost heart, even though he remained speaker of the house. He also made Brown his second in command, effectively tapping him as his successor. For his part, Brown's influence increased as he became chair of the assembly's powerful Ways and Means Committee and as he continued to fight California's Republicans on the Vietnam War, on the legality of campus demonstrations, and on the Republican's efforts to gut the budget for the state's university system. Brown promoted affirmative action programs in hiring, gave a rousing speech at the 1972 Democratic National Convention, and was well-positioned to be chosen as speaker of the house in 1974, with Unruh no longer in charge.

When a rival faction of Democrats blocked Brown's election as house speaker in 1974, and then snubbed him in subsequent leadership appointments, it appeared that Brown's political career was just about over, but it was not. Brown bided his time and began to work behind the scenes with California Republicans, effectively cutting a deal. The Republicans would help to put Brown in the speaker's chair, and in return Brown would give Republican leaders many of the plum committee assignments. In 1980, the deal was done. Brown became speaker (the first African American speaker), and rival Democrats watched in rage as the new "Democratic" speaker gave the Republicans their due. Brown's demise was not forthcoming, as many angry Democrats predicted. Instead, he stayed in command of the assembly for 15 years, a state record. He spent much of his political capital in the 1980s seeking to end all California investments in South Africa, which was clinging to its system of apartheid. He also moved into the environmental movement. In the 1994 elections, Republican conservatives took over the U.S. Congress and the California legislature. Brown fought them for a short while, delaying their takeover temporarily, and then he stepped down from the speakership.

For Brown, however, stepping down in Sacramento did not mean stepping out of politics. Far from it. He soon announced his candidacy for mayor of San Francisco, and he won in a landslide in 1995. At about the same time Tom Bradley finished his 20 years as L.A.'s mayor, Willie Brown began a long season as head of the City by the Bay. Stylish as always, still in good health, and still occasionally outlandish in his rhetoric and political deals, Brown continues the good fight for civil rights and inner-city improvements. Forty years after first being elected, Brown is still going strong.

SPORTS AS THE GREAT EQUALIZER?

In 1981, the same year Reagan took office and initiated his cuts in welfare spending, the L.A. Lakers signed rookie Earvin "Magic" Johnson to a 25-year contract worth $25 million—a record contract at that time, and one that sparked a wild enthusiasm in L.A. Johnson proved to be a huge hit, on and off the court, and gave rise to the fast-break "Show Time" style of Lakers basketball. The Lakers won the NBA championship that year, with Magic starring at both guard and center and being named the most valuable player of the playoffs. There were four more

NBA championships, all in the 1980s. All of this occurred at the same time the inner city of L.A. was in decline.

Magic Johnson himself would become an important player in addressing the economic decline of South Central L.A. In 1991, Johnson tested positive for HIV and announced his immediate retirement in a press conference that stunned the nation. At the time, HIV usually led to the onset of AIDS, which virtually always resulted in death. Johnson would beat the odds, and his HIV has not yet resulted in AIDS. He would actually play a bit more for the Lakers and for the U.S. Olympic Team, but his basketball career was effectively finished. Magic's autobiography, published soon after his retirement, confessed that he had had sex with so many women that he had no way of knowing when or from whom he had contracted HIV. In recounting his sexual escapades, Johnson provided rather more information than some readers cared to know, and he came under criticism for it. But he weathered the storm, remained very popular, and began a new career as an economic developer for inner-city neighborhoods—including those in L.A. He has also been active in HIV/AIDS awareness and prevention at the national and international levels. He continues to live in Southern California and is an active supporter of the Democratic Party in California.

In contrast to Magic Johnson's ongoing popularity was the public antipathy toward baseball star Barry Bonds, who became, in the words of a recent biographer, an "anti-hero." Bonds was the product of Southern California, raised in Riverside, the son of Bobby Bonds, a former baseball great for the San Francisco Giants. Immensely talented and outspokenly arrogant, Barry went on to star for the University of Arizona before moving on to a career in Major League Baseball. He played for Pittsburgh, developing a love-hate relationship with both the city and his teammates. In 1993, he came back west, to his father's former team in San Francisco. He brought immediate life to the slumping team and won the affection of local fans with his spectacular talent for hitting home runs. He also verbally abused his teammates and became the kind of player opposing fans love to hate. He finally led the Giants to the World Series in 2002. At turns lovable and hatable, Bonds remains an enigmatic figure.

Bonds now holds the coveted record for career home runs, but the latter years of his career, during which he chased the long-standing home run mark set by Hank Aaron, were dogged by allegations of steroid doping. The allegations involved Bonds's involvement with BALCO (Bay Area Laboratory Cooperative), a sports-training facility for high-level athletes. Bonds was one of those athletes, and when BALCO was hauled to court on charges of steroid distribution, Bonds was called to testify to a federal grand jury. Bonds publicly denied taking steroids. Later, his testimony was illegally leaked to the press (the leak came from a BALCO attorney, who was later convicted for his crime, a felony) and seemed to indicate that Bonds had been taking performance-enhancing drugs. This gave opposing fans even more reason to hurl verbal abuse at Bonds, and more reasons for him to be hounded by the media.

Did fans and the media heap abuse on Bonds because he was an openly rude and arrogant man, or because he was a rude and arrogant *black* man? It is tempting to take the former view because so much progress has been made in the mainstream acceptance of full black participation in American life. In an earlier era, Willie Mays was greeted lovingly by fans in San Francisco as soon as he arrived, but he was prevented from buying the home he wanted, which was located in a white neighborhood. Barry Bonds, hated in L.A., lives in a very high-priced gated community in Beverly Hills. Plus, American fans have shown that they can turn on white sports stars at the drop of a hat. That said, and taking the long historical view, it would be foolish to underestimate the power of race in shaping the public reputation of Barry Bonds.

A more edifying success story came in a sport with a long history of racial exclusiveness—tennis—and it came in the form of the Williams sisters, Venus and Serena, who grew up in Compton. They learned the game from their father, Richard, on public courts near the mean streets. They were also coached some by their mother, Oracene, who continues to coach them to this day. Theirs was a stable, disciplined home, dedicated to the faith of the Jehovah's Witnesses. The parents kept a close hold on the sisters' development, avoiding the usual Junior Circuit because Richard disliked what he considered to be the obsessive intensity and thinly veiled (sometimes unveiled) racist sentiments of the other tennis parents. Eventually, though, Venus and Serena were invited to the famous Florida training camp for tennis prodigies, Rick Macci's Tennis Academy. Their parents consented, and they all moved together to Palm Beach Gardens.

Icons of professional tennis and fashion, Venus Williams (left) and younger sister Serena grew up playing on the public courts in Compton, California. (Shutterstock)

In the beginning, Venus was practically the whole story, with the outspoken Richard coming in close second. Serena was not really on the media radar until the late 1990s. Technically, both sisters turned professional in turn when they reached the age of 14, but they seldom played in tournaments until they were older. When they finally came on the scene in full during the late 1990s, interest in women's tennis soared, and of course the media placed the race issue front and center, not without reason: for one thing, Richard's critical comments about traditional tennis culture kept putting it there. He also became a lightning rod for critics because he openly boasted that his daughters would beat everyone. When they began to do so, Richard began to quiet down a bit, and the sisters themselves became the focus of the media. They proved from the beginning to be well-spoken, well-rounded people, with plenty of interest beyond tennis, most especially in fashion. The sisters remained best friends and almost inseparable.

Soon both of them were at or near the top, and sometimes they played one another in the final match of a tournament. Venus beat Serena easily for a year or two, then Serena blasted her way to the top spot. Serena won the U.S. Open in 1999, the first African American to do so since Althea Gibson (of Harlem) won it in 1958. Venus would later win Wimbledon several times over. Serena became the world's number one player in 2002.

In 1998, Richard Williams referred to his daughters proudly as his "Ghetto Cinderellas," and so they were, but the ghetto unexpectedly took its toll on the family in 2003, when Venus and Serena's oldest sister, Yetunde, was shot and killed in Compton. Yetunde's young children then moved in with the rest of the family, and the Williams sisters entered a long grieving process. For a family that closely knit, and one whose ghetto origins were a point of pride, this loss ran deep and set Serena in particular into a fight against depression. For her part, Venus let tennis slide while she focused on fashion school, where she recently earned her degree. Both Venus and Serena have their own line of clothes, ranging from red-carpet gowns to athletic wear. Both have worked as models and have worked in television. And tennis remains. In May 2007, Serena came back from tennis obscurity and won the Australian Open. And since Venus committed herself to fashion, she has won Wimbledon twice more.

The other great breakthrough in sports came in golf, with the rise of Tiger Woods. Tiger was a legendary amateur golfer and made an even greater impact when he turned pro. He quickly won two tournaments and drew large galleries, who followed his every shot. He hit the ball a mile off of the tee box, made seemingly impossible shots look easy, and made putts from everywhere. He also possessed the kind of energetic charisma that was made for live television. Then came the Masters tournament in April 1997. The most famous tournament in America, the Masters is staged at and by Augusta National golf club in Augusta, Georgia. The Masters had a deep reputation for its social and racial conservatism. Augusta National and its powerful all-male membership had fully subscribed to (and, as people of power, helped to uphold) Jim Crow segregation in the South. Tiger Woods was not the first black man to play in the Masters—that "first" fell to Lee Elder in the wake of the civil rights movement—but Tiger was the first African American to win the Masters, and he won it famously, beating the field by a record 12 strokes—and doing so before a cheering, mostly white crowd and a mesmerized television audience. The rest of the Tiger Woods story is so widely known that it needs little telling. Suffice it to say that Woods has dominated professional golf ever since and has justifiably gained a huge global following (see the sidebar on page 296).

And yet neither tennis nor golf have experienced a further surge of African Americans into the top ranks, at least not yet. The Williams sisters remain at or near the top of the game, but other African Americans, male or female, are even now seldom seen on the WTA (Women's Tennis Association) tour. Tiger changed the face of golf, to be sure; the galleries at tournaments became more ethnically diverse and golf's popularity among the black middle-class and professional class shot upward. So far, however, Woods is *still* the only African American to have made the PGA tour. And currently, there are no African American women on the LPGA (Ladies Profession Golf Association) tour. It may well be that the Williams sisters and Tiger Woods have already opened doors at the youth level and that the two traditionally white sports will become more naturally mixed in the years ahead. Woods himself is aiming for that, sponsoring programs to promote golf in the inner cities through the Tiger Woods Foundation, which focuses its energies on innovation in education.

TIGER WOODS

Born in 1975 and raised in Southern California, Eldrick "Tiger" Woods would become one of the greatest golfers of all time and, in terms of global recognition, easily the most famous. Tiger is the son of Earl Woods, an African American, and Kultida Woods (nee Punsawad), a native of Thailand. The nickname "Tiger" came from his father, who, during his tour of duty in Vietnam, admired a South Vietnamese soldier with that name. Earl claimed some Chinese and American Indian heritage, and Kultida's ancestry included Chinese and Dutch. Tiger embraces both his identity as an African American and his multiracial heritage.

Tiger's earliest golf was the stuff of legend. At age two, he appeared on *The Mike Douglas Show*, a popular television program. He won three straight U.S. Junior National Championships. Then he won three consecutive U.S. Amateurs, all televised, all dramatic. He left Stanford University after two years to turn professional and, before hitting a ball as a professional, signed a $20 million deal with Nike that was seen as an outrageous gamble by the corporation at the time (but as a great investment since). Earl was the quiet, ubiquitous presence at all of Tiger's matches and, after every championship, would wrap his son in a bear hug and sob unapologetically. Earl promised greatness from Tiger, on and off the course, and Tiger has delivered.

Woods won as a professional almost immediately and then, in spring 1997, rocked the golfing world with a dominating victory at that most conservative and important of tournaments, the Masters. This was the first of 14 major tournament victories, and at one point he held all four major titles at once—dubbed "The Tiger Slam." In total majors, he trails only Jack Nicklaus, whose record 18 majors Tiger continues to chase. Off the course, he dealt gracefully with an unprecedented media crush, kept his private life mostly private (he is married and has a daughter, Sam), and handled the grief of his father's death with unerring dignity. More than a decade after winning the Masters in 1997, he is, for many people throughout the world, the model global citizen.

SUBURBANIZATION

Tiger Woods grew up in Orange County, California, which may be thought of as one big suburb. He was not the only African American growing up in the suburbs of the West. After the 1960s, black movement out of the cities and into the suburbs began. The trend began slowly during the 1970s, picked up steam in the 1980s, and became noticeable to the general public in the 1990s. It is a trend that continues today, as more and more African Americans can afford to live in the suburbs and as fewer whites in the suburbs have problems with the arrival of black neighbors. As governor of California in 1967, Ronald Reagan championed white homeowner resistance to blacks as a "basic human right" (Wiese, *Places*, 212, citing a quote from the *New York Times*). With that kind of rhetoric coming from the governor, laws prohibiting housing restrictions against African Americans were not particularly effective.

Slowly, conditions began to change in the 1970s as blacks began to move into suburban neighborhoods that were predominantly white—without witnessing a panicked white flight from those neighborhoods. In Denver and Phoenix, for example, a majority of African Americans who moved into the suburbs were moving into housing districts that were at least 90 percent white. In metropolitan Los Angeles, black suburbanization outpaced that in any other metropolitan region. Less dramatically, black suburbanites became more common in the Bay Area as well. The rising incomes and expectations of affluent blacks, combined with the deterioration of the inner cities, were the basic causes of this suburban movement.

The suburbanization of African Americans in the West was not widely seen or understood, in part because the suburbs blacks were moving to were not really in the public consciousness—as the cities of the Great Migration had been. The suburbs blacks were moving to in Southern California included West Covina, Chino, Tustin, Fountain Valley, Mission Viejo, Vista, Carlsbad, and Spring Valley—places most people in major cities had never heard of, much less could locate on a map. So the process took place mainly out of sight from the mainstream media, which was, not without reason, focused on the problems of the inner cities. With so much attention focused on South Central Los Angeles, it often went unnoticed that the African American population in that part of the city was declining rapidly, even as large numbers of Latinos and Asians were moving into those neighborhoods.

Clearly, this suburban shift was progress for African Americans in the West, who had worked so hard for so long to be able simply to buy a home in a neighborhood of their choice, without white people blocking their path. Schools were better in the suburbs, and many of these outlying communities were experiencing rapid growth, which fostered prosperity for African Americans who moved there. Looking at this trend from the other direction, the addition of African Americans to these areas helped to diversify communities that were badly in need of diversity. Some closed minds began to open. Even so, both the parents and children of black suburbanites often felt ambivalent about their move.

For these upwardly and geographically mobile African Americans, the amenities of suburban life came at a cost—a growing sense of isolation. Suburban police, not accustomed to black residents, tended to stop the newcomers, inquiring what they were doing in that area. And some police did worse than that. Perhaps the bigger problem involved a sense of being disconnected from the traditional networks of black acculturation and fellowship. In the beginning, there were not many black churches in the suburbs or many social clubs or neighbors who could really identify with black America. Young African Americans attended the good schools their parents had wanted for them, and they tended to do well in those schools, but many young people felt somehow cut off from their own heritage, felt that somehow they were missing out on an important aspect of their lives. Some black parents felt that way, too, especially when they heard their own children express negative views of the inner city, or when their own children seemed not to appreciate the sacrifices that earlier generations of black activists had made in order for them to be in this kind of home, in this kind of environment. Black suburbanites seldom found that they were shunned; they made friends and generally found common interests with their nonblack neighbors, but skin color and history, as influences in everyday life, never went away.

The dream of the West, it seemed, kept moving just beyond reach. And more than that, the American Dream seemed to be moving out of the West.

LEAVING THE WEST

By the 1990s, the national influence of the black West had begun to wane. The region was no longer the epicenter of African American politics and culture. That era was coming to an end, and for several reasons. To begin with, the long period of black migration *out* of the South and into the North and West was over. Between 1980 and 1990, more African Americans actually moved *to the South* than left it. The South had changed; the civil rights revolution had changed it for the better. The urban North and West had lost their novelty and their major comparative advantage: they were no longer freer places to live than the South. The children and grandchildren of the Great Migrations began to return home—to family, to roots, and to a region that, in many respects, was new and exciting.

The larger cities in particular were magnets for African Americans: Atlanta, Charlotte, Nashville, and Jacksonville. By the end of the century, blacks from the West and North would be moving into these southern cities by the hundreds of thousands, and the cities were rolling out the welcome mats, because these newcomers were not the desperate poor looking for industrial jobs or low-wage employment. These migrants were mostly members of the much-expanded black middle-class or the black professional class—including, especially in Atlanta, professional athletes, who might play for teams in another part of the country but made their home in "the ATL." This generation of blacks moving into the South brought with them money, entrepreneurship, technical skills, and enthusiasm for this newest "New South"—one finally worthy of the name.

Another reason for the decline in western influence—and there is no escaping the point—was that the West Coast produced too many negative influences, too much violence, to remain a place of American dreams. Looking to the West for inspiration, Americans adopted too many trends that were destructive and divisive. Other cities, other regions found they had better things to offer. The Rodney King riot of 1992 offered the people of the United States a crisis around which they could forge new ways of life, new political outlooks, and new understandings of the national experience. Americans had done just that back in 1965, when they responded so powerfully to the Watts Rebellion—emulating it, condemning it, and struggling to come to grips with it. In 1992, many observers

RETURNING TO THE SOUTH

From roughly 1890 to 1970, millions of black southerners left Dixie to seek better lives in the North and the West. First there was the Talented Tenth Migration (ca. 1890–1915), in which middle-class blacks left the South while they still had something to lose. Then there was the Great Migration of World War I, which continued through the 1920s. Both of these bursts of migration sent more Afro-southerners to the urban North than to the West. Finally, there came the Second Great Migration, which brought millions of African Americans into the West in the generation after 1940.

During the 1970s, given the civil rights victories in the South and the urban riots in the North and West, black outmigration from Dixie slowed. More accurately, *net* population loss declined. Blacks were still leaving the South in large numbers, but now blacks from the North and West were also beginning to move *to the South*. The trend intensified in the 1980s, and by 1990, it was clear that the great southern exodus had ended.

The African Americans who left the West and the North for the South were, as they often said, "returning" to their true home—to their family roots—even if they had never been to the South themselves. These return migrants were the descendants of those who had, quite literally, made the Great Migrations of old. The big cities of the South were the main beneficiaries of the Return Migration, and the African Americans who were moving there were largely middle class and professional class. They had a choice. The South had changed, and so had the West. New frontiers awaited (Gregory, *The Southern Diaspora*).

believed the Rodney King conflagration would be repeated in other cities across the nation, but while there were some violent flash points, nothing like the L.A. Riot occurred elsewhere. The rest of the nation's cities did not follow L.A.'s lead. Perhaps African Americans back East had stopped taking political cues from the urban West.

A final reason was simply the passing of time. The power of different regions to shape the national experience has varied over time from one region to another. In African American life, the influence of the West was strong between 1965 and 1990, and rather tightly focused on California's metropolitan areas. But things change. The cultural and political power of any region or big city waxes and wanes, and the black West had its time of influence. But when Shaq arrived in L.A. in the mid-1990s, was it in any way a "western" event? Or were the nation's cities more or less interchangeable now? Indeed, were the regions themselves basically the same? Nationalization and globalization were having their say; regional lines were beginning to blur.

BIBLIOGRAPHIC ESSAY

The opening vignette on Shaquille O'Neal was compiled from several newspaper articles, all of which are available on the Internet; many libraries carry online newspaper subscriptions. Steve Chase's views are from an article published in Minneapolis (a good indication of what a big story this was nationally): Rachel Blount, "Shaq Quake," *(Minneapolis, MN) Star Tribune*, September 29, 1996. On the reaction in local newspapers, see Steve Springer, "Shaq-zamm! He's a $120-Million Laker," *Los Angeles Times,* July 19, 1996; Chris Kraul, "Nothin' But Net," *Los Angeles Times*, July 20, 1996: D1; Howard Rosenberg, "Coming to You Live and in Color: Shaqvision," *Los Angeles Times,* July 24, 1996; and Chris Baker, "Lean and Mean O'Neal Begins a New Chapter," *Los Angeles Times*, August 24, 1996.

The inner-city crisis in the West has been studied from various angles. A powerful case study is Robert O. Self's *American Babylon: Race and the Struggle for Postwar Oakland* (Princeton, NJ: Princeton University Press, 2003). See also Gretchen Lemke-Santangelo, "Deindustrialization, Urban Poverty, and African American Community Mobilization in Oakland, 1945 through the 1990s" in Lawrence B. de Graaf, et al., *Seeking El Dorado: African Americans in California* (Seattle: University of Washington Press, 2001), 343–376. The essays by journalist Lynell George—collected in *No Crystal Stair: American-Americans in the City of Angels* (New York: Verso, 1993)—bear careful attention. On street gangs, a journalistic account is Leon Bing, *Do or Die* (New York: HarperCollins, 1991). An example of the gangster memoir is Kody Scott, *Monster: The Autobiography of an L.A. Gang Member* (New York: Atlantic Monthly Press, 1993).

On the Rodney King events, starting points include Lou Cannon, *Official Negligence: How Rodney King and the Riots Changed Los Angeles and the LAPD* (New York: Random House, 1997), and Gerald Horne, "Black Fire: 'Riot' and 'Revolt' in Los Angeles," in de Graaf, et al., *Seeking El Dorado*, 377–404.

Rap music and hip-hop culture is scarcely old enough to be "history" yet, so a fully realized history of the West Coast gangsta rap movement of the late 1980s and 1990s will require more scholarly distance, but the essential starting point for gangsta rap and many other aspects of black urban culture is Robin D.G. Kelley's work, especially *Race Rebels: Culture, Politics, and the Black Working Class* (New York: The Free Press, 1994); and *Yo' Mama's DisFUNKtional! Fighting the Culture Wars in Urban America* (Boston: Beacon Press, 1997). A breezier treatment is in Larry Starr and Christopher Waterman, *American Popular Music from Minstrelsy to MP3*, 2nd Edition (New York: Oxford University Press, 2007), chapters 12 and 14.

Willie Brown's career is ably covered in James Richardson, *Willie Brown: A Biography* (Berkeley: University of California Press, 1996), which should be read alongside John Jacobs, *A Rage for Justice: The Passion and Politics of Phillip Burton* (Berkeley: University of California Press, 1995), which opens a window on the passion of California liberals in the 1960s and offers a revealing look at California's freewheeling old-boy political system of that era.

On sports and the larger question of racial equality, see Matthew C. Whitaker, *African American Icons of Sport: Triumph, Excellence, and Courage* (Westport, CT: Greenwood Press, 2008); and Arthur Ashe Jr., *Long Road to Glory: A History of the African American Athlete since 1946* (New York: Amistad Press, 1993). Few of the sports figures mentioned in this chapter have received serious scholarly analysis, for the simple fact that not enough time has passed and most of their careers are still in motion. Magic Johnson's autobiography is *Magic Johnson: My Life*, published by Random House in 1992. There is a pile of books on Magic, beginning with a "biography" of him published during his rookie year with the Lakers and extending into life after HIV. Shortly after his HIV announcement, Johnson published *Unsafe Sex in the Age of AIDS*, which has since been updated and republished as *What You Can Do to Avoid AIDS*. Serena Williams's depression after Yetunde's death is briefly mentioned in Sean Gregory, "Slam, Glam, Serena," *Time*, May 28, 2007, 52. Books about the sisters are beginning to be published; see Jacqueline Edmondson, *Venus and Serena Williams: A Biography* (Westport, CT: Greenwood Press, 2005); and the sisters' own co-authored book of life lessons: *Serving from the Hip: 10 Rules for Living, Loving, and Winning* (New York: Houghton Mifflin, 2005). On Tiger, a solid work is Lawrence J. Londino, *Tiger Woods: A Biography* (Westport, CT: Greenwood Press, 2005).

On black suburbanization, see Lawrence B. de Graaf, "African American Suburbanization in California, 1960 through 1990," in de Graaf, et al., *Seeking El Dorado*; and Andrew Wiese, *Places of Their Own: African American Suburbanization in the Twentieth Century* (Chicago: University of Chicago Press, 2004), 405–449. On blacks returning to the South, see James N. Gregory, *The Southern Diaspora: How the Great Migrations of Black and White Southerners Transformed America* (Chapel Hill: University of North Carolina Press, 2005), chapter 9.

Chapter Ten

HISTORIOGRAPHY
AND CURRENT ISSUES

In 1988, the Gene Autry Western Heritage Museum opened in Los Angeles (it now goes by the name Autry Museum of Western Heritage). In the 1930s and 1940s, Gene Autry had been one of Hollywood's first and most popular "singing cowboys." A Texan, Autry's films portrayed a simple, mythic West—where the good guys were good and wore white hats, and the bad guys were bad and wore black hats. Although Hollywood made a few black singing cowboy films for black audiences, the old black-and-white westerns of Autry's day were, well, pretty darn white, and Autry remained nostalgically linked with the traditional Hollywood westerns. Whatever Autry's own views about race, the films he starred in featured a virtually all-white heritage in the West, and the Autry Museum's original exhibits reflected that traditional view of things.

So it was important that, in 1990, only two years after the Autry Museum opened its doors, it offered the public a Black History Month program. The program featured one of the pioneering historians of African Americans in the West—Loren Katz—who gave two lectures: one titled "The Black Cowboys" and the other "Black Indians." Both lectures packed in the patrons, and the Autry Museum continued to expand its coverage of colored peoples in the West. At the beginning of the 21st century, the Autry Museum sponsored the publication of a landmark book of historical essays in black western history—Lawrence B. de Graaf, Kevin Mulroy, and Quintard Taylor, eds., *Seeking El Dorado: African Americans in California* (Los Angeles: Autry Museum of Western Heritage, in association with the University of Washington Press, 2001).

In the preface of *Seeking El Dorado*, the director of the Autry Museum's research center, Kevin Mulroy, took stock of the Autry's innovative and popular programs on black western history, and he predicted continued innovation into the new century. "The Autry Museum," he wrote, "is seeking its own El Dorado: an inclusive view of the West in which the importance of African American history is recognized, understood, and collected" (xiii). And again to emphasize the point, this is from the Gene Autry Museum. For historians of African Americans in the West, this was a very good sign indeed.

Perhaps the most important thing about the Autry's interest in and promotion of black western history, however, was that it was not unique. During the 1990s, there was something of an explosion in the production of African American history in the West. The point to be emphasized here is that this trend was in no way limited to academic scholars. The public seemed almost hungry for the topic, and not just the African American public. Throughout the American West, black history was being collected and presented in museums and libraries—large and small, old and new.

Part of this process was simply recovering stories that had been left out of the traditional western history books. This is a vital contribution to scholarly and public knowledge, but once enough verifiable information is available, scholars inevitably begin to disagree about it—about what that information means, what it all adds up to. The interested public is no less likely to disagree. Mulroy saw this very thing at the Autry's lectures, especially among African Americans who themselves had come to California. Did California really offer a better life for African Americans, or was this El Dorado just fool's gold after all? There was disagreement in the audience, and that was as it should have been, for the meaning of the past is too important to accept uncritically.

Professional historians seldom accept anything about the past without critical scrutiny. This chapter surveys what has been written about black western history in recent decades and points out some of the arguments over interpretation that have emerged among historians. The chapter's final section sketches some current issues facing African Americans in the West and suggests some ways to think about these issues in light of historical trends.

THE HISTORIOGRAPHY OF THE BLACK WEST

Written history has its own history. What historians choose to write about and how they write about it changes over time. For example, a history of the West written in 1876, the nation's centennial, would be quite different from one written for the nation's bicentennial in 1976. Even when historians are writing books at about the same time, they may present different interpretations of the same people or events. Different schools of thought find their way into print. Studying the differences in written history and how it has developed through time is called the study of "historiography." By briefly surveying the historiography of the black West here, this chapter seeks to provide readers with a better sense of where this book fits in the broader study of western history.

The first historians of the black West were the black pioneers themselves. These authors were, more often than not, pioneers of the urban West, not the rural west. In the early 20th century, Delilah Beasley published *The Negro Trail Blazers of California* (Los Angeles: California Eagle Publishing Company, 1919), which is a sprawling compilation highlighting African American accomplishments in, and contributions to, California. Beasley, a journalist from the Bay Area, wanted to show Californians that African Americans had been part of the story. Her task was to overcome the tendency of white journalists and historians to ignore or marginalize the black presence. Other individuals offered memoirs or biographies to achieve the same goal. A few writers spun yarns of their western adventures to sell to the reading public, adding a touch of color to the conventional stories of the Wild West.

Among professional historians, however, studies of the black West were very rare until recently. Historians of the West were preoccupied with Frederick Jackson Turner, attacking or defending his famous thesis. African Americans seldom figured into their debates. At the same time, historians of the African American experience basically ignored the West. With some justification, they directed their research toward the slave South and the ghetto North, so black history and western history were moving along separate tracks that never intersected.

That began to change in the 1970s. By the late 1960s, the civil rights movement in the South and the "long hot summers" of race riots in the

North had sparked unprecedented interest in the historical experiences of black Americans. In that context, the historian William Loren Katz began researching the black experience in the West. In the process, he spoke briefly with Langston Hughes, himself a westerner by upbringing, who gave a fervent piece of advice: "Don't forget the cowboys!" Katz did not forget, and indeed the primary thesis of his book, *The Black West,* 3rd ed., rev. and expanded (Seattle: Open Hand Publishing, 1987), was to remind Americans, with example after example, that blacks were also part of America's frontier experience. In effect, Katz was offering his own fervent piece of advice: Don't forget the blacks.

More influential in the long run was work by the historian Lawrence B. de Graaf. In 1970 he published a pioneering and influential article in black western historiography, "The City of Black Angels: Emergence of the Los Angeles Ghetto, 1890–1930" *Pacific Historical Review* 39 (August 1970): 323–352. De Graaf situated his work squarely in the new and growing field of American urban history—no tip of the hat to Turner was even necessary— and he raised the question of ghettoization in the West. De Graaf argued that Los Angeles was unusually open to black opportunity during the late 19th and early 20th centuries, but only temporarily. Opportunities for black Angelenos became more constricted over time, he emphasized. Using census data and focusing on housing patterns, de Graaf argued that the 1910s and 1920s brought increased racial concentration—primarily because of white-led real estate restrictions on blacks—which put in place the essential ingredients of ghettoization. His article thus pointed toward western distinctiveness during the formative period of the urban west (ca. 1890–1910) and a convergence with national norms as the city matured (1910–1930).

In keeping with de Graaf's emphasis on the black urban West, Henry Douglas Daniels published *Pioneer Urbanites: A Cultural and Social History of Black San Francisco* (Philadelphia: Temple University Press, 1980), which offered the first book-length study of African Americans in a western city. His work on black San Francisco was one of the earliest community studies to focus on the black middle class and, as its title suggested, was partly an effort to flip Turner on his head, suggesting that African Americans played a vital role in pioneering modern urban life. That same year, Emory Tolbert's *The U.N.I.A. in Los Angeles: Ideology and Community in the American Garvey Movement* (Los Angeles: UCLA Center for

Afro-American Studies, 1980) gave a western twist to Marcus Garvey's famous Universal Negro Improvement Association, which had long been viewed from its headquarters in New York. Like de Graaf's "Black Angels," Tolbert's study gave evidence of both western distinctiveness and nationwide parallels. Thomas Cox's *Blacks in Topeka, Kansas, 1865–1915: A Social History* (Baton Rouge: Louisiana State University Press, 1982) brought a needed urban perspective on the African American experience in Kansas. Historians such as William Lang and Quintard Taylor examined African American settlers in small western towns rather than larger cities, further extending the meaning of the black urban west.

Black western historiography deepened throughout the 1980s. Fresh and creative studies spanned the regional panorama, from Jacqueline Cogdell DjeDje's studies of gospel music in Los Angeles (including—a good place to begin—"Gospel Music in the Los Angeles Black Community: A Historical Overview" *Black Music Research Journal* 9 [Spring 1989]: 35–79) to Nell Irvin Painter's *Exodusters: Black Migration to Kansas after Reconstruction* (original 1977, reprinted New York: W.W. Norton, 1986). Katz had offered a pioneering chapter on black women in the West in the early 1970s, but the larger analysis of gender gained its momentum in the 1980s. New leaders in western history, such as Virginia Scharff and Peggy Pascoe, emphasized both gender and race in their work. De Graaf himself contributed an important overview in "Race, Sex, and Region: Black Women in the American West, 1850–1920" *Pacific Historical Review* 49 (1980): 285–313; and Ann M. Butler's article "Still in Chains: Black Women in Western Prisons, 1895–1910" *Western Historical Quarterly* 20 (February 1989): 19–36, demonstrated the insights that could be gained through new and creative approaches. At decade's end, Richard White, one of the most influential historians of the West, declared that race (the region's multiracial character) was the most distinguishing feature of the American West. This statement, accepted without notable controversy in 1989, would have seemed oddly out of place in western historiography only 20 years earlier.

In the 1990s, the field seemed to explode with new and exciting work. Albert S. Broussard brought out *Black San Francisco: The Struggle for Racial Equality in the West, 1900–1954* (Lawrence: Kansas University Press, 1993), which offered a community study that called into question the city's liberal reputation. Quintard Taylor's *The Forging of a Black Community: Seattle's Central District from 1870 through the Civil Rights Era* (Seattle: University of Washington Press, 1994), which appeared the following year, marked a culmination of his persistent examination of African Americans in the Northwest and, like Broussard's work, emphasized themes from African American history and urban studies, leaving Turnerian concerns behind. Gretchen Lemke-Santangelo, *Abiding Courage: African American Migrant Women and the East Bay Community* (Chapel Hill: University of North Carolina Press, 1996) brought issues of gender and regional identity to the forefront of her rich study of northern California. Jacqueline Cogdell DjeDje and Eddie S. Meadows, eds., *California Soul: Music of African Americans in the West* (Berkeley: University of California Press, 1998), pulled together a treasure trove of material on West Coast jazz, the blues, gospel, and R&B. Gerald Horne, *Fire This Time: The Watts Uprising and the 1960s* (Cambridge, MA: Da Capo Press, 1997), offered a major reassessment of the Watts riot.

Meanwhile, Taylor followed up his book on Seattle with a milestone work in black western historiography: his 1998 book, *In Search of the Racial Frontier: African Americans in the American West, 1528–1990* (New York: W.W. Norton, 1998). In it he posits the key theme of black western history as a series of questions. "Did the West represent the last best hope for nineteenth- and twentieth-century African Americans?" he asks. "Was it a racial frontier beyond which lay the potential for an egalitarian society? Or did the region fail to match the unobtainable promise imposed upon it by legions of boosters, to provide both political freedom and economic opportunity? Perhaps black Americans, in their desire to escape the repression of the East and South, simply exaggerated the possibilities in the region. Did western distinctiveness apply to race?" Taylor is quick to add that "such questions defy easy, immediate answers," and his richly detailed study successfully avoids oversimplification (Taylor, 1998, quotes 17).

Taylor decisively positions his survey of black western history as an exploration of *region*—of place rather than process, of section rather than frontier. Like historians of the American South, he connects his key themes to questions about sectional distinctiveness and the relationship between myth and reality. Yet he also brings the notion of frontier back into the story, as both his book title and his second question emphasize.

This is not the Turnerian frontier, a band of expanding westward settlement that transforms its inhabitants; instead, it is a promised land of uncertain promise. Nonetheless, there is a powerful expectation in this frontier, a hope connected to the West itself.

A superlative book on the multicultural West appeared only a year after Taylor's synthesis. This was the historian Walter Nugent's magisterial work, *Into the West: The Story of Its People* (New York: Alfred A. Knopf, 1999). Nugent's synthesis of migration and settlement patterns in the western region is remarkable in its scope. It covers the experiences of virtually all ethnic and racial groups. Chronologically, it ranges from antiquity to the end of the 20th century. It is a must read for anyone interested in the multicultural West. For readers most interested in the African American experience, Nugent not only deals with that topic but also, more important, allows us to place the black experience in a larger ethno-racial perspective.

The essential question raised by Taylor and Nugent may be stated simply: Could the West live up to its egalitarian promise? This theme continued to drive black western historiography into the twenty-first century. The *Seeking El Dorado* anthology, discussed above, appeared in 2001 and foreshadowed the wide-ranging books on black California that would soon appear. Shirley Ann Wilson Moore, *To Place Our Deeds: The African American Community in Richmond, California, 1910–1963* (Berkeley: University of California Press, 2001), enhanced our knowledge of the East Bay, as did Robert O. Self, *American Babylon: Race and the Struggle for Postwar Oakland* (Princeton, NJ: Princeton University Press). Work on Los Angeles included Douglas Flamming, *Bound for Freedom: Black Los Angeles in Jim Crow America* (Berkeley: University of California Press, 2005), which covered the half century before World War II, and Josh Sides, *L.A. City Limits: African American Los Angeles from the Great Depression to the Present* (Berkeley: University of California Press, 2003).

Fascinating work appeared on special topics. Looking back into the nineteenth century, DeEtta Demaratus, *The Force of a Feather: The Search for a Lost Story of Slavery and Freedom* (Salt Lake City: University of Utah Press, 2002), offered a haunting and beautiful telling of the Hannah Smith-Biddy Mason story. Quintard Taylor and Shirley Ann Wilson Moore, eds., *African American Women Confront the West, 1600–2000*

(Norman: University of Oklahoma Press, 2003), brought a wide chronological and geographical scope to this vital aspect of black western history. R. J. Smith's *The Great Black Way: L.A. in the 1940s and the Lost African-American Renaissance* (New York: Public Affairs, 2006) brought the old Central Avenue jazz scene to life.

Thus, the history of African Americans in the West continues to bloom. New books and articles continue to appear regularly, and there have been many public history programs, museum exhibitions, and conferences exploring the African American past in the West. There is good reason for this. Black western history sheds light on vitally important issues: race, region, and the promise of America.

A NEW WAVE OF MULTIRACIAL HISTORY?

In recent years, a succession of new books have been published that deal not only with African Americans in the West but also with black westerners' relationships with other ethnic and racial minorities in the region. Previous historians had not really ignored the topic; all of the early works noted the essential point: Race relations in the western region have never been just black and white. There were American Indians, of course, and not just those on reservations. More than that, however, there were large numbers of people from Asian countries: the Chinese, Japanese, and Filipinos were all well represented in the West before World War II, and that meant African Americans who moved to the West before and during the war found themselves in a different kind of racial environment than they had faced in the Jim Crow South and the ghetto North. Then there were Latinos—mostly of Mexican descent.

This point was obvious to all, but efforts at multiracial histories proved difficult. When the field of black western history began to take off in the 1990s, historians studying the topic had all they could handle in merely telling the basic story: What happened here? Pushing toward a fuller multiracial history was just too big a task at that time. Just reconstructing the basic foundations of black western history was in itself quite challenging.

What's more—and this puzzled all who were working in the field, including myself—the multiracial story of the West seemed reluctant to reveal itself. There were moments when black leaders openly considered the multiracial environment in which they found themselves, and there were even times when different racial and ethnic groups would join together as allies in the fight for everyone's civil rights, but these moments were scattered; they were few and far between. In most cities, people of different racial and ethnic minority groups were living side by side and sending their kids to the same schools. Without a doubt, African Americans, Asian Americans, and Mexican Americans were living alongside one another in mixed neighborhoods. Quintard Taylor's study of black Seattle devoted a chapter to a discussion of the Japanese community and the African American community. He was able to compare certain aspects of life, such as home ownership, but he also found little significant interaction between the groups.

It is still not entirely clear what difference these mixed neighborhoods actually made in the history of western race relations. Community studies of Mexican Americans have found that ethnic Mexicans viewed their living situation in relation to the dominant white community, and, in their efforts for civil rights they almost always dealt with white leaders; politically, they seldom interacted with Asians or African Americans. Studies of Asian communities have found the same thing; as outsiders looking for equal access and opportunity, Asians dealt directly with white political leaders and seldom with the black or brown populations. Community studies of black communities have found the same thing again. It was almost as if the minority groups who were living side by side in the urban West were acting in parallel universes that rarely came together.

Recent books on race in the West are beginning to address this question in fresh and innovative ways. It is too soon to judge whether these books will come to be seen as a new wave of historical scholarship, but it is certainly worth considering. One recent example is Kevin Allen Leonard, *The Battle for Los Angeles: Racial Ideology and World War II* (Albuquerque: University of New Mexico Press, 2006). In this illuminating work, Leonard carefully examines local newspapers of whites, African Americans, Mexican Americans, and Japanese Americans. In doing so, he provides unique insights into the ways in which the language of "race," as expressed in public, was complex and dynamic—and became entwined with American war aims and competing visions of the postwar future.

Another example, also focused on L.A., is Scott Kurashige, *The Shifting Grounds of Race: Black and Japanese Americans in the Making of Multiethnic Los Angeles* (Princeton, NJ: Princeton University Press, 2008). This is a fascinating and compelling book. Kurashige is not merely comparing the groups; he is examining how the fate of one group was bound up with the fate of another, usually because of government actions for or against each group, during and after World War II. For example, during the war, it was in the U.S. government's interest to intern the Japanese and to promote the industrial wage-earning opportunities for African Americans, and both groups were profoundly affected by these government actions. After the war, however, equal opportunities for African Americans sank as a federal priority, while in contrast, the U.S. government wanted the Japanese to rebound nicely and to be integrated into American life—in order to highlight U.S. democratic society during the ideological Cold War with the Soviet Union. One need not accept all that Kurashige argues to appreciate the importance of his work in the multiracial history of the West.

Outside the cities, intriguing new work is appearing on the history of black and Indian relationships—both during black slavery and after it was abolished. Kevin Mulroy, the historian whose involvement at the Autry Museum led off this chapter, has authored two fascinating studies on the Seminole Indians of Florida and the African Americans who, having escaped from slavery, encountered the Seminoles and developed a complex and unique relationship to the Indian tribe. Mulroy emphasizes that the black Seminoles should be considered, as they and their descendants considered themselves, as a separate and independent ethnic group, neither African American nor Seminole but, rather, as the Seminole Maroons. Mulroy's *Freedom on the Border: The Seminole Maroons in Florida, the Indian Territory, Coahuila, and Texas* (Lubbock: Texas Tech University Press, 1993) is an important and readable book, which tells the story of a Maroon group that escaped from Indian Territory and fled to Mexico.

A wide-ranging collection of essays is James F. Brooks, ed., *Confounding the Color Line: The Indian-Black Experience in North America* (Lincoln: University of Nebraska Press, 2002). The geographical focus of these essays is not the western region; indeed, most of the pieces concern the eastern half of the United States or some slice of the early frontier experience. One of the essays analyzes Afro-Indian whaling crews in old

New England. That will get one thinking! Contributors to the Brooks anthology are from multiple disciplines: history, anthropology, law, political science, and literature. That bodes well for black-Indian studies, and for the multiracial history of the West.

A "Minority Majority"?

The growth of the Latino and Asian populations has grown rapidly in the West in recent decades. Soon, the three major "minority" groups—African American, Latino, and Asian—will be the majority of the population. This eventuality has given rise to the notion of a "Minority Majority"—in which the minority groups of the past collectively make up the majority of the population. In fact, the U.S. Census Bureau has made projections about what the national population might look like in 2050, and the "middle" estimate (not the high or low) saw the proportion of whites (not counting Latinos) dropping from about 70 percent of the national total to just over 50 percent of the total. That's in 2050, and that's national. The proportion of "minority" populations in the West is considerably higher, especially in California and the American Southwest.

It is not clear how these different minority groups could come together to form a collective "majority" that would shape the law, economy, and culture of the West. Consider, for example, the Asian population of Los Angeles County in 1990. Rounding off the numbers for the general picture, the largest Asian group was the Chinese, with nearly 250,000 residents in the county. Filipinos numbered about 220,000; Koreans, 145,000; Vietnamese, 65,000; Indians from India, 45,000; Cambodians, 30,000; and Thais, 20,000—and of course there are others, such as the Hmong, the Laotians, and a wide array of Pacific Islanders, to say nothing of the Japanese. It does not take much consideration of these figures to see that the category "Asian" is too big an umbrella to have much cultural or political meaning. And these figures say nothing about the basic divide within the Chinese population—namely, those whose roots lay in Taiwan (i.e., their families had fled the communist takeover in 1949) and those who, more recently, have emigrated directly from mainland China. What about Native American Indians: the L.A. metropolitan region has more Indian residents than any other urban area in the nation (about 90,000). Where would they fit into the Minority Majority?

A major divide among Latinos (what the U.S. Census Bureau calls Hispanics) is between people from Mexico and the various nationalities from Central America, who have arrived in the United States in large numbers during recent decades. In 1990, two years before the L.A. riots had broadcast the huge and diverse—and poor—Latino population taking to the streets, the U.S. Census for the city counted some 400,000 people from Guatemala and El Salvador. Growing numbers of Puerto Ricans and other Spanish-speaking people from the Caribbean complicate the Latino mix as well.

People with roots in Mexico remain the largest Latin group and have achieved the most political clout. This politicization was largely due to the fierce anti-immigrant movement led by white conservatives during the 1990s, which led to the explosive battle over California Proposition 187. The official title of Proposition 187 was the "Save Our State" initiative—which meant, basically, save white, English-speaking California from Mexican immigrants. The provisions called for barring illegal immigrants from public schools and state-sponsored medical services, such as the maternity wards in public hospitals, and it made California's citizenry liable to arrest should they know about such use and not report it. The proposition was passed by California's voters by an easy 70 to 30 margin.

California courts invalidated Proposition 187 on the grounds that it violated rights guaranteed by the Fourteenth Amendment, but the struggle over the law continued in California and spread across the Southwest. Arizona voters passed their own version of Proposition 187 in 2004. On the one hand it seemed that these white against brown campaigns united Latinos in self-defense, but on the other hand, it appeared that long-standing divisions between older Mexican Americans and new Latino immigrants prevented such political unity. By one estimate, for example, 23 percent of California's Latino population voted *for* Proposition 187.

The African American population of the West has been a more cohesive political bloc, but divisions do exist and will not soon disappear from the horizon. One of the more interesting divisions is cultural and involves the gay and lesbian movement. On this question of sexuality, most African Americans remain culturally conservative and generally support the Republican Party's efforts to prevent gay marriage—or to render it unconstitutional, as did California's Proposition 8 in the election of 2008, a proposition that won easily in a state that otherwise voted overwhelmingly for Barack Obama. Other black activists argue that the gay civil rights activism of the present day is based on the same principles of liberty and equal rights that drove the movement for black civil rights.

Another division among blacks in the West will probably involve the growing number of immigrants from Africa who are arriving in the American West. These have immigrated mostly to the major cities, where traditional black political power has been strongest. Will African Americans welcome newcomers from Africa or will they view them as competitors in the job market and as people who too naively embrace the American Dream? Ethiopians, Nigerians, Liberians, Sudanese, and more—these new immigrants have often narrowly escaped Africa's civil wars and ethnic conflicts. They will have a different outlook on life, on African Americans, and on the West. What will that outlook be? Will they strengthen African American political power or dilute it?

These paragraphs have only considered divisions within the Asian, Latino, and black populations without touching the larger issue, which is the triangular relationship among the three groups. To what extent can there be common cause among them in the future when common cause among them has been so rare in the past? And there are other reasons to be pessimistic about harmony among these groups. The black–Korean conflicts that *predated* the L.A. riots of 1992 were an ill omen. So was, in a less violent but nonetheless startling way, a political uprising of Latinos in Compton seeking to throw out the entrenched black political establishment, who, the Latino critics claimed, paid no attention to the problems afflicting Latinos in Compton. Fights between blacks and Latinos in the public schools throughout the region contributed to doubt about cross-ethnic alliances.

Scott Kurashige's *Shifting Grounds of Race* considers these complicated questions in the conclusion of his book. He holds up two events as metaphors for what might happen. One was the organization of young black youth in L.A.'s Crenshaw District against the coming of Latinos into the neighborhood. They organized the Crispus Attucks Brigade for this purpose; the reference is to the black patriot and martyr of the American Revolution, who fell to British bullets in the Boston Massacre. These new black patriots invited to Crenshaw a white, far-right paramilitary group called the Minutemen, who infamously and without government sanction began to patrol the border with Mexico in the early years of the 21st century. In 2006, the all-black Crispus Attucks Brigade and the all-white Minutemen group gathered in the Crenshaw District for an issue-oriented protest against Mexican immigration. Both organizations were fringe groups within their own communities, but their temporary alliance cast doubt on the possibility of a black–brown alliance.

On a more positive note, Kurashige posits the story of Crenshaw's Holiday Bowl (not to be confused with the famous Hollywood Bowl theater). The Holiday Bowl was a bowling alley and cafe that served both soul food and Asian foods—one could have grits and gravy, or Japanese noodle soup, and no one would bat an eye either way. By the year 2000, the Holiday had long been a multicultural spot for locals, a place in which blacks and Asians could hang out, together or separately, and imbibe the best of both worlds as they bowled a few games. In that year, however, the real estate went up for sale and a strip mall was slated to replace it. What happened next was interesting: black and Asian patrons of the Holiday Bowl gathered in front of the old building to prevent its demolition. Preservationists joined the band, and the Coalition to Save the Holiday Bowl gave the old building a longer life. A dual-minority coalition had saved a place that had contributed to true interracial interaction.

Kurashige closes by asking the question that is now facing, and will continue to face, African Americans in the West. What will the future hold for the West's racial and ethnic minorities: a Minuteman-style conflict between minority groups, with white power called to bear on the matter, or a Holiday Bowl of harmonious interaction between minority groups? Almost surely, the West of the future will witness both. But perhaps, to borrow the words of Lincoln, the better angels of our nature will arise. The dream of an egalitarian West, a place where freedom really does exist for all, is still alive—and remains to be realized.

CHRONOLOGY

This list includes events that were of general significance for the history of the United States and the American West, as well as events that had more direct importance for the history of African Americans in the West.

1492   Christopher Columbus's first expedition reaches the Caribbean Islands. European colonization of the Americas follows.

1519   The African slave trade begins. Portugal initiates the slave trade to the Americas; Spain, England, France, and Holland gradually join in. The trade peaks in the 18th century (1700–1800) and is gradually abolished over the course of the 19th century. Africans are sold into all parts of the Americas. In all, about 12 million Africans are sold into slavery during a 350-year period.

1600–1630   England begins to colonize the North American mainland on the Atlantic Coast, establishing Virginia and Massachusetts.

1619   Slaves arrive in Virginia. The first purchase of African slaves in England's mainland colonies occurs in the Chesapeake Bay area.

1776   The 13 American colonies declare their independence from Great Britain. The Declaration of Independence asserts that "all men are created equal."

1781   New Spain founds Los Angeles, in which most settlers are of African descent.

In the Battle of Yorktown, the United States and France defeat Great Britain decisively, securing American independence—and American slavery.

1783   The Treaty of Paris marks the formal end of the American Revolution. Great Britain surrenders its mainland colonies, giving the United States all lands westward to the Mississippi River.

1787   The U.S. Constitution approved. It implicitly protects slavery but also sets a 20-year limit on the importation of slaves.

Congress passes the Northwest Ordinance, which sets rules for the development of states in the western territories: north of the Ohio River there will be no slavery, but south of the Ohio River, slavery is legal.

1803   With the $15 million Louisiana Purchase, the United States acquires a massive amount of land from Napoleon's France, thereby expanding America's western frontier.

1814   The War of 1812 ends. This settlement sparks a massive migration of Americans into the trans-Appalachian frontier. In the southern territories, slavery spreads rapidly westward.

1820   The Missouri Compromise temporarily settles the political crisis over slavery in the territories beyond the Mississippi River.

1821   Mexico gains independence from Spain and takes possession of the far north provinces. Mexico outlaws slavery.

1830s   The United States creates Indian Territory. At different times, the major tribes of the Southeast are forced off their homelands and into Indian Territory (today's Oklahoma). These tribes own black slaves, who are taken to the territory.

1836	The Republic of Texas is established. Americans and Tejanos living in the Mexican province of Texas declare their independence from Mexico and win it militarily. A slaveholding republic is born.
1846–1848	U.S. president James K. Polk calls for war against Mexico, ostensibly over a boundary dispute. The U.S. victory results in the Treaty of Guadalupe Hidalgo (1848), which cedes Mexico's far north provinces, including California, to the United States.
1849	During the California gold rush, many free blacks in the United States move to California. Slaves are taken there, too.
1850	California attains statehood. The territorial legislature petitions to be admitted to the United States as a free state, prompting an outcry of protest from the South and strengthening the abolitionist movement. The Compromise of 1850 consists of a series of laws passed by the U.S. Congress that are intended to settle the crisis over slavery in the New West.
1854	The Kansas-Nebraska Act, introduced by Democratic senator Stephen Douglas of Illinois, holds that the people of any territory had the "popular sovereignty" to decide the question of slavery there, potentially opening all American territories and states to slavery. Northern anger over the Kansas-Nebraska Act leads to the creation of a new political party, the Republican Party, whose main object is to prevent the spread of slavery into the New West.
1855–1860	At the California Colored Conventions, black leaders in the Bay Area promote civil rights through political petitions to the California legislature.
1857	In the *Dred Scott* decision, the U.S. Supreme Court not only upholds the Fugitive Slave Act but also states that

"blacks have no rights whites are bound to respect" and that Congress has no constitutional right to prohibit slavery in any part of the United States.

1858   The Lincoln-Douglas debates take place. Abraham Lincoln of Illinois narrowly loses his unlikely bid to take Stephen Douglas's seat in the U.S. Senate. These debates over slavery receive national attention and make Lincoln the nation's best-known Republican Party leader.

1860   Lincoln is elected president. The Deep South states secede from the Union even before he is inaugurated in March 1861.

1860–1890   The United States wages the Indian Wars, the collective name for U.S. wars against the Indian tribes of the Great Plains. In 1866, the U.S. Army creates four all-black regiments who fight in these wars, marking the origins of the Buffalo Soldiers.

1861–1865   The American Civil War is waged.

1863   The Emancipation Proclamation is Abraham Lincoln's formal declaration that bondsmen held in Confederate territory are free. Technically, the proclamation frees no one, but it transforms the Civil War from a war to restore the Union into a war to end slavery.

1865   The Thirteenth Amendment to the U.S. Constitution is ratified. It abolishes slavery and involuntary servitude in America.

1865–1890   Black cowboys participate in open-range cattle drives out of Texas, up the Great Plains to rail lines in Kansas and Nebraska, and to other points north.

1868   The Fourteenth Amendment to the U.S. Constitution is ratified. It makes former slaves full citizens and requires equal protection under the law.

1869	The completion of the Transcontinental Railroad leads to an era of Pullman Coach travel and the creation of the all-black Pullman porters. It also sparks the rise of the black community in Oakland, the western terminus of the Transcontinental Railroad.
1870	The Fifteenth Amendment to the U.S. Constitution is ratified. It forbids race as a means for political disfranchisement.
1875–1880	This period marks a mass movement of African Americans, called "Exodusters," out of the South and into Kansas. The Southern Pacific Railroad connects the South with Los Angeles and leads to the rise of black Los Angeles.
1890s	Black voters are disfranchised through methods such as poll taxes and literacy tests laws that sweep across the South, forcing blacks out of the political system. Formal Jim Crow segregation laws follow, which are backed up by unchecked lynchings of African Americans. In the Talented Tenth Migration, middle-class blacks begin to leave the South for the urban North and West.
1898	The Spanish-American War, a brief war between the United States and Spain, is waged over Spanish treatment of Cubans. The war places African American troops at the center of the war in Cuba, where they fight alongside Teddy Roosevelt's Rough Riders.
1906	The Brownsville incident refers to President Roosevelt's dishonorable discharge, without trial, of African American soldiers stationed in Brownsville who will not provide evidence regarding a local shootout.

1914   World War I begins in Europe.

The First Great Migration takes place. When the war cuts off labor migration from Europe, American industrialists recruit black workers from the South, sparking the Great Migration to the urban industrial North.

1915   *The Birth of a Nation*, the first blockbuster Hollywood film, premieres. In the film, director D. W. Griffith portrays blacks in a viciously stereotyped manner and glorifies the Ku Klux Klan. The movie sparks the first major protest of the National Association for the Advancement of Colored People (NAACP), which seeks to ban the film.

1917   Buffalo Soldiers sent to camp in Houston face repeated attacks from whites. This leads to a black counterattack and a white riot. Many soldiers are hanged or sentenced to life in prison as a result of their participation in the race riot.

In a race riot, a white mob virtually wipes out the black community of East St. Louis.

The United States enters World War I. President Wilson calls for war against Germany, promising to "make the world safe for democracy."

1918   World War I ends after U.S. troops, including segregated black troops, stop the final German offensive on France.

Frederick M. Roberts becomes the first black person elected to the state assembly in California. He has biracial (black and white) support on the Republican Party ticket.

1919   Race riots occur in many American cities, including the western city of Omaha. White mobs storm black communities, but emboldened by the war and angry that their patriotic service has not resulted in democracy at home, many blacks fight back.

1920–1925	The second Ku Klux Klan is active in the West.
1920s	This decade sees the Harlem Renaissance arts movement, the Jazz era, and the rise of Hollywood.
1921	A race riot erupts in Tulsa, Oklahoma.
1928	The Los Angeles branch of the NAACP hosts the national NAACP convention at the new Somerville Hotel, after promising and delivering a beautiful new hotel for the delegates. It is the first NAACP convention held in the West.
1929	The stock market crashes, marking the beginning of the Great Depression.
1932	Franklin D. Roosevelt wins the presidency in a landslide; the liberal wing of the Democratic Party gains importance.
1933	FDR takes office and the New Deal begins.
1934	Augustus "Gus" Hawkins, a black Democrat, defeats black Republican incumbent Frederick Roberts in the election for the California statehouse.
1936	FDR is reelected, and there are massive shifts of black voters into the Democratic Party in the North and West. Black southerners are still disfranchised.
1939	Hitler invades Poland. This German offensive, the last straw for Europe's democracies, sparks World War II in Europe.
1940	War production for England sparks industrial boom in the United States, which increases when the United States begins a military draft and production for its own army. The Great Depression ends.
1941	Led by A. Philip Randolph, blacks participate in a national protest against the exclusion of African Americans in defense plant jobs. In response, FDR issues

Executive Order 8802, which prohibits discrimination on account of race in any factory that has a government military contract. This action also leads to the creation of the Equal Employment Opportunity Commission.

Japan bombs Pearl Harbor on December 7, bringing the United States into the war in both the Pacific and Europe.

1942–1945   In the Second Great Migration, the wartime defense boom ignites another mass movement of African Americans from the South to the North and West. For the western cities, this was effectively their *first* Great Migration.

The Japanese are removed from western cities and relocated to internment camps. In Los Angeles, black newcomers change Little Tokyo into Bronzeville.

1945   World War II ends. Germany surrenders first in Europe. In August, the United States drops atomic bombs on Japan, prompting its surrender.

1945–1950   The Cold War develops between the capitalist United States and the communist Soviet Union, sparking the McCarthy-era Red Scare and weakening or destroying left-wing and liberal civil rights organizations.

1947   Jackie Robinson of Pasadena, California, breaks the color line in Major League Baseball, playing for the Brooklyn Dodgers.

1948   The Democratic Party convention officially calls for civil rights legislation. Delegates from some Deep South states leave the party and form the State's Rights Democratic Party (often called "Dixiecrats"). Truman wins with heavy support from black voters.

In *Shelley v. Kraemer*, Loren Miller of Los Angeles leads the NAACP court case to strike down racially restrictive real estate covenants. The U.S. Supreme Court rules covenants unenforceable. A 1953 follow-up case, *Barrows v. Jackson*, further weakens the legal force of restrictive covenants.

1950–1953   During the Korean War, Truman desegregates the U.S. Army, a first in U.S. history.

1952   Charlotta Bass, the owner-editor of the *California Eagle*, is chosen as the candidate for vice president for the left-leaning Progressive Party—the first African American to be nominated to run for that office on a national ticket.

1954   In *Brown v. Board of Education of Topeka, Kansas*, the U.S. Supreme Court rules that the old "separate but equal" loophole for segregation is unconstitutional. A follow-up ruling in 1955 demands that schools integrate with "all deliberate speed."

1955   Martin Luther King Jr. rises to prominence during the year-long Montgomery Bus Boycott in Alabama. The Southern Christian Leadership Conference (SCLC) is formed out of this Massive Resistance movement.

1956–1963   During this period, blacks see major gains in civil rights laws in California, the result of a biracial coalition in the legislature and support from Democratic governor Harold Brown.

1960   The student sit-in movement begins in North Carolina, leading to the organization of the Student Nonviolent Coordinating Committee (SNCC).

1960–1965   The southern civil rights movement dominates national news and politics.

1963   During the March on Washington, Martin Luther King delivers his famous "I Have a Dream" speech to the nation.

President Kennedy calls for a civil rights law.

Kennedy is assassinated in Dallas in November.

President Johnson urges the nation to continue Kennedy's agenda and promotes the civil rights act.

Three African American men, including future mayor Tom Bradley, are elected to the Los Angeles City Council, a breakthrough in local representation.

1963–1965   California's Fair Housing Act prompts white backlash.

1964   The Civil Rights Act is passed. This important legislation makes racial segregation illegal. In addition, the act prohibits employment discrimination on account of race and sex, providing a major boost to employment opportunities for white women.

1965   Protests for the right to vote in Selma, Alabama, lead to an attack on peaceful marchers by Alabama state troopers and the local sheriff's posse. National outrage follows the television broadcasts of the "Bloody Sunday" attacks. President Johnson calls for voting rights legislation in a live broadcast, saying "We Shall Overcome."

Voting Rights Act of 1965 is passed.

President Johnson sends U.S. Marines to Vietnam.

The Watts Rebellion takes place.

1965–1970   "Black Power!" becomes the slogan of young activists. Black Panthers and United Slaves organize in California, popularizing militant black nationalism.

1968   In this year of turmoil, political conflict, urban violence, and assassination were common in the United States and throughout the world. Martin Luther King is assassinated in Memphis, sparking race riots nationwide.

Bobby Kennedy is assassinated in Los Angeles. Antiwar riots explode in Chicago. Republican Richard Nixon is elected president on a law and order platform.

In the Summer Olympic Games, held in Mexico City, two American sprinters on the winners' stand give the Black Power salute during the national anthem, sparking massive controversy.

1972   The music-making giant Motown moves from Detroit and shifts from popular music to Hollywood films. Its first picture, *Lady Sings the Blues* (1973), is a box-office success.

1973   The U.S. war in Vietnam ends, but Nixon's Watergate troubles begin, leading him to resign the presidency in 1974.

1980   The Reagan era begins. Ronald Reagan, former governor of California, is elected president of the United States and gives a famous inaugural speech saying that "government is not the solution; government is the problem." Federal social welfare programs for inner cities experience drastic budget cuts.

1980s   Street gangs, predominantly the Bloods and Crips of Los Angeles, grow large and increasingly violent.

1980–2000 This 20-year period is an era of black suburbanization. Throughout the urban West, increasing numbers of African Americans move out of the inner cities and into mostly white suburbs.

Millions of African Americans in the North and West, the children and grandchildren of the earlier Great Migrations, begin to move back to the South, where they reconnect with their roots. The South appears to have better economic and racial conditions than other parts of the country.

1988–1998	Gangsta rap, a product of the West Coast ghettos, becomes popular nationally. Although it is initially considered underground music, it becomes mainstream.
1991	Rodney King, a resident of Altadena, California, is beaten by L.A. Police Department (LAPD) officers after a high-speed chase. The incident is captured on video and sparks outrage.
1992	The trial of the LAPD officers involved in the Rodney King beating is moved to the conservative Simi Valley area, where an all-white jury acquits all of the officers on all charges.
	Soon after the Simi Valley verdicts are announced; violence, arson, and looting rage through L.A. for about one week, with Americans watching most of the riots on live television.
	Bill Clinton, a southerner popular among African American voters, is elected president on the Democratic ticket.
2008	For the first time in U.S. history, an African American is nominated for, and then elected to, the presidency. Western states strongly support Barack Obama.

GLOSSARY

Afro-American Council   An American civil rights organization founded in the 1890s; often seen as precursor to the NAACP.

aridity   Aridity and semiaridity refer to desert or near-desert environments.

Black Nationalism   An ideal among African Americans that blacks should be self-governed and in control of their cultural and economic destiny.

Black Panther Party   A black nationalist organization established in Oakland, California, in 1966.

Buffalo Soldiers   African American units in the U.S. Army that were stationed in western forts during the Indian Wars (ca. 1866–1900). There were four units: The Ninth and Tenth Cavalry units; and the 24th and 25th Infantry units.

California Colored Conventions   The first civil rights conclaves in the American West, these conventions were held in San Francisco and Sacramento during the 1850s.

chattel slavery   The form of slavery Europeans developed for Africans enslaved in the Americas. In chattel slavery, the offspring of slaves are also slaves.

coffle   Collars made of wood, rope, or iron used to shackle together a line of slaves being marched overland or transported by ship.

Congress of Racial Equality (CORE)   National civil rights organization active during the 1950s and 1960s.

direct-action protest   A strategy of protest in which an offensive law or custom is confronted by direct personal violation of that law or custom.

disfranchisement   Taking the vote away from an identifiable group of people.

Double-V campaign   Blacks used this phrase during World War II to emphasize their determination to win victory against the fascist overseas and victory for civil rights at home.

Executive Order 8802   A presidential directive issued by Franklin Roosevelt in 1941; it forbade employment discrimination on account of race in defense plants with federal contracts.

Exodusters   The name generally applied to African Americans who moved in large groups from the South to Kansas during the late 1870s—especially the group from Mississippi.

Garveyism   Black nationalist movement of the late 1910s and early 1920s; led by Marcus Garvey, it emphasized economic self-reliance.

ghetto   The term dates to the Italian Renaissance, when Jewish people were forced to live in walled-off "ghettos" within cities. In late 19th-century America, the term was applied to poor European immigrants who packed into northern cities. In the 20th century, it was mostly applied to black sections of American cities.

Great Migration   During World War I, roughly half a million African Americans migrated from the American South to the large industrial cities of the urban North. This migration missed the urban West. A Second Great Migration occurred during World War II and strongly affected the urban West.

Harlem Renaissance   During the 1920s, a flowering of African American art and literature that was centered in the mostly black Harlem district of Manhattan.

Jim Crow   A term applied to both legal and informal forms of forced racial segregation, exclusion, or subordination.

Juneteenth   Unofficial African American holiday to celebrate the day emancipation was announced in Texas at the end of the Civil War—June 19, 1865.

Kwanzaa   A holiday created in Los Angeles in 1966 that was intended as an Afrocentric alternative to Christmas. Kwanzaa celebrates the "first fruits"—the blessings of harvest, family, and African values and heritage— over a seven-day period.

literacy test   A method used to disfranchise black and poor voters in the New South.

Manifest Destiny   The idea, popular among white Americans during the 1830s and 1840s, that U.S. expansion westward was a divine mandate.

March on Washington, 1941   A campaign to protest hiring discrimination in defense plants by holding a mass demonstration in the nation's capital. To prevent the march, President Roosevelt issued Executive Order 8802, which, in principle, gave blacks the right to employment in defense work.

March on Washington, 1963   Also known as the March for Jobs and Freedom, this March on Washington had strong support from the Congress of Industrial Organizations (CIO) labor leaders as well as civil rights organizations. It was the site of Martin Luther King's "I Have a Dream" speech and helped inspire President Kennedy's civil rights bill.

McCone Commission   The state-level commission established to investigate the Watts Rebellion of 1965—the commission's findings were widely criticized by African American leaders.

National Association for the Advancement of Colored People (NAACP)   Major civil rights organization still in operation today. Established in New York in 1911 as a biracial (white and black) association to promote black civil rights within America.

98th meridian   A longitude line that marks the unofficial divide between the eastern and western halves of the United States. East of the 98th meridian, average rainfall is abundant; west of the 98th meridian, rainfall is scant. The humid and well-forested East is quite different from the mostly arid and open country of the West.

poll tax   An annual tax that was used in the postbellum South to disfranchise large numbers of blacks and poor whites.

Progressivism   Name designating a general reform movement that swept American politics circa 1900–1920. The Progressive Party was organized in 1912 around Teddy Roosevelt's unsuccessful bid to regain the White House; this party was short-lived. After World War II, a very different Progressive Party was established; this left-leaning party nominated Charlotta Bass—an African American newspaper publisher and civil rights activist from L.A.—as its candidate for vice president.

Proposition 187   A 1994 California proposition that sought to deny social services, such as public schools and emergency hospital care for illegal immigrants and their children.

race papers   Term used in the black community for black-owned newspapers.

race riot   From roughly 1865 to 1965 the term "race riot" meant a white mob attacking a black section of a town or city. After the Watts Riot of 1965, the term came to mean a black uprising within the ghetto itself.

Reconstruction Amendments   The Thirteenth (1865), Fourteenth (1868), and Fifteenth (1870) Amendments to the U.S. Constitution, abolishing slavery, giving citizenship rights to former slaves, and seeking secure voting rights for black men. These were key expressions of the Republican Reconstruction era, circa 1865–1877.

Rosie the Riveter   Appreciative name given to women who worked in defense plants during World War II.

Southern Christian Leadership Conference (SCLC)   Civil rights organization established during the Montgomery, Alabama, Bus Boycott of 1955–1956. Its early leader was Martin Luther King Jr., who typified the middle-class, integrationist, church-centered nature of the SCLC.

Student Nonviolent Coordinating Committee (SNCC)   The young people's arm of the southern civil rights movement, a biracial organization established in the wake of the sit-in movement of 1960. After 1965, SNCC expelled its white membership and adopted a black nationalist agenda.

Talented Tenth   A term coined by black civil rights leader W. E. B. Du Bois in the early 20th century. It referred to the college-educated black leadership—the "talented tenth" of the race—that he hoped would lead blacks toward full civil rights.

trans-Appalachian frontier   Historians use this term for the lands lying between the Appalachian Mountains and the Mississippi—the nation's first major frontier area.

Treaty of Guadalupe Hidalgo   This 1848 treaty between the United States and Mexico ended the Mexican War and gave the United States its present-day Southwest.

United Slaves Organization (also called US Organization)   Black nationalist organization established by Ron Karenga of Los Angeles after the Watts Rebellion of 1965.

SELECTED BIBLIOGRAPHY

Bogle, Donald. *Bright Boulevards, Bold Dreams: The Story of Black Hollywood*. New York: Ballantine Books, 2006.

Bontemps, Arna. *Black Thunder*. New York: Macmillan, 1936. Reprinted with an introduction by the author. Boston: Beacon Press, 1968.

Brooks, James F., ed. *The Indian-Black Experience in North America*. Lincoln: University of Nebraska Press, 2002.

Broussard, Albert S. *Black San Francisco: The Struggle for Racial Equality in the West, 1900–1954*. Lawrence: University of Kansas Press, 1993.

Broussard, Albert S. *African-American Odyssey: The Stewarts, 1853–1963*. Lawrence: University Press of Kansas.

Brown, Elaine. *A Taste of Power: A Black Woman's Story*. New York: Anchor Books, 1992.

Bryant, Clora, Buddy Collette, William Green, Steven Isoardi, Jack Kelson, Horace Tapscott, Gerald Wilson, and Marl Young, eds. *Central Avenue Sounds: Jazz in Los Angeles*. Berkeley: University of California Press, 1998.

Cannon, Lou. *Official Negligence: How Rodney King and the Riots Changed Los Angeles and the LAPD*. New York: Times Books, 1997.

Chamberlain, Charles D. *Victory at Home: Manpower and Race in the American South during World War II*. Athens: University of Georgia Press, 2003.

Conot, Robert. *Rivers of Blood, Years of Darkness*. New York: Bantam Books, 1967.

Cox, Thomas. *Blacks in Topeka, Kansas, 1865–1915: A Social History*. Baton Rouge: Louisiana State University Press, 1982.

Crouchett, Lawrence P., Lonnie G. Bunch, III, Martha Kendall Winnacker. *Visions Toward Tomorrow: The History of the East Bay Afro-American Community, 1852–1977.* Oakland: Northern California Center for Afro-American History and Life, 1989.

Daniels, Henry Douglas. *Pioneer Urbanites: A Social and Cultural History of Black San Francisco.* Berkeley: University of California Press, 1990.

Davis, Angela. *Angela Davis: An Autobiography.* 1974. Reprinted with a new introduction by the author. New York: International Publishers, 2006.

De Graaf, Lawrence B., Kevin Mulroy, and Quintard Taylor, *Seeking El Dorado: African Americans in California.* Seattle: University of Washington Press, 2001.

Demaratus, DeEtta. *The Force of a Feather: The Search for a Lost Story of Slavery and Freedom.* Salt Lake City: University of Utah Press, 2002.

Deverell, William, ed. *A Companion to the American West.* Malden, MA: Blackwell Publishing, 2004.

DjeDje, Jacqueline Cogdell, and Eddie S. Meadows. *California Soul: Music of African Americans in the West.* Berkeley: University of California Press, 1998.

Durham, Philip, and Everett L. Jones. *The Negro Cowboys.* Lincoln: University of Nebraska Press, 1965.

Ellsworth, Scott. *Death in a Promised Land: The Tulsa Race Riot of 1921.* Baton Rouge: Louisiana State University Press, 1982.

Flamming, Douglas. *Bound for Freedom: Black Los Angeles in Jim Crow America.* Berkeley: University of California Press, 2005.

Fogelson, Robert M., compiler. *Mass Violence in America: The Los Angeles Riots.* New York: Arno Press and the New York Times, 1969.

Franklin, Jimmie. *Journey Toward Hope: A History of Blacks in Oklahoma.* Norman: University of Oklahoma Press, 1982.

Garceau-Hagen, Dee, ed. *Portraits of Women in the American West.* New York: Routledge, 2005.

Gatewood, Willard B. *Aristocrats of Color: The Black Elite, 1880–1920.* Bloomington: Indiana University Press, 1990.

George, Lynell. *No Crystal Stair: African Americans in the City of Angels.* New York: Verso, 1992.

Glave, Dianne D., and Mark Stoll, eds. *"To Love the Wind and the Rain": African Americans and Environmental History.* Pittsburgh, PA: University of Pittsburgh Press, 2006.

Green, A. C. *900 Miles on the Butterfield Trail.* Denton: University of North Texas Press, 1995.

Greenberg, Cheryl Lynn. *"Or Does it Explode?": Black Harlem in the Great Depression.* New York: Oxford University Press, 1991.

Gregory, James N. *The Southern Diaspora: How the Great Migration of Black and White Southerners Transformed America.* Chapel Hill: University of North Carolina Press, 2005.

Hirsch, James S. *Riot and Remembrance: The Tulsa Race War and Its Legacy.* Boston: Houghton Mifflin, 2002.

Horne, Gerald. *Fire This Time: The Watts Uprising and the 1960s.* Cambridge, MA: Da Capo Press, 1997.

Howe, Daniel Walker. *What Hath God Wrought: The Transformation of America, 1815–1848.* New York: Oxford University Press, 2007.

Hudson, Lynn. *The Making of "Mammy Pleasant": A Black Entrepreneur in Nineteenth-Century San Francisco.* Urbana: University of Illinois Press, 2003.

Hughes, Langston. *Not Without Laughter.* New York: Alfred A. Knopf, 1969.

Iber, Jorge, and Arnoldo De Leon, *Hispanics in the American West.* Santa Barbara, CA: ABC-CLIO, 2008.

James, Michael E. *The Conspiracy of the Good: Civil Rights and the Struggle for Community in Two American Cities, 1875–2000.* New York: Peter Lang, 2005.

Johnson, Marilynn S. *The Second Gold Rush: Oakland and the East Bay in World War II.* Berkeley: University of California Press, 1994.

Jones, Kirkland C. *Renaissance Man from Louisiana: A Biography of Arna Wendell Bontemps.* Westport, CT: Greenwood Press, 1992.

Katz, William Loren. *The Black West.* 3rd ed., revised and expanded. Seattle, WA: Open Hand Publishing, 1987.

Kurashige, Scott. *The Shifting Grounds of Race: Black and Japanese Americans in the Making of Multiethnic Los Angeles.* Princeton, NJ: Princeton University Press, 2008.

Lapp, Rudolph M. *Afro-Americans in California.* 2nd ed. San Francisco: Boyd and Fraser Publishing Company, 1987.

Leckie, William H. *The Buffalo Soldiers: A Narrative of the Negro Cavalry in the West.* Norman: University of Oklahoma Press, 1967.

Lemke-Santangelo, Gretchen. *Abiding Courage: African American Migrant Women and the East Bay Community.* Chapel Hill: University of North Carolina Press, 1996.

Leonard, Kevin Allen. *The Battle for Los Angeles: Racial Ideology and World War II.* Albuquerque: University of New Mexico Press, 2006.

LeSeur, Geta. *Not All Okies Are White: The Lives of Black Cotton Pickers in Arizona.* Columbia: University of Missouri Press, 2000.

Lewis, David Levering, ed. *The Portable Harlem Renaissance Reader.* New York: Viking, 1994.

Love, Nat. *The Life and Adventures of Nat Love.* Los Angeles: Wayside Press, 1907. Reprinted with an introduction by Brackette F. Williams. Lincoln: Bison Books, University of Nebraska Press, 1995.

McPherson, James M. *Battle Cry of Freedom: The Civil War Era.* Cambridge, UK: Oxford University Press, 1988.

Moore, Shirley Ann Wilson. *To Place Our Deeds: The African American Community in Richmond, California, 1910–1963.* Berkeley: University of California Press, 2001.

Mulroy, Kevin. *Freedom on the Border: The Seminole Maroons in Florida, the Indian Territory, Coahuila, and Texas.* Lubbock: Texas Tech University Press, 1993.

Nobles, Gregory H. *American Frontiers: Cultural Encounters and Continental Conquest.* New York: Penguin Books, 1997.

Nugent, Walter. *Into the West: The Story of Its People.* New York: Alfred A. Knopf, 1999.

Painter, Nell Irvin. *Exodusters: Black Migration to Kansas after Reconstruction.* New York: W.W. Norton, 1992. First published 1977.

Palgon, Gary Mitchell. *William Alexander Leidesdorff: First Black Millionaire, American Consul and California Pioneer.* Atlanta: privately published, 2005.

Pearlman, Jeff. *Love Me, Hate Me: Barry Bonds and the Making of an Antihero.* New York: Harper Collins, 2006.

Rampersad, Arnold. *The Life of Langston Hughes.* Vol. I, *1902–1941, 'I, Too, Sing America'.* New York: Oxford University Press, 1986.

Ravage, John W. *Black Pioneers: Images of the Black Experience on the North American Frontier.* Salt Lake City: University of Utah Press, 1997.

Richardson, James. *Willie Brown: A Biography.* Berkeley: University of California Press, 1996.

Robinson, Rachel. *Jackie Robinson: An Intimate Biography.* New York: Harry Abrams, 1996.

Rohrbough, Malcolm J. *The Trans-Appalachian Frontier: People, Societies, and Institutions, 1775–1850.* New York: Oxford University Press, 1978.

Schubert, Frank N. *Voices of the Buffalo Soldier: Records, Reports, and Recollections of Military Life and Service in the West.* Albuquerque: University of New Mexico Press, 2003.

Self, Robert O. *American Babylon: Race and the Struggle for Postwar Oakland.* Princeton, NJ: Princeton University Press, 2003.

Sides, Josh. *L.A. City Limits: African American Los Angeles from the Great Depression to the Present.* Berkeley: University of California Press, 2003.

Smith, R. J. *The Great Black Way: L.A. in the 1940s and the Lost African-American Renaissance.* New York: Public Affairs, 2006.

Sonenshein, Raphael J. *Politics in Black and White: Race and Power in Los Angeles.* Princeton, NJ: Princeton University Press, 1993.

Taylor, Alan. *American Colonies: The Settling of North America.* New York: Penguin Books, 2001.

Taylor, Quintard. *The Forging of a Black Community: Seattle's Central District from 1870 through the Civil Rights Era.* Seattle: University of Washington Press, 1994.

Taylor, Quintard. *In Search of the Racial Frontier: African Americans in the American West, 1528–1990.* New York: W.W. Norton, 1998.

Taylor, Quintard, and Shirley Ann Wilson Moore. *African American Women Confront the West, 1600–2000.* Norman: University of Oklahoma Press, 2003.

Thurman, Wallace. *The Blacker the Berry . . . : A Novel of Negro Life.* New York, 1929. Reprinted. New York: Macmillan, 1970.

Tygiel, Jules. *Baseball's Great Experiment: Jackie Robinson and His Legacy.* New York: Oxford University Press, 1983.

Utley, Robert M., and Wilcomb E. Washburn. *Indian Wars.* New York: Houghton Mifflin, 2002.

Wheeler, B. Gordon. *Black California: The History of African-Americans in the Golden State.* New York: Hippocrene Books, 1993.

Whitaker, Matthew C. *Race Work: The Rise of Civil Rights in the Urban West.* Lincoln: University of Nebraska Press, 2005.

White, Richard. *It's Your Misfortune and None of My Own: A New History of the American West.* Norman: University of Oklahoma Press, 1992.

Wiese, Andrew. *Places of Their Own: African American Suburbanization in the Twentieth Century.* Chicago: University of Chicago Press, 2004.

Wild, Mark. *Street Meeting: Multiethnic Neighborhoods in Early Twentieth-Century Los Angeles.* Berkeley: University of California Press, 2005.

Wright, Donald R. *African Americans in the Colonial Era: From African Origins Through the American Revolution.* Arlington Heights, IL: Harlan Davidson, 1990.

Wright, Donald R. *African Americans in the Early Republic, 1789–1831.* Arlington Heights, IL: Harlan Davidson, 1993.

INDEX

ABOUT THE AUTHOR

Douglas Flamming is a professor of history at the Georgia Institute of Technology in Atlanta. His early research focused on the history of the American South, and his first book, *Creating the Modern South: Millhands and Managers in Dalton, Georgia, 1884–1984,* won the 1992 Philip Taft Labor History Award for the best book in labor history published that year. He then shifted his research to the American West, with a particular interest in the history of the African American community in Los Angeles. He has published numerous essays and given many talks on the subject to both scholars and the general public. His most recent book is the highly regarded work *Bound for Freedom: Black Los Angeles in Jim Crow America* (2005).